Chrétien de Troyes was one of the most important medieval writers of Arthurian narrative. A key figure in reshaping the "once and future fictions" of Arthurian story, he was instrumental in the late twelfth-century shift from written and oral legendary traditions to a highly sophisticated literary cultivation of the Old French verse romance. While examining individually each of Chrétien's five Arthurian romances, Donald Maddox looks at their coherence as a group, suggesting that their intertextual relations lend a harmony of meaning and design to the ensemble as a whole. Central to his argument is the focus on customs, which provide unity within as well as among the works while conveying an acute sense of the vulnerability and dissolution of feudal institutions in an age of social crisis and transition.

The Arthurian Romances of Chrétien de Troyes

CAMBRIDGE STUDIES IN MEDIEVAL LITERATURE 12

General Editor: Professor Alastair Minnis, Professor of Medieval Literature,
University of York

Editorial Board
Professor Piero Boitani (Professor of English, Rome)
Professor Patrick Boyde, FBA (Serena Professor of Italian, Cambridge)
Professor John Burrow, FBA (Winterstoke Professor of English, Bristol)
Professor Alan Deyermond, FBA (Professor of Hispanic Studies, London)
Professor Peter Dronke, FBA (Professor of Medieval Latin Literature,
Cambridge)
Tony Hunt (St. Peter's College, Oxford)
Dr Nigel Palmer (Lecturer in Medieval German, Oxford)
Professor Winthrop Wetherbee (Professor of English, Cornell)

This series of critical books seeks to cover the whole area of literature written in the
major medieval languages – the main European vernaculars, and medieval Latin and
Greek – during the period *c.* 1100–*c.* 1500. Its chief aim is to publish and stimulate
fresh scholarship and criticism on medieval literature, special emphasis being placed
on understanding major works of poetry, prose and drama in relation to the
contemporary culture and learning which fostered them.

The Arthurian Romances of Chrétien de Troyes
Once and future fictions

DONALD MADDOX

Professor of French, University of Massachusetts, Amherst

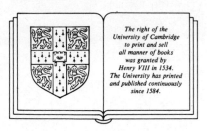

The right of the
University of Cambridge
to print and sell
all manner of books
was granted by
Henry VIII in 1534.
The University has printed
and published continuously
since 1584.

CAMBRIDGE UNIVERSITY PRESS

Cambridge

New York   Port Chester   Melbourne   Sydney

Published by the Press Syndicate of the University of Cambridge
The Pitt Building, Trumpington Street, Cambridge CB2 1RP
40 West 20th Street, New York, NY 10011, USA
10 Stamford Road, Oakleigh, Melbourne 3166, Australia

First published 1991

Printed in Great Britain at the University Press, Cambridge

British Library cataloguing in publication data
Maddox, Donald
The Arthurian romances of Chrétien de Troyes: once and
future fictions (Cambridge Studies in Medieval Literature: 12).
1. Poetry in Old French. Chrétien de Troyes
1. Title
841.1

Library of Congress cataloguing in publication data
Maddox, Donald,
The Arthurian romances of Chrétien de Troyes: once and future
fictions/Donald Maddox.
p.   cm. – (Cambridge studies in medieval literature: 12).
Includes bibliographical references and index.
ISBN 0 521 39450 3
1. Chrétien, de Troyes, 12th cent. – Criticism and interpretation.
2. Arthurian romances – History and criticism. 1. Title.
11. Series.
PQ1448.M33   1991
841'.1 – dc20   90–38037 CIP

ISBN 0 521 39450 3 hardback

This book is dedicated to
Howard and Allene Maddox

Contents

Acknowledgments

This book was written in Europe, during a prolonged, relatively private encounter with Chrétien de Troyes, so there were few who shared in its unfolding. I am deeply grateful to those who kindly read the entire typescript, Tony Hunt, Rosemary Morris, and Linda Paterson, from whose sensitive and meticulous readings I learned so much, and to my editor, Kevin Taylor, wise beyond his years in the ways of the word. I would also like to thank Matilda Bruckner for helpful comments on an initial incarnation of Chapter 2; Emmanuèle Baumgartner, Christiane Marchello-Nizia, and Cesare Segre, for inviting me to share some of my ideas with their students in Paris and Pavia; and Elspeth Kennedy for many stimulating discussions of Arthurian literature over the years. In countless ways this study benefited immeasurably from the wise counsel of my wife, Sara, whose interest and encouragement were forthcoming from the earliest phases through completion.

Abbreviations

Abbreviations

Dict	*Sémiotique: Dictionnaire raisonné de la théorie du langage*, ed. A. J. Greimas and J. Courtés, vols. I and II (Paris: Hachette, 1979; 1986)
Mél. LeGentil	*Mélanges de langue et de littérature médiévales offerts à Pierre LeGentil*, ed. J. Dufournet and D. Poirion (Paris: SEDES, 1973)
Mél. Lejeune	*Mélanges offerts à Rita Lejeune*, vols. I and II (Gembloux: Duculot, 1969)
Mél. Lods	*Mélanges de littérature du Moyen Age au XXe siècle, offerts à Mademoiselle Jeanne Lods* (Paris: Ecole Normale Supérieure de Jeunes Filles, 1978)
Sower	*The Sower and his Seed: Essays on Chrétien de Troyes*, ed. R.T. Pickens (Lexington, KY: French Forum, 1983)
St. Siciliano	*Studi in onore di Italo Siciliano*, vols. I and II (Florence: Olschki, 1966)

Introduction

According to a popular commonplace whose currency owes as much to modern fiction and cinema as to medieval legend and literature, King Arthur is a "once and future" ruler – *Rex quondam rexque futurus* – who will someday return from the remote, enchanted isle of Avalon. According to the mid-twelfth-century poet Wace, it was the prophet Merlin who had affirmed that rumors of Arthur's demise were premature, thus inspiring among the credulous Bretons an enduring climate of anticipation.[1] Perhaps a medieval avatar of the "dying and reviving gods" long ago described by Sir James G. Frazer in *The Golden Bough*, Arthur has lived on in the popular imagination for centuries, but largely as a monarch *absconditus*, much like the ethereal old king in the next room at the Grail Castle, invisible yet alive, miraculously sustained. Meanwhile, during the prolonged period of Arthur's absence, the Arthurian legend has retained its arresting openness, idling somewhere between the mortally wounded monarch's evanescence and his second coming, healed and hale, to the great hall at Camelot. Moreover, within that indeterminate, ever-lengthening span of centuries separating the legend's conventional end from its promised new beginning, the stories of King Arthur and the Knights of the Round Table comprise a long and venerable tradition of rewriting and recycling, an ever-expanding corpus of "once and future fictions."

The present contribution returns to the late twelfth century in order to examine in depth the moment at which a recently burgeoning Arthurian tradition achieved its first extensive literary incarnation. Thus it returns to Chrétien de Troyes: after Master Wace had cast doubt on Merlin's assertion of the fabled monarch's eventual return, Chrétien was the first in a long series of authors who sought to reanimate the world of King Arthur, supplementing his prolonged absence by rewriting the fictions of his life and rule according to new designs. Chrétien's five Old French romances comprise the first multi-textual series of Arthurian fictions by a single author. They represent the consummation of a monumental shift from a complex array of written and oral legendary traditions evoking a nebulous past to a highly sophisticated literary cultivation of the Matter of Britain, one whose legacy would profoundly influence the future of Arthurian narrative for centuries thereafter.

Chrétien began his career as a narrative poet at a moment when, for the first time, a sharply delineated figure of the monarch had just been introduced into the Arthurian tradition.[2] Oral and written strands of the legend had only recently coalesced in the first extensive depiction of his reign: Geoffrey's *Historia* of 1137 and its French counterpart of 1155, Wace's *Roman de Brut*, translated from the Latin of Geoffrey.[3] In these pseudo-historical chronicles Arthur is portrayed as an ideal monarch, on a par with the Charlemagne or the Alexander who preceded him in medieval French narrative. In the *Brut*, his virtues are extolled at considerable length:

> Les teches Artur vos dirai,
> Si que de rien n'an mantirai;
> Chevaliers fu molt vertueus,
> Molt prisanz et molt glorieus;
> Contre orguelleus fu orgueilleus
> Et contre humble dolz et piteus;
> Forz et hardiz et conqueranz,
> Larges donerres, despandanz;
> Et se besoigneus le requist,
> S'eidier li pot, ne l'escondist.
> Molt ama pris, molt ama gloire,
> Molt volt ses fez metre an memoire;
> Servir se fist cortoisemant
> Et si se tint molt noblemant.
> Tant com il vesqui et regna
> Toz altres princes sormonta
> De corteisie et de noblesce
> Et de vertu et de largesce.[4]

I will tell you about the good qualities of Arthur; about none of them will I lie. He was a most valiant knight, exalted and renowned. Toward the arrogant he was pitiless; toward the humble, gentle and compassionate. Mighty and bold and conquering, liberal in his gifts, and generous. He never denied the appeal of the indigent, when it was within his means. He desired esteem and glory and that his deeds be remembered. Toward those in his service he was courteous, and bore himself nobly. As long as he lived and reigned, he surpassed all other princes in courtliness and nobility, in strength and generosity.

This portrait attributes to Arthur all the initiative, strength, bravado, generosity, and compassion that one might expect of a charismatic leader with a loyal following. Indeed, in the Arthurian tradition as represented by Geoffrey and Wace, Arthur is a dynamic, quasi-epic conqueror with a crusade-like sense of mission. He guides his warriors to victory over Saxons, Norwegians, and Danes, carries on a nine-year campaign in France, and defeats the armies of the Roman Emperor. His march on Rome itself is forestalled only by Mordret's treason in Britain, and Arthur falls in civil strife; in Wace's version, he is borne off to Avalon whence, it is said, he may one day return. Throughout Wace's account of his reign as inspired by Geoffrey, this "once and future king" illustrates the remarkable characteristics detailed in the portrait cited above.

Chrétien's renewal of the myth of Arthur appears to have modified it profoundly, leaving neither king nor court unchanged. Scarcely a generation after Wace had vernacularized a remarkably *dynamic* Arthur, Chrétien produced five major romances in which the Arthurian court and a new, far more sedentary Arthur make an appearance only at intervals in order to witness the departure of knights in search of adventure or to herald their return with festive accolades.

Introduction

Apart from these moments, king and court recede into obscurity as the heroic intrigue comes into prominence. When it does appear, this court is always already a functioning polity; gone are the phases of societal maturation portrayed by tradition. There are few explicit indications as to the social and political nature of this sometimes contradictory, seemingly unstable society, and no explanations as to why it receives only intermittent, often unflattering attention. It is as if in what was to be the auspicious rebirth of legend as literature, a potentially crippling deformity has crept in. The contrast between Chrétien's frequently disrupted Arthurian community and the far more vigorous and efficient communities of his immediate predecessors could hardly be more acute, and the critical question to ask is why such an abrupt modification occurred. Indeed, a major concern of this study will be to determine what new coherence emerges from Chrétien's representation of the Arthurian world.

Rather than focus exclusively on the particularities of Chrétien's narratives at this particular point in the tradition, one might of course consider him as the initiator of one of two dominant, apparently contrary, currents that run throughout the later medieval Arthurian tradition. On the one hand, the considerably idealized Arthur in the synoptic narratives of Geoffrey and Wace is recalled in some later contexts, so that by the fourteenth century he had earned a place among the Nine Worthies.[5] On the other hand, after Chrétien, many romances in verse and prose depict Arthur as a problematic figure who, depending upon which of the many texts is considered, is not uncommonly depressed, lethargic, hesitant, powerless, concupiscent, incestuous, short-sighted, or even apparently senile.[6]

The likelihood of identifying a stable intertextual portrayal of the renowned realm as we move from Chrétien to later writers is thus diminished by the fact that there was no consistently held, canonically "medieval" attitude toward Arthurian story and its regal protagonist. During the Middle Ages, the Arthurian matter proved itself adaptable to a wide array of positive and negative schemes.[7] As a result of the incessant *mouvance* of the myth, heirs of the rich legacy of Chrétien and of *his* precursors repeatedly appropriated and reinvested the tradition in ways that were not always in harmony with those of their forebears.[8] Consequently, there is no monolithic medieval portrayal of Arthur or of his reign, no invariable signification attributable to its principal emblems such as the Round Table and the grail, no single idea of order equally pertinent to all Arthurian works. Despite the wealth of detail shared by these narratives, they do not disclose a consistent or homogeneous world-view encompassing the entire medieval Arthurian tradition,[9] and we must avoid the pitfalls of undue generalization. It cannot be assumed, for example, that the objectives of Chrétien's continuators were necessarily those of the author of *Le Conte du graal*, or that the representations of customs in the prose *Quête du saint graal* provide an adequate gloss for those in the earlier verse romances.[10] Nor should the uniqueness of a specific work be overlooked in an effort to locate intertextual coherence shared among a plurality of texts, whether such a work belongs within a set of texts produced by a single author like Chrétien de Troyes or is part of a cycle involving multiple authorship.

Introduction

How, then, do we undertake to read the Arthurian world of Chrétien de Troyes? While this essay is by no means the first to deal with all of Chrétien's Arthurian romances, it is undertaken in recognition of a certain number of issues that have not been fully addressed in previous discussions. One of these has to do with the numerous suggestions throughout the five romances that the individuality of each poem conveys not only its comprehensive meaning as an independent entity, but also its signification as part of a coherence developed progressively through the five works and perceptible only on the basis of a reading of the ensemble as a whole. In the history of fictive forms, it was during the nineteenth century, not the twelfth, that vast interrelated textual ensembles developed in a grandly self-conscious fashion. The *Comédie humaine* of Balzac, Zola's *Rougon-Macquart*, and numerous later multi-novel ventures all attest to a conscious and persistent effort to locate the discrete textuality of a given novel within a global coherence gradually made apparent by the cumulative revelations concerning it as they emanate from successive works in the series. While Chrétien left no treatise nor any explicit mention of a transtextual design – certainly nothing akin to, say, Balzac's Preface to *La Comédie humaine* – we should remember that it was his immediate successors who witnessed the rise of a powerful intertextualizing mentality, one which already foreshadows the post-Romantic novel's assimilation to massive narrative cycles. In the verse *Continuations* of the *Roman de Perceval*, the verse and prose versions of Robert de Boron's narratives, the Vulgate Cycle of Arthurian Romances, and cycles of the later *chansons de queste*, to cite only a few salient examples, there is ample evidence that highly intricate types of multi-textual organization had already reached advanced stages of development. Given Chrétien's proximity to these developments, we might well expect to identify ways in which his works, considered as an ensemble, anticipate them.

While that issue pertains to Chrétien's anticipation of the future of medieval Arthurian fiction, another concerns his relationship to its past. Previous inquiries have occasionally pondered Chrétien's apparently ambivalent attitude toward his immediate precursors, Geoffrey and Wace, acknowledging his sporadic indebtedness to them while also emphasizing notable contrasts.[11] Yet there remains a need to inquire further into the "why" of Chrétien's significant change of course in contrast to the direction already taken by his predecessors, and here it is especially important to weigh the consequences of an apparently revisionary attitude for his reconceptualization of tradition.

While situating Chrétien's Arthurian world within this dual context of fictions future and fictions past, we must also see how the *intra*textual cohesiveness of each of his works participates in the elaboration of an *inter*textual coherence that brings them all into harmony with a larger design. Once again previous scholarship helps to point the way: many studies have shown that the heroic intrigues in these works characteristically involve their principals in a monumental individual crisis midway through their exploits, so that much of the overall narrative dynamic is invested in the development and eruption of this dramatic interlude, followed thereafter by its progressive resolution. At the same time, however, the courtly microcosm of Arthur and his subjects is itself repeatedly disrupted by crises on a

4

collective scale, and these moments, as well as their connections with the individual crises of the heroic protagonists, have so far received much less attention than they deserve. Thus, in addition to a *textuality of crisis* which organizes the heroic intrigue, there is also an evident *intertextuality of crisis* elaborated in successive depictions of the Arthurian court, and this, too, calls for more attentive scrutiny.

Recent demonstrations of the close relationship between ethics and poetics during the Middle Ages, as well as the identification of affinities between poetic and legal fiction from Antiquity to the Renaissance, further underline the importance of examining more fully this aspect of medieval vernacular narrative,[12] and in particular the role played by legal themes in the development of intertextual coherence among medieval narratives. R. Howard Bloch has recently suggested that Chrétien's works anticipate the frequent depictions of deposition and inquest in later medieval French Arthurian romance.[13] An important aspect of the juridical dimension in Chrétien's works is determined by the prominence in each of customs, to which Erich Köhler called our attention more than a quarter of a century ago. Köhler's treatment of the question, however, was cursory and ultimately reductive in its rigid adherence to a socio-historical thesis that too often remained insensitive to textual detail;[14] the significance of customs to Chrétien's Arthurian world remains an open question in need of more detailed study.

These perspectives will govern the elaboration of the present study. On the basis of specific analytical criteria, the Arthurian community and its relationship to the depicted careers of its chivalric heroes will be traced through the series in Chapters 1 through 4. Emphasizing the two earliest works, *Erec et Enide* and *Cligés*, Chapter 1 will detail how Chrétien, early in his career as an Arthurian poet, effected an ostentatious and emphatic turn away from the Arthurian world depicted by Geoffrey and Wace while also laying out the parameters of an Arthurian "anterior order" more commensurate with the issues to be emphasized throughout his own works. Under the rubric of the "anterior order," two related perspectives help to identify aspects of the Arthurian society with which they are fundamentally concerned. In one, "anterior" designates the dominant social and political features represented in this fictive world, with particular emphasis on the kinds of attitudes, situations, and events that lead to the outbreak of its collective crises. The term seems particularly apt in a second sense, moreover, for behind Arthur's precarious, crisis-prone exercise of royal functions lies the influential anterior order of his father, Utherpandragon. Although rarely evoked within the corpus, this antecedent reign is nonetheless identified, in *Erec et Enide* and *Le Conte du graal*, as a juridical substratum of Arthur's own kingship, thus becoming a significant point of reference to circumstances prior to those narrated within the linear chronology of a story.[15] In short, *rex quondam*, as the first chapter will suggest, designates both the legacy of Uther and that aspect of Arthur which stands within the shadow of the absent father.

While Chapter 1 will show how Chrétien in his early poems reworks the Arthurian matter in terms of a significantly new orientation, Chapters 2 through 4 will take up in turn the three later romances – *Lancelot, ou le chevalier de la charrete*,

Yvain, ou le chevalier au lion, and *Perceval, ou le conte du graal* – in order to consider how this question is developed through the rest of the ensemble.[16] These three romances, along with *Erec et Enide*, will frequently be referred to as Chrétien's *customal romances* because of their extensive and prominent depiction of customs. In studies of medieval European institutions, the term "customal" is more familiar as a noun, used interchangeably with "customary" in the nominative, to designate the collections of written customs that began to emerge shortly after Chrétien's works had appeared.[17] The use of "customal" as an adjective in referring to these works will thus serve to underline their frequent evocations of literary customs, at the very moment, moreover, when repositories of written versions of customs – or customals – were soon to proliferate. We shall see that it is precisely the customal dimension which lends special shape and significance to Chrétien's Arthurian romances, both individually and as an ensemble.

Drawing upon the insights that emerge from these analyses of individual works, Chapter 5 will assess the intertextual relationships in Chrétien's Arthurian world, taking up in turn, under the rubrics of "crisis" and "custom," the two most important determinants of this larger coherence. Earlier analyses of the crises confronted individually by chivalric heroes and collectively by the court will now provide a means of tracing the progressive decline of the Arthurian community through the ensemble. It will also become apparent that this descending curve is directly related to the importance of customs which, within individual works as well as on an intertextual scale, serve to integrate and unify the aesthetic and the ethical import of these poems while also highlighting Chrétien's originality with regard to the reigning poetics of contemporaneous courtly authors. Moreover, we shall see that in the last, unfinished work the significant contrast between two orders of custom, reflecting two contrasting ideas of order, retrospectively establishes the transtextual coherence of the *œuvre* as a whole.

Finally, the Conclusion will consider how Chrétien's imaginative, literary usage of customs prompts a reconsideration of socio-historical issues. Instead of the optimistic solidarity between the monarch and his "questing" upholders and guardians of custom that Erich Köhler had perceived in these works, there emerges an essentially negative appraisal of customs on the part of the poet. A number of episodes throughout the series cumulatively indicate that customs, which rely exclusively on oral tradition, actually entail interruption of juridical continuity and imperil social and political stability. Whence Chrétien's innovative use of Arthurian fiction in order to animate a possible world that mounts a nuanced critique of contemporaneous institutions, one which significantly anticipates the early thirteenth-century trend toward the establishment of written records of customal procedures.

In the light of the synthesis elaborated in Chapter 5 and the Conclusion, the notion of "once and future fictions" will assume a twofold coherence. In more general terms, it will have designated the development of Arthurian narratives from one incarnation to the next, as in the literary-historical dynamic that distinguishes Chrétien from his precursors while anticipating his successors. In a more restricted sense made possible by the findings of this study, it will

Introduction

comprehend the aesthetic and poetic achievements as well as the ethical and socio-cultural concerns of a major poet within the Arthurian tradition. From this latter perspective, it is Chrétien's customs that are perceived as the "once and future fictions" which underlie his intertextuality of crisis. While animating and unifying his Arthurian world, they become the hallmark, both of his criticism of feudal institutions, and of his originality and maturity as narrative poet.

Rex quondam: Arthurian tradition and the anterior order

The portrayal of King Arthur in the romances of Chrétien de Troyes contains scant evidence of a vigorous rise to power or of a glorious *regnum*, as in the magnificent career recorded by Geoffrey of Monmouth and Wace. These forerunners are not entirely obscured in Chrétien's narratives, however. Indeed, they are emphatically brought to mind in the first part of *Cligés*. An examination of Arthur and his court as they initially appear in what some critics have viewed as the least Arthurian of all of Chrétien's romances will enable us, in the first part of this chapter, to see how *Cligés* provided a means of effecting a dramatic turn away from the powerful example set by immediate precursors. The rest of the chapter will reveal how in his first work, *Erec et Enide*, Chrétien was from the very outset of his career already reconceptualizing the Arthurian world, in an effort to delineate a fictive *anterior order* against the background of which to set forth a fresh portrayal of Arthur as a complex, often ineffectual figure. In sum, we shall begin to see in this chapter how *Cligés* and *Erec* offer two different yet complementary departures from the earlier twelfth-century tradition that together orientate Chrétien's subsequent development of Arthurian romances in a significantly new direction.

ANTECEDENT TRADITION AND CHRETIEN'S REVISIONARY DESIGN: CLIGES

In *Cligés*, it is the universal renown of Arthur and his court that prompts Alexandre and his Byzantine companions at arms to journey to England, to receive knighthood at Arthur's hand "or not at all" (vv. 336ff.). The Arthur of Geoffrey and Wace had sent all of Europe into a frenzy and set Rome on the defensive; the fame of Chrétien's Arthur has extended even farther, to the very hub of the Eastern Empire. In his presence, the young foreigners find themselves "Devant le meillor roi del mont/Qui onques fust ne ja mes soit" ("Before the world's greatest king, that ever was or ever will be," vv. 304-5)[1] From without, Arthur's kingdom is perceived as the paragon of order, its chivalry *nec plus ultra*, the ideal exemplar of knighthood; in the ensuing developments, the Arthurian court will delegate its standards of chivalry to aspirants from the rim of the known world and extend its lineage to the throne of Constantinople. Through the good offices of the queen and the imperious constraints of Amor, Alexandre will marry into the Arthurian court, united with Soredamors, Gauvain's sister and Arthur's niece. Their son Cligés will retrace his father's itinerary and tourney his way to recognition by his Arthurian kin; eventually, he and Fénice will appeal to the Arthurian court as arbiter of their grievance against his paternal uncle Alis, whose death forestalls the clash of East and West, an Arthurian world war. Through all of this, the Arthurian realm remains a respected and powerful domain to whose standard the world is drawn.[2] For those outsiders mesmerized by its glory, it is not their land but Arthur's which promises adventure. When Alexandre expresses a desire to seek out alien lands – "la terre estrange" (v. 148) – he is mindful not of the wonders of the forest, but of the marvels of courtliness and prowess awaiting him at Arthur's court. There is much here to suggest, then, that Chrétien has taken his cue for the Arthurianization of *Cligés* from his immediate predecessors, for whom Arthur was also the greatest "Qui onques fust ne ja mes soit."

This impression is intensified by the way in which Chrétien contextualizes the nascent love of Alexandre and Soredamors within the civil crisis at Arthur's court. For reasons which remain wholly unexplained, Arthur decides upon a prolonged stay in Brittany, and on the advice of his baronial council he designates Angrés, the Count of Windsor, as regent during his absence (vv. 416ff.). Description of the court's long and peaceful months in Brittany is limited to what transpires in the minds of Alexandre and Soredamors as each ruminates on the joy and pain of unavowed love (vv. 435–1038). After word arrives that Angrés, intent upon usurping Arthur's authority (vv. 1041ff.), has assembled an army and seized London, Arthur's militant return to England and his response to this act of treason are developed at length. Chrétien describes Arthur's siege of Angrés' stronghold at Windsor Castle in a long passage laden with topographical detail and military strategy, featuring the triumphant cunning and prowess of Alexandre (vv. 1625–2169). Nowhere else in his works does Chrétien come as close to the pseudo-historical, epic style of Wace.[3] Moreover, the episode is concluded by an Arthur who resembles Wace's forceful monarch. Knowing that the king would unhesitatingly execute his prisoners, Alexandre submits the first four to the queen instead. Arthur intervenes, however, convening his knights to deliberate their fate (vv. 1333ff.), and while they consider various forms of punishment, he himself determines that the traitors will be mercilessly drawn before Windsor Castle, as an appropriate warning to the enemy within. Later, after Alexandre has captured the last of the outlaws, he counsels them to put themselves humbly at Arthur's mercy, to avoid execution. Arthur is indeed swayed by their humility, while toward Angrés, the instigator of the insurrection, he acts swiftly:

> Et li rois n'a plus atandu
> Que lors n'an face sa justise.   (vv. 2170–1)

And the king waited no longer to exact his justice.

Thus he conforms to Wace's portrait of the monarch:

> Contre orguelleus fu orgueilleus
> Et contre humble dolz et piteus.   (*Brut*, vv. 479–80)

Toward the arrogant he was pitiless; toward the humble, gentle and compassionate.

9

The primary model for this long episode, as scholars have often pointed out, is Mordret's treason in the *Roman de Brut*.[4] Pelan likens the role of Angrés to that of Mordret, observing that Chrétien "thus brought into his romance ... a pseudo-historical event, contenting himself simply with substitution of an invented name, Angrés, for the real name of the rebel".[5] It will be recalled from circumstances depicted by Geoffrey and Wace that their Arthur had at this point risen to near the apogee of his career as a military conqueror, and had but to seize Rome in order to make it complete. The reversal of his fortune involved a double betrayal: not only had his nephew Mordret seized the realm, with the help of Saxons, Scots, Picts, and Irish; Guenevere had espoused the traitor and his cause. As in *Cligés*, Arthur returned from the Continent to reclaim his kingdom. In the earlier works, however, he was to confront not Angrés but his own nephew, Gauvain's brother, in successive battles, in the first of which Mordret was routed but Gauvain died, while Guenevere took refuge in a convent. Arthur pursued Mordret through a second pitched battle, until in a third he killed his treacherous kinsman; he himself sustained mortal wounds and, in Wace's version, was spirited off to the isle of Avalon to be healed.

These antecedents allow us to measure the degree of Chrétien's indebtedness. The intertextual recall is unmistakable, but what stand out are the contrasts. In the two earlier texts, this moment marks the greatest peripeteia of the entire account of Arthur's monarchy, the shattering trauma that will, with dizzying rapidity, alter forever the course of Arthur's fortunes and bring his reign to an end in a maelstrom of treason, adultery, incest, and murder. Why, then, of all the potentially useful episodes from the Arthurian universe created by Geoffrey and Wace, would Chrétien have chosen to evoke precisely the one which so abruptly ushered in the tragic outcome of an otherwise glorious story? Why did Chrétien recast an episode with such apocalyptic overtones – as thirteenth-century authors would recognize – into a charming interlace of love and war with a comic dénouement?[6]

In Chrétien's return to the great traumatic moment in the earlier twelfth-century synoptic account of Arthur's reign, we may recognize a project of rewriting at the basic "fault" of Arthurian fiction, to evoke a geological metaphor, that is, a project which reinforces that point in the edifice which is most vulnerable to stress and which when disturbed may provoke a major upheaval involving structural breakdown. In choosing this critical moment rather than some other, Chrétien would seem to be singling out the fault line, as it were, in the comprehensive traditional version, set into memory as recently as the preceding generation, so as to reduce the traditional weight it bears and thus reduce its potentially negative influence on his own re-fictionalization of Arthur's reign. For that last, long crossing from the Continent to Britain had been a harbinger of the inexorable end, of Arthur's futile effort to "at least set [his] lands in order" (Eliot), to *tenir terre*. It is now rewritten with a wholly positive outcome: Mordret again dies, in the guise of his double, Angrés, but this time Arthur remains masterfully in charge of meting out justice, while the faithful queen discourses on the virtues of marital love and Gauvain thrives among the living. As if to underline more emphatically the contrast with earlier tradition, the Arthur in *Cligés* will offer Alexandre any recompense "Fors las corone et la reïne" ("except the crown and the queen," v. 2185), precisely the two entities wrested from him in the traditional analogue of this episode. Thus does Chrétien ensure that *his* Arthurian fiction will not be that of his precursors. At issue is a denial of the Arthurian cycle's crepuscular phase, its turn toward the twilight of closure. The tragic finality of the former fiction will not mar the future of Chrétien's fictive portrayal of "the greatest king that ever was *or ever will be.*"

The episode devoted to the treason of Angrés in *Cligés* thus appears to be the product of a *revisionary design* on the part of the Champenois poet. In it we may also recognize what Harold Bloom has called the "anxiety of influence" which, in his view, is frequently at the origin of such designs in the evolving history of traditions.[7] Among the revisionary types, or "ratios," identified by Bloom, this description comes close to identifying the revisionary dynamic apparent in this instance: "A poet swerves away from his precursor . . . This appears as a corrective movement in his own poem, which implies that the precursor poem went accurately up to a certain point, but then should have swerved, precisely in the direction that the new poem moves".[8] Here is the revisionist tactic of the "strong poet" coming to terms with the potentially stifling influence of the strong "Poetic Father" by executing a salutary change of course: "the true history of modern poetry would be the accurate recording of these revisionary swerves."[9] What about the history of the medieval Arthurian tradition? It would be of the utmost interest to ponder the successive "swervings" as we go from, say, *Le Conte du graal* to the Continuations, from verse to prose in the works of Robert de Boron, or even from work to work in the Vulgate Cycle. In the case at hand, the tradition of the Father (and, indeed, the Grandfather) of French Arthurian fiction will be assumed by the son, but only through the strong intertextual statement of turning away from the trail they had blazed. The heritage of the earlier authors is thus modified by their immediate heir. In order to give Arthur new life, Chrétien must kill Mordret again, in the form of his fictive double, while radically altering the circumstances of his death. The anterior literary order must be altered to ensure the future of the fiction. A Promethean challenge: it is a matter of the son's unbinding himself from the sinews binding, and thus closing off, the fiction of the father. To what end, then? If not Arthur's tragic mortality, as in Geoffrey, nor his potential return, as in Wace, what is the objective of this change of course which forecloses on the basic fault and pre-empts the traditional endings? Why, in short, is Chrétien's Arthur not the *rex quondam* of Geoffrey and Wace, why does Chrétien's account of Arthur's era contrast so markedly with the account by his predecessors?

On the limited evidence provided by the substitution of Angrés for Mordret, a seemingly plausible answer might be that Chrétien was rejecting the fatal turning point in the Arthurian tradition as part of a larger effort to replace the internally flawed world of Arthurian society in Geoffrey and Wace with a new, idealized, non-problematic, possibly even utopian Arthurian society. After all, in his rewriting of the treason of Mordret, Chrétien substitutes for an embattled monarch a vigorous, decisive, effective agent of sanction. According to this view, Chrétien would have gone straight back to the basic fault, this time in the ethical sense of the term, in order to redeem it.

Such an hypothesis becomes untenable, however, as soon as the rewritten episode is considered against the background of *Cligés* in its entirety and, *a fortiori*, within the entire corpus of Chrétien's Arthurian romances. In *Cligés*, there is a hint that Arthur's severity in dealing with the first four prisoners is excessive, at least in the estimation of Alexandre and the queen (vv. 1337ff.). Moreover, in addition to the many ironies at other levels of this work, this very episode sets up the Arthurian court as the greatest standard of chivalric excellence the world has ever known, and then proceeds to award all of the accolades to the shrewd stratagem and chivalric brilliance of the newcomers from afar. If Arthur is indeed the agent of sanction, the lawgiver and adjudicator of this society, it is the outsider, the Greek, who assumes *active* responsibility for the viability of its values. This detail provides an ironic recall of the *westward* progression of political and intellectual supremacy – from Greece, thence to Rome and France – as evoked in the Prologue, vv. 28ff.[10] The military aspect of the topos of *translatio studii et imperii* is literalized by the migratory chivalry of Alexandre and his men![11] A much later episode again casts Arthur in a less than flattering light. After Cligés and Fénice have been denounced to Alis, the couple turn for help to Arthur, who immediately prepares to launch a full-scale war of succession with Greece. As in the earlier portrayal of Arthur beneath the walls of Windsor Castle, there is a hint here of impulsiveness, suggesting a propensity to excessive measures.

Within the larger context of the five romances, of course, it is readily apparent that the vision of Arthurian society presented by Chrétien is profoundly problematical. While some readers have emphasized the idealized nature of the Arthurian polity,[12] or adduced evidence of certain positive or even utopian qualities,[13] one also finds through the corpus an apparent intensification of the problems confronted by Arthur's realm and those in proximity to it. Chrétien's Arthur never really represents "the ideal king of an ideal realm,"[14] nor does the Round Table signify – at least not in Chrétien – "the embodiment of a peaceful and prosperous community."[15] On the other hand, critics sometimes delineate the problematic aspects of Chrétien's Arthur in excessively general terms. Thus one observer sees Arthur as "weak – either petty or impotent – although . . . a cultivated gentleman [whose] time is passed entirely on leisure pursuits . . . He is surrounded by knights, not by counselors, by self-seeking individualists, not by loyal subjects."[16] Another notes: "Only in *Cligés* does Arthur wage war personally in the campaign against Angrés, the Ganelon or Mordred of that romance . . . Chrétien's Arthur is not only a figurehead, a static monarch, but a 'roi fainéant' whose weakness the poet mentions again and again and not without humor."[17] Of Chrétien's figure of Arthur as a *rex inutilis*, yet another says that the king "often appears helpless as much from literary convention as from any political bias on the part of the poet or his audience"[18] – although one wonders, in the light of positive portrayals by Geoffrey and Wace, what specific antecedents establish the "convention" allegedly in use by Chrétien.

On balance, over the course of these works there does occur an intermittently negative appraisal of both Arthur and his court, one that seems to be the most acute when a naïve Perceval encounters a speechless Arthur for whom the immediate circumstances are out of control (*Le Conte du graal*, vv. 909ff). These developments have been variously interpreted, as, for example, the products of Chrétien's increasingly severe "view of Arthur's spiritual limitations";[19] as the depiction of a king "unworthy of his brilliant reputation";[20] as a gerontological problem;[21] as a result of the poet's change from royal to noble patronage in the course of his career;[22] even as evidence of a desire to damage or have done entirely with the legend of a millennial or allegedly historical personage.[23] These views cumulatively reveal that no consensus has emerged concerning the nature of Chrétien's monarch, that no single depiction of Arthur runs unmodified through these romances, and that the vigorous and emphatic Arthur of *Cligés* contrasts with his portrayal elsewhere, particularly in later works.

The problem is compounded by divergent attitudes toward the monarch within a single work. The most striking example of the coexistence of favorable and unfavorable perspectives is his mother's evocation, addressed to Gauvain in *Le Conte du graal*, of her son's profile as a Puer Senex:

> —Biax sire, fait ele, et li rois
> Artus, coment se contient ore?"
> —"Miex qu'il ne fist enques encore,
> Plus sains, plus legiers et plus fors."
> —"Par foi, sire, ce n'est pas tors,
> Qu'il est enfes, li rois Artus;
> S'il a cent ans, s'en a pas plus,
> Ne plus n'en puet il pas avoir."　　(*Conte du graal*, vv. 8164–71)

"Good sir," she says, "and King Arthur, how is he nowadays?" "Better than ever, more healthy, agile and strong." "In faith, sir, that must be true, for he's but a child, King Arthur. If he's a hundred, he's no older, nor can he be any older."

Here, in Chrétien's last work, we find Arthur both seemingly "worse than ever," as Perceval first encounters him, and yet "never better," according to Gauvain. Chrétien's general tendency, however, is toward portrayal of an Arthur who, as he recedes into the background behind his illustrious knights, either slumbers or is reduced to anguished silence. Slightly altered, the words of General MacArthur are broadly descriptive of Chrétien's ruler: "Old Arthur never dies; he just fades away."

It is evident at least that the constitutive properties of Chrétien's Arthurian universe cannot adequately be defined merely in contrast with antecedent literary tradition, nor at this point can they be formulated in a comprehensive characterization. Although in *Cligés* one finds persuasive evidence of a revisionary swerving away from precedents within the tradition, the clues as to why this occurred and to its significance are more likely to emerge from an attentive examination of the corpus as a whole. This necessitates a change of perspective, from the antecedent tradition of literary history to the anterior order within the fictive dimension of Chrétien's poems. Turning from the traditional Arthur reflected in *Cligés* to the Arthur contextualized in *Erec et Enide* by the anterior order of Uther, it will become apparent that submission to the law of the father and subversion of the anterior tradition go hand in hand.

Arthur and Erec

Let us begin at the end of *Erec*, with the magnificent *descriptio* of a coronation that brings the romance to a close (vv. 6585–878). This event occurs at Nantes on Christmas Day, amidst the largest assembly of nobility and clergy ever convoked for the sacring of a king. Our attention is directed to the coronation robe, to details depicting the Quadrivium. Geometry measures the heavens, plumbs the depths of the sea, and spans the firmament; Arithmetic numbers, one by one, drops of water, stones, leaves, and stars; Music harmonizes the instruments of mankind; while Astronomy, chief among the arts, takes wise counsel of sun, moon, and stars concerning past and future (vv. 6682–728). In the right hand of the newly anointed king is an emerald sceptre which bears likenesses of all earthly creatures, fish and fowl, beast and man (vv. 6808–23). With the regal synecdoches of orb and gown, throne and crown, Chrétien elaborates a symbolic portrait of the king as mediator of heaven and earth, divine and human law, nature and culture. Around this static figure crystallizes the idealized image of the monarch as the measure of the universe. What is more remarkable still in this, the most self-consciously lavish description of royalty in all of Chrétien's romances, is that the king thus arrayed is Erec and not Arthur, whose accessory function it is to invest this young ruler with his patrimony and sponsor the festive coronation (vv. 6485ff.). The narrative had followed Erec as he won a bride, then succumbed to a phase of idleness before transcending his former glory in the achievement of an exemplary, communally beneficial knighthood. Now as he at last accedes to the throne of his late father, similarity conceals contrast. He and Arthur together merely *seem* to represent a nearly complete cycle of kingship: as Erec, the nascent hero-king, and Arthur, the avuncular sovereign, converge in the former's coronation, there is a largely formal veneer suggestive of continuity and of tradition preserved.

For this scene does not substantiate the claim that Arthur is "the symbol of an ideal feudal state represented as a guarantor of a perfect human order."[24] The events leading up to the coronation make this an unduly optimistic assessment. Initially, Arthur is identified as an hereditary monarch whose father, Utherpandragon, had established the principles of his own reign, including the supposedly beneficial Custom of the White Stag which Arthur at the outset intends to maintain. He vigorously defends this position with a solemn discourse on the duties of the monarch, who must uphold not only custom, but truth, faith, justice, law, order, and equity.[25] As I have shown at length elsewhere,[26] however, the Custom of the White Stag which opens the romance dramatizes a basic ideological rift. On one side stands a monarch whose lineally founded feudal order depends for its vitality and harmony on the collective support of his vassals; on the other, there

14

has emerged a newer chivalric mentality which self-servingly sets aside collective support of the monarchy's principles of order in favor of individual distinction according to the values of courtly chivalry.

The volatile knights at Arthur's court, each of whom is eager to further his own interests at the expense of the traditional observance of the royal custom, bring to mind the youthful chivalric ambition of the twelfth-century "jeune" described by Georges Duby.[27] Their presence at court creates an enduring situation of potential anarchy that threatens the viability of authority based on communal assent. Much later in the course of the romance, Erec demonstrates that the tension between monarchy and chivalry can be overcome: in the "Joie de la Cort" episode, he places courtly chivalry at the service of a disrupted monarchy while revealing that such service may nonetheless satisfy a chivalric need for self-esteem. While Erec's coronation thus consecrates the compatibility of monarchy and chivalry, Arthur has been identified with an *anterior order* whose juridical institutions clash with the individualistic aspirations of his knights. It is thus the mediatory experience of Erec, rather than the precarious order of Arthur, which is ceremoniously recognized at the end of *Erec et Enide*.[28]

Sovereign sponsorship

The problematic situation of Arthur in *Erec* will be examined in further detail later in this chapter. It is already apparent, however, that Chrétien's initial romance creates a dichotomy between the ultimate significance of the hero's achievement and the values and concerns of the Arthurian monarchy. The fact that Erec, in his principal exploits, is not exclusively or even primarily in service to Arthur's objective of perpetuating unmodified an idealized anterior order hints at the possibility that there is no perfect congruence between the heroic sphere of values and those that comprise the most cherished political ideals of this monarch. While it certainly cannot be maintained that the overall impression generated by the final scene of Chrétien's first romance is one of incompatibility between the two spheres, this scene does raise questions as to the nature of Arthur's relationship to Erec and, by extension, to the protagonists of later works, where further discrepancies of outlook between king and hero are apparent. There is thus a need at this point to evaluate the status of Arthur with regard to the narrative dynamic within which Chrétien develops the heroic protagonist's sphere of actions. A preliminary analysis of the degree to which Arthur participates, in terms of functions and values, in the narrative organization of the heroic intrigues is indispensable to a satisfactory understanding of his crucial role in "Li premiers vers" of *Erec*; it will also be helpful in assessing his general significance in all five romances.

Prior to assessing the import of King Arthur to the intrigues of Chrétien's Arthurian romances, they can be considered briefly in terms of their presentation of an heroic career. Examining them in this fashion, one begins to see that they all tend to divide roughly into two sections comprising multiple episodes, so as to create an overall form which modern scholars have often discussed under the rubric of "bipartition."[29]

In each of the first four romances, this bipartite pattern is implemented in a unique way. At the end of an overlong honeymoon following upon Erec's winning of a bride and the accolades of the Arthurian court, Enide's fateful *parole* makes him aware of his dereliction of chivalric duty and sends the couple into a new series of adventures leading to recovery and then transcendence of their former glory.[30] The first half of *Cligés* establishes Cligés as heir-apparent to the throne of Constantinople, then suddenly undermines this prospect when Alis takes Fénice as his bride; resolution of this crisis begins at the precise numerical midpoint of the romance, with the narcotically induced delusion of Alis, followed in the second half by further ruses and reversals that eventually place Cligés and Fénice on the Byzantine throne.[31] The consequences of a broken promise occasion the madness that initiates Yvain's long crisis, after which he will eventually recover Laudine's good graces through his chivalric exploits under an assumed identity.[32] Lancelot's initial itinerary in the direction of the queen is completed despite the many obstacles imposed by Meleagant; after the hero's nocturnal tryst, however, Meleagant's accusatory intervention reactivates and further complicates the juridical crisis that Lancelot will resolve only at the end of a second itinerary, this time in the direction of Arthur's court, though again despite the formidable obstacles contrived by his adversary.[33] Although incomplete, Chrétien's final romance embodies a *double* implementation of the pattern. Perceval's initial series of adventures culminates in his triumphant return to Arthur's court, where the Hideous Damsel's excoriation of his failure at the Grail Castle provokes the pivotal crisis that sends him off in an effort to rectify his error. Yet this scene also *initiates* the adventures of Gauvain, whose crisis occurs later on: just after he has successfully ended the enchantments at the castle of his maternal kin, his misgivings concerning assumption of the seigneurial duties at this remote refuge initiate a new series of qualifying trials that remain incomplete when this romance breaks off.

This brief survey of the comprehensive narrative organization of Chrétien's Arthurian fictions will suffice to suggest that each work in its own unique way tends to develop what might appropriately be identified as a *textuality of crisis*, according to which each poem relates two fictive phases through a median crisis.[34] While it may vary in length, this critical transition is always located temporally between two complementary series of episodes, the former developing toward some problem that provokes the crisis, the latter discovering the means of its resolution in a sequel. The crisis is invariably a major turning point for the protagonist, whose experience prior to this moment is abruptly marked, in retrospect, by a negative evaluation that brings new awareness of a need for change. Accordingly, structural and thematic details in the post-crisis phase frequently evoke those in the pre-crisis counterpart, so as to show, by contrast, how the protagonist's later development rectifies specifically the problematic aspects of his exploits prior to the crisis.

It is not a matter here of examining Chrétien's hero-centered textuality of crisis at length, but rather of evoking it as a basis for discussion of Arthur's participation in the elaboration of the heroic intrigues that make up these works. We might well assume that his involvement would be considerable. If one thinks in terms of the much simpler types of folk narrative that were not at all unfamiliar to medieval audiences, it must be admitted that a monarch's sponsorship and evaluation of heroic performance in these tales is far from uncommon. Thus might the king in a folktale initially enjoin the hero to rescue the realm from the ravages of a dragon, motivating the hero's performance by emphasizing his own concern for upholding the ideals of the realm against the threat of malevolent and destructive influences from afar. When the hero returns with the slain dragon's tongue, the king, now in a role which is less catalytic and more adjudicative, awards due recognition of the hero's performance, as well as appropriate accolades – marriage to his daughter, property, gold, and so on – as a positive evaluation of the exploit. This rudimentary example of an intrigue characteristic of popular prototypes of romance shows how heroic endeavor can be closely allied to the significant interventions of the monarch. Rather than evolving in complete autonomy from the communal sphere and its values, the hero is initially motivated to perform by, and ultimately recognized for his performance on behalf of, this sphere as it is represented to him through the offices of the monarch. Whence a remarkable degree of solidarity, indeed, of reciprocity, between hero and king in the folktale.

In modern narrative theory, this intimate relationship has in fact been described by A. J. Greimas in terms of a general model of agency in narrative. This model identifies as "actants" six functional categories – subject, object, addressor, addressee, adjuvant, opponent – involved in the accomplishment or undergoing of an act.[35] In this context, the *subject* – represented by the hero in folktales – is said to assume and to perform "contractual" obligations which, when accomplished, are judged favorably or unfavorably.[36] The subject is not typically the contracting or sanctioning agent, however. The latter role is fulfilled by the *addressor* or *sender* (Fr. *destinateur*),[37] typically represented in folktales by the king. In fact, as we have seen in our example from a folktale, the actantial role of the addressor involves *two* distinct functions, one before and one after the subject's performance. Initially, the addressor is said to transform, through various forms of manipulation, an *addressee* or *receiver* (Fr. *destinataire*) into a competent *subject*. If the subject acts at its own behest, thus also assuming the function of the addressor, then only one, compound role is involved, as when the king is also the hero. Otherwise separate "actors" assume the distinct roles of addressor and addressee-turned-subject. In our folktale, for example, the hero is constituted as subject by virtue of the king's efforts, as *instigative addressor* or sender, to invest the role of the subject with an actor whose superlative qualities will ensure the success of the perilous encounter with the dragon. Upon the hero's completion of this mission, the king, now in the role of *sanctioning addressor*, evaluates this accomplishment: at the outset the king had *mobilized* the heroic subject; now he becomes the *adjudicator* that *sanctions* positively the subject's heroic performance.

Mindful of both the relation of solidarity between hero and king in the folktale and the more formal description of this type of relationship from a theoretical perspective, we may usefully rephrase the question of Arthur's relationship to the heroes in Chrétien's romances: is it in the doubly powerful role of the addressor, who initially motivates the hero's performance and ultimately rewards its completion with positive sanctions, that Arthur finds his place in the narrative organization of Chrétien's poems? In the antecedent tradition represented by Geoffrey and Wace Arthur is to a considerable extent both addressor and subject – a hero acting at his own behest as king. Has Chrétien removed Arthur from this double role which dominated the depictions of him by Geoffrey and Wace, in order to distribute the regulatory (and regal) functions of the addressor and the heroic performative functions of the subject between two different actors?

Some details in these five romances lend support to such a view. Consider the representational status of Arthur's court.[38] It is an intermittent feature, rarely dominating the action. Its locations vary among specific towns – Cardigan, Nantes, Winchester, Cardiff, and so on – and temporary locations, such as the banks of the Thames below Windsor Castle, an encampment in the wilderness, or Laudine's manor. In addition, it is less frequently the site of crucial events than a clearing-house of vital information: the hero or his captives hasten there to give account of their adventures, or the court itself moves elsewhere in search of information pertaining to its knights, as when Arthur visits Yvain and Gauvain after their year of tourneying or searches for the long-absent Perceval. This Arthurian court thus pertains more to the cognitive order than to the order of events *per se*. It bears many of the earmarks of a locus at which heroic performance is instigated and later evaluated.

In addition, within the conventional representational space of this court, Arthur does indeed display characteristics of the addressor. In *Erec*, he is the *lawgiver* who proclaims the traditional hunt and delivers an oration on the duties of kingship. He assumes an instigative and regulatory role in *Cligés* as well, initiating the counter-offensive against Angrés and, later, against Alis; in *Le Chevalier au lion* he declares after having heard Calogrenant's story that the court must visit the fountain; in *Le Conte du graal* he mandates the court's search for Perceval. His role as an agent of various types of sanction is even more frequently in evidence. He brings the Custom of the White Stag to a peaceful resolution and convenes his vassals for public functions at which he presides; he takes swift and severe measures against Angrés and upholds the rightful succession to the throne of Constantinople; when the judicial combat between Yvain and Gauvain is at an impasse, he intervenes and imposes a settlement of the legacy disputed by two sisters. He recognizes the merits – and lineage – of Cligés after the tournament at Oxford and witnesses the accusations against Yvain, Perceval, and Gauvain; it is in his presence, appropriately enough, that Meleagant is beheaded. Even as the last romance breaks off, he is being summoned to witness the combat between Gauvain and Guiromelant. In all, an impressive inventory of evidence that, if Chrétien's Arthur almost never occupies the heroic role of the subject, he often appears in the role of addressor, both as instigator of heroic endeavor and as arbiter of its positive sanction.

Does the contrast between the Arthur of Geoffrey and Wace and Chrétien's Arthur therefore stem merely from a shift in the king's actantial status? Whereas they cast him in the glorious double role of the hero and king, of subject and addressor, according to the paradigm of the mythic hero-ruler, did Chrétien instead portray him in the authoritative role of the addressor, in keeping with the paradigm of the king who mandates and rewards the hero, as in the folktale? Is their hero-king of action to be contrasted with Chrétien's donor-king of obligation and judgment? After all, the heroic dynamic in which the subject achieves extraordinary objectives and receives positive sanctions for his achievements presupposes an addressor whose values motivate his efforts and reward his successes. While Chrétien's Arthur does at times play such a role, these are the crucial questions: Is Arthur the *only* addressor in this fiction? If not, is he the *primary* or *critical* addressor with regard to the subject's functions in Chrétien's textuality of crisis?

A brief sampling from each of the works suffices to show that he is *not* the only addressor in evidence, nor is he frequently even a primary one. As instigator, the addressor's function is to motivate the performance of a given subject in accordance with a specific system of values.[39] It has been shown that this role can be invested not only by individuals but by social, even cosmic forces.[40] Such is frequently the case in Chrétien's romances. In *Cligés*, Amor is the addressor of the nascent love of Alexandre and Soredamors (vv. 450, 464) identified by the narrator as well as in the lovers' monologues:

> "D'amor, qui justisier me vialt" (v. 481)

> "from Love, which seeks to control me"

> "Cest mal me fet Amors avoir" (v. 658)

> "Love causes me to have this illness"

> "S'Amors me chastie et menace
> Por aprandre et por anseignier,
> Doi je mon mestre desdaignier?" (vv. 674–6)

"If Love warns and threatens me so as to instruct and teach me, should I disdain my master?"

Amor plays a similar role in the story of Cligés and Fénice.[41] For both Alexandre and Cligés, the father is originally the primary addressor, as he equips his son or informs him to seek out Arthur (vv. 175ff., 2565); the role is then assumed, partly by Arthur as he bestows knighthood and motivates prowess, partly by Amor as the love intrigues take shape, and thereafter Love and Sovereignty motivate the plot, with Arthur playing only an incidental, ephemeral role in the second couple's bid for the Byzantine throne. In the *Charrete*, Amor is clearly Lancelot's primary addressor, either allegorically, as in the debate between Reison and Amors (vv. 360ff.), or as incarnated in the queen; the next chapter will comment further on the weakness of Arthur as an addressor in this work. In *Le Chevalier au lion*, both Amors and Haine motivate Yvain in the final combat, while, as will be seen in Chapter 3, Arthur provides no positive sanction for the heroes in this ultimate struggle.

Los, or reputation, is also frequently an instigator. At the beginning of *Erec et*

Enide, Erec alone among the knights has not obeyed Arthur's call to the hunt. When he soon finds himself involved in a quest to avenge his shame at having failed to protect the queen's maidservant from a dwarf's insult, it is this catalyst, not Arthur's, which takes him to his future bride, and after the couple's marriage it is Enide's admonition that he recover his "premier los" that reactivates him. Yvain, too, sets out to avenge shame, that of his cousin, and wins a bride in the process; thereafter, he encounters a series of addressors – Gauvain, Laudine's messenger, a hermit, a healing damsel, Lunete, various imperiled individuals and groups – but Arthur is not among them.[42] In both parts of the *Conte du graal*, the hero gradually becomes aware that an ultimate addressor is Sovereignty, invested in a community apart from the Arthurian court, while a number of intermediary addressors – Gornemanz, Blancheflor, the Hideous Damsel, Guingambresil, the Pucele as Mances Petites – serve at intervals to motivate specific heroic endeavors.

Where, then, in these heroic *Arthurian* narratives is any prominence given to Arthur as an effective addressor? As Paul Ricœur has observed with regard to the concept of addressor, the term *destinateur* emanates from the language of communication and evokes "the notion of message, thus of dispatching, thus of setting into motion, of dynamization."[43] Apart from his catalytic role in the first part of *Cligés*, Arthur is *not* the dispatcher who sends the hero into his principal and glorifying trials. Yet in all of the works, including *Cligés*, the heroic subject is marked from the very outset by a common bond with Arthurian chivalry. If at the beginning of his narrated career the hero is not already one of Arthur's knights, then he is – as is the case with Alexandre, Cligés, and Perceval – an ardent aspirant to this status and subsequently attains it (though lamely in the case of Arthur's defective knighting of Perceval)[44] – *before* moving into his principal exploits. Here, then, is where Arthur most extensively plays the role of addressor-catalyst: without exception, this occurs in the formative stage of the hero, prior to his principal exploits. The one quality all of Chrétien's heroes share is that they have all received the preliminary sanction of a type of knighthood broadly commensurate with Authurian standards by the time their principal adventures take place. Arthur thus fulfils the role of instigator in his capacity as a maker of knights. But only after this moment of the hero's deepest bond with Arthur, his greatest communicative sharing of the latter's values, does the principal narrative line begin to develop, and, as it does, it invariably involves the hero in some problematic apart from his formal intersubjective and symbolic relationship with Arthur.

It has often been suggested that Chrétien's Arthurian realm is a magnetic, "centripetal" locus, and indeed it is, to the extent that its fame attracts aspirants eager for conferral of knighthood at Arthur's hand. Yet this centripetal moment is but the prelude to the centrifugal itinerary that leads toward ultimate objectives that lie elsewhere. While the itinerant Arthurian knight may send captives back to the court, sojourn overnight or even celebrate his crowning achievements there, one invariably has a sense that his assistance to this court, no less than his involvement with its system of values, is secondary to concerns that ultimately lie beyond the sphere of this social universe.

The anterior order: *Erec et Enide*

From beginning to end, moreover, there is frequently a sense that the principal positive values of the heroic subject stem from other orders with which he is initially identified or to which his adventures will ultimately take him. All of Chrétien's protagonists, even Arthur's own nephew Gauvain, are at some point identified with a lineage or an origin apart from the court: Erec, son of King Lac; Alexandre and Cligés, sons, respectively, of a Byzantine emperor and of his heir-apparent; Yvain, son of Urïen; Perceval, son of a knight maimed in battle; Gauvain, son of Lot; even Lancelot "del Lac." In every instance of the heroic pattern identified earlier, the initial series of episodes take these heroes *away* from the court, be it to Carnant or Constantinople, the fountain realm, Gorre, the Castle of the Grail, or the Castle of Marvels. As for the crises, the negative sanction that initiates them by making the hero aware of his earlier shortcomings or his currently untenable situation emanates from some source other than the Arthurian court. Enide, Alis, Laudine's messenger, Meleagant, the Hideous Damsel, Guiromelant: all are figures who in some way help to disclose the negative import of the subject's situation with respect to an ultimate objective – reputation, love, matrimony, or sovereignty – that does not pertain directly to the Arthurian court or its well-being. Erec and Cligés will finally reign in their native lands, while Yvain will return to residence in the realm of the fountain. Perceval and Gauvain both seem destined to sovereignty in the realms of matrilineal kin. In the *Charrete*, the crisis initiates a second series of heroic adventures whose covert – and unrealized – objective is not ultimately Arthur's: while Lancelot does rid the court of Meleagant, he has amply demonstrated his passion for the queen and sworn abiding allegiance to King Bademagu's daughter in Gorre (vv. 6582ff.).[45]

Given this propensity to involve the subject-hero in the valorization and pursuit of objectives that stand apart, in more than a merely topographical way, from those identified by the Arthurian court, one begins to wonder about the precise significance of that court to this fiction. If the hero's stories are not a major part of Arthur's story, whatever *that* might be, if their textuality of crisis is not his, then what, once again, constitutes the internal dimension of Arthur and his court in this Arthurian fiction? Since consideration of Arthur in the role of addressor does not provide an answer, we may examine the opposite category in the actantial model, that of the *addressee* (Fr. *destinataire*).

The sovereign audience

Consider the lull following the climactic "Joie de la Cort" in *Erec et Enide*, where we find a dejected Arthur surrounded by a "mere" five hundred retainers (vv. 6364–438). Never had the court been so empty, says the narrator (perhaps ironically), nor the king so disconsolate. Whereupon the arrival of a messenger with news of the approach of Erec, Enide, and Guivret sends the court into a flurry of anticipation, culminating in the king's great joy as he greets the three of them. Calling for silence, the king appeals to Erec for news of his adventures, and when the noise abates Erec begins his story of the events preceding his arrival. At this point, the narrator intervenes and addresses *his* listener:

Mes cuidiez vos que je vos die
quex acoisons le fist movoir?
Naie; que bien savez le voir
et de ice, et d'autre chose,
si con ge la vos ai esclose:
li reconters me seroit griés,
que li contes n'est mie briés,
qui le voldroit recomancier,
et les paroles ragencier
si com il lor conta et dist...   (vv. 6420-9)

Do you assume, then, that I'll now tell you why he set out in the first place? Certainly not, for you know about this and much more, just as I have disclosed it to you. It would be a real chore to tell it all again, for the story is by no means so brief that anyone would want to begin anew and reiterate all the words just as he told it to them...

The story Erec is now telling Arthur is the very same one the narrator has just told his listener. Erec's fictive listener, Arthur, belongs to the category of the *narratee*, and it is in this role that he accedes to the actantial category of the addressee.[46]

In the works of Chrétien there are many occasions like this one, where a knight or one of his captives arrives and recounts events that took place elsewhere. In this same text, Yder, the queen's prisoner, tells the court how Erec defeated him (vv. 1183ff.), while after his arrival the latter explains Enide's background and the conditions upon which they took leave of her family (vv. 1534ff.); later, Erec slays two giants and sends the couple he rescued to report this incident to Arthur (vv. 4488ff.). In *Cligés*, a messenger tells Arthur of Angrés' betrayal (vv. 1045ff.), and Arthur listens to Cligés' grievance against Alis (vv. 6552ff). Upon hearing the queen retell the story of Calogrenant in *Yvain*, Arthur vows that the court will visit the marvelous fountain within a fortnight (vv. 649-72), and Gauvain's niece later tells Arthur how "le Chevalier au lion" saved her from captivity by the giant Harpin (vv. 4740ff.). Upon his return from Gorre, Lancelot explains to Arthur how Meleagant had held him captive in a tower and how he was released (*Charrete*, vv. 6854ff.). In the *Conte du graal*, Perceval sends Clamadeu des Illes and his seneschal to report to Arthur after defeating them (vv. 2313ff., 2692ff., 2831ff.).

These instances together show how frequently Arthur serves as the sovereign audience of chivalry. The purpose of these reiterations and recalls is *not* to inform the reader, who in every instance is already aware of what has transpired. Their main function is to inform the king, to make *him* the ultimate addressee of the knights' stories. R. Howard Bloch has shown how important this motif, adumbrated in Chrétien, will become in subsequent French Arthurian romance, in conformity with the "legal model" of "inquisitory deposition."[47] Having restored order elsewhere, the hero either sends back to court or returns with a "verbal record" of this achievement, so that, according to this view, "the hero is, in essence, one who becomes capable, through his accomplishments, of telling the tale which we read."[48] This formulation again reveals that, even in the aftermath of adventure, the heroic paradigm is subject-centered: the doer of remarkable deeds becomes in turn their narrator. The question remains, however, as to why *Arthur* is the narratee of these accounts. Is there truly a legal model in evidence here, which makes it important that Arthur sanction his knights' restoration of rectitude in remote locales?

Although Arthur is frequently an attentive narratee, his simply hearing an account of the hero's adventures, or even rewarding them with positive sanctions, is not his sole, or even his primary, concern at these moments. Consider again, briefly, Erec's narration of his feats. At first, this would seem to be an authentic *mise en abyme* – or internal duplication – of the narrator's story, up to the point where Erec begins to retell it to Arthur. It soon becomes apparent that this is not the case, for Erec told them

> des trois chevaliers qu'il conquist,
> et puis des cinc, et puis del conte
> qui feire li volt si grant honte;
> et puis des jaianz dist aprés;
> trestot en ordre pres a pres
> ses avantures lor conta
> jusque la ou il esfronta
> le conte qui sist au mangier,
> et con recovra son destrier. (vv. 6430–8)

about the three knights he conquered, then about the other five, then about the count who sought to shame him so; and then he spoke afterward about the giants; he told them his adventures in their precise order up until he confronted the count who sat at table, and how he recovered his charger.

Surprisingly, he stops short of narrating the most remarkable and significant adventure of all, the "Joie de la Cort," not because he wants to leave it out, but because Arthur abruptly cuts him off and changes the subject entirely:

> Erec, dist li rois, biax amis,
> or remanez an cest païs
> en ma cort, si con vos solez. (vv. 6439–41)

"Erec," said the king, "dear friend, stay in this country now, at my court, as you used to."

One might well expect that Arthur would eagerly hear about and positively sanction Erec's performance in the one adventure demonstrating how chivalric initiative, far from disrupting the court, can serve its interests – an account that might have held special interest for Arthur, whose juridical imperatives had clashed in "Li premiers vers" with his knights' individualistic objectives.[49] Thus Erec's mediation of such a contradiction in the "Joie de la Cort is now eclipsed by Arthurs preoccupation with whether or not he will remain. This suggests that the king is less concerned about the success of his knights in restoring order to remote lands than he is with augmenting numbers at his court. Indeed this was, according to the narrator, precisely the cause of his anguish prior to Erec's arrival (v. 6370).

This scene partakes of a more general affective tendency on Arthur's part. Distraught when his favorite knights are afield and no news has arrived as to their well-being, he is singularly euphoric when they or their captives augment his retinue. In *Erec*, Arthur agrees to pardon Yder on condition that he remain at court (vv. 1221ff.). Assembling all of his barons for the wedding of Erec and Enide, on account of which he "molt an fu liez en son corage" ("was exceedingly glad at heart," v. 1962), to heighten the "joy" of the occasion he knights a hundred apprentices and offers them splendid accoutrements. Joy is thus proportional to the number of Arthurian subjects present. The leitmotif of "joy" echoing through the account of the throngs at Erec's and Enide's coronation is another case in point, and the romance ends with the narrator's avowal of his incapacity to tally the number of kings, dukes, counts, and knights in attendance.[50] This attitude does not diminish in later works. In the opening scene of the *Charrete*, Arthur is justifiably dismayed by Meleagant's progressive decimation of his court (vv. 55ff.). When he first appears in *Le Conte du graal*, the king is angry because many of his esteemed companions of the Round Table have opportunistically departed for castles that offer "a better sojourn" (vv. 853ff.). Later, rather than learn from Clamadeu and his seneschal how Perceval had saved Blanchefleur's castle and liberated her vassals, he is preoccupied with the well-being of their conqueror, and chides Kay for having alienated him from the court with his sarcasm (v. 2878).

These moments would seem to suggest that if Arthur is indeed concerned about the performance of his knights in the maintenance of "a perfect human order," as some have maintained, it is above all else with *his own court* that he is so concerned, and not with those that lie beyond this relatively circumscribed, egocentric locus. Chrétien's heroes do bring justice and order to distant realms and remote wilderness settings. Yet there is little real concern on Arthur's part that his "heroes, like the historical *chevalier*, bring the law of Camelot – a sense of justice, prohibitions against senseless killing, theft, and rape – to the forest, a zone governed by the laws of chance and of the strongest."[51] The king would seem instead to betray a relative insensitivity to this process, except insofar as it contributes directly to the maintenance of local serenity within large assemblies of those who have received knighthood at his hand. The only time he actively undertakes to investigate a distant customal practice, that of the tempestuous fountain in *Le Chevalier au lion*, he does so with no concern for its ethical significance, but out of curiosity, to "see" (*veoir*) the rainfall activated by this marvel (vv. 649ff.). When he later resolves a disputed inheritance in favor of the younger of two sisters (vv. 6335ff.), an episode examined extensively in Chapter 3, his manipulative intervention suggests his desire to rid his own community of potential loss on account of a dispute that only indirectly concerns the court. While his knights often grow, during their post-crisis adventures, in their awareness of the value of altruistic service, Arthur's concern is consistently with the solidarity of his own court.

In sum, consideration of Arthur in the role of the addressee further underlines his negative depiction throughout the corpus. If in this role he does eventually participate in the narrative dimension of the heroic subject, this involvement is strictly indirect, entails no active role on his part, and seldom leads to positive sanction of the ethical or juridical import of his knights' principal achievements. If he initially sanctioned their identity as "Arthurian knight" by conferring knighthood upon them, his subsequent involvement is largely restricted to their maintenance of *the centripetal ideal of his realm*, that is, the ideal which brought them to him in their youth and which he fervently hopes will keep them with him after they return.

The anterior dimension: Arthur and Uther

Arthur's participation in the heroic dynamic of his knights is thus doubly problematic, in that he neither "receives" the stories of their victories in any full and consequential way nor "sends" many significant mandates or sanctions for their endeavours. As indicated above, Arthur's concern with the scope and significance of his court is restricted to its immediate constitution at any given moment. The least evidence of attrition suffices to provoke a negative reaction on his part, ranging from a kind of listless melancholy to an apparent anxiety for the well-being of the absentee.[52] This attitude could be summed up as the need for a *plenary presence*. The plenary occasions in Chrétien's romances are usually festive ones, sometimes coinciding with feast days in the liturgical calendar or involving major social functions; at other moments, when the focus shifts away from the court, Arthur is often typified by a motif of passivity, which could be called *the motif of the waiting king*, waiting, impatiently, for the return of the hero and the social – if not particularly ethical – reanimation of the court.

What need, other than festive animation, might be met by the plenary presence that Arthur perennially desires? The answer may suggest reasons why Arthur as both addressor and addressee often gives the appearance of being quite aloof from the heroic processes of his most illustrious companions. Arthur delivers his longest discourse in the entire corpus on one such occasion, at the end of "Li premiers vers" in *Erec*. Its immediate concern is whether or not Enide is to be the recipient of Arthur's ritual kiss, as prescribed by the custom. Yet this oration also broaches other, more general matters, and thus merits careful scrutiny in its entirety:

> Puis dist as chevaliers: "Seignor,
> que dites vos? Que vos an sanble?
> Ceste est de cors, de vis ansanble,
> et de quanqu'estuet a pucele,
> et la plus gente? et la plus bele?
> ne qui soit des la, ce me sanble,
> ou li ciax et la terre asanble?
> Je dis que droiz est antresait
> ceste l'enor del blanc cerf ait.
> Et vos, seignor, qu'an volez dire?
> Savez i vos rien contredire?
> Se nus i vialt metre desfanse,
> s'an die or androit ce qu'il panse.
> Je sui rois, si ne doi mantir,
> ne vilenie consantir,
> ne fauseté ne desmesure;
> reison doi garder et droiture,

qu'il apartient a leal roi
que il doit maintenir la loi,
verité, et foi, et justise.
Je ne voldroie an nule guise
fere deslëauté ne tort,
ne plus au foible que au fort;
n'est droiz que nus de moi se plaigne.
Et je ne voel pas que remaigne
la costume ne li usages
que siaut maintenir mes lignages.
De ce vos devroit il peser,
se ge vos voloie alever
autre costume et autre lois
que ne tint mes peres li rois.
L'usage Pandragon, mon pere,
qui rois estoit et emperere,
voel je garder et maintenir
que que il m'an doie avenir.
Or me dites toz voz talanz,
de voir dire ne soit nus lanz:
se ceste n'est de ma meison,
ele doit bien et par reison
le beisier del blanc cerf avoir;
la verité an voel savoir."

(vv. 1736–76)

Then he said to the knights: "Lords, what say you? What is your opinion? Is she not, in both body and countenance, and all that beseems a maiden, the noblest and the most beautiful that might be, I think, this side of where heaven meets earth? I say that it is absolutely right that she receive the honor of the white stag. And you, my lords, what say you? Have you any objection? If anyone wishes to forbid it, let him say now what he thinks. I am the king, and therefore must not lie, nor brook baseness, falsehood or excess. I must preserve reason and justice, for it befits the just king that he uphold the law, truth, faith, and justice. In no manner do I wish to do that which is disloyal or wrongful to either weak or strong. It is not right for anyone to have cause to complain of me. Nor do I desire that the custom and the practice that my forebears maintained go unobserved. It should weigh heavily upon you if I were to impose upon you customs and laws other than those kept by my father the king. I wish to keep and maintain the practice of my father Pandragon, who was king and emperor, at all costs to myself. So make your wishes fully known, be not slow to say the truth. Though the maiden is not of my household, she ought well and reasonably to receive the kiss of the white stag: I wish to know the truth of the matter."

This is Arthur's most extensive and formal plenary discourse in any of Chrétien's works, as well as his most direct statement concerning the duties of a monarch. A number of assumptions, both implicit and explicit, make it both difficult and revealing. Particularly striking is the fact that the entire intervention is constructed on a limited number of aspectual categories, within each of which there is an opposition of two terms: *mood* (declarative vs. interrogative); *degree* (absolute vs. contingent); *temporality* (timeless vs. temporal, past vs. present); *place* (presence vs. absence); *lineage* (self vs. ascendant); *modality* (duty, *devoir* vs. desire, *vouloir*).[53] What is most extraordinary about this speech, moreover, is that the oppositions in these categories are semanticized in such a way that neither term is wholly privileged.

There is, rather, either vacillation between the two, or drift from one to the other. We may consider them in turn:

Mood (declarative vs. interrogative): one dominant purpose of Arthur's speech is to declare his wishes concerning the custom. Just before he turns to address the assembly of barons, he agrees with the queen that even though Enide, won in another land, was not one of the damsels of the court when the enactment of the custom began, she is the most beautiful of those within the court, indeed in "the whole world." Moreover, she was won by chivalric initiative (vv. 1721–32). Yet each of the local knights had been eager to impose his own local favorite, again by chivalric means (vv. 49ff.). Arthur is aware of the potential for objection to a relative outsider's being honored. He privately *declares* his intention to designate Enide, "unless I am challenged" (vv. 1734–5), but recognizing the delicacy of the situation, he shifts from the declarative to the *interrogative* as he turns to the barons: 'Lords, what say you?" Implied is that the decision is to be theirs. It is only after this interrogative opening that he uses the *declarative*: "Je dis que droiz est antresait / ceste l'enor del blanc cerf ait" ("I say that it is absolutely right that she receive the honor of the white stag"). He quickly gives contingence to the categorical *antresait* by anaphorically returning to the interrogative refrain, "And you, my lords, what say you?" Presumably, this will be a mutual decision, befitting a feudal monarch as *primus inter pares*, although his remark before the hunt began had suggested his fondness for edicts: "parole que rois a dite/ne doit puis estre contredite" ("the king's world should not thereafter be disputed," vv. 61–2). Whence his careful qualification: "If anyone wishes to forbid it, let him say now what he thinks"; yet further on, he *declares* that he intends to maintain his father's usage, which includes the custom, "at all costs" (*que que il m'an doie avenir*).

Degree (absolute vs. contingent): having named what is *absolutely* right (*droiz antresait*) while at the same time making its choice *contingent* upon opinion, his *and* that of his barons, he turns to matters that bear more generally on the nature of monarchy: "Je sui rois". – I *am* the king. This phrase is *absolutist* and non-contingent; recourse to such an utterance as "I *am* the king" (as to its modern counterpart, "I *am* the President") has the effect of assimilating a *contingent* human presence to a presumably immutable category invested with authority.

Temporality (timeless vs. temporal): to the seemingly absolute, static social category of "king" are assimilated the values highlighted by an aura of absolute and *timeless stability*: "truth, faith, justice." Interestingly, this abstract trio follows yet another abstract term, the only one of the four preceded by a definite article: *the* law – "*la* loi". These seemingly timeless, transcendent values, however, are situated in time by Arthur's delineation of his duties and obligations. As for the temporal axis (past vs. present), the present reign is aligned with the one immediately preceding it and, apparently, more powerful still, for Pandragon was "emperere" as well as "rois." The single image of *the* law – with no indication as to whether divine, natural, or human, though presumably the latter in harmony with the other two – is rendered plural by the evocation of past *usages* and customs.[54] Against immutably timeless values applied in the seeming plenitude of the present, there is nonetheless an acute awareness of the passage of time, as well as of the past as being directly tributary to the present.

Place (presence vs. absence) and *lineage* (self vs. ascendant): the evocation of the royal father and his "lineage" as sources of authority undermines the notion of kingship as an authority *present* unto itself. The connotation of authority as a plenitude *in praesentia* is thus challenged in the image of forebears absented by death. Selfhood predicated as an absolute, present, non-contingent category – "Je sui rois" – is offset by the image of royal selfhood invested by the alterity of the father, who "rois estoit," and by the indeterminate anteriority of "mes lignages."

Modality (duty, *devoir* vs. desire, *vouloir*):[55] Here a more extensive analysis is required. In laying out his functions and prerogatives as monarch, Arthur first discusses duties and obligations, then passes to a discussion of what he desires. Under the deontic, or ethical, modal verb *devoir*, he divides his inventory of obligations between acts which are proscribed (*devoir ne pas faire*) and those which in his view are prescribed, and indeed obligatory (*devoir faire*). The proscriptions are consequent upon his being "the king":

"Je sui rois, *si* ne doi..."

"I am king and *therefore* must not. ..."

At the top of this list is mendacity – *ne doi mantir*. The implication for the matter at hand is powerful: if Arthur is king, and he knows that the king must not lie, then his having said that Enide *absolutely must* be honored cannot *not* be true. The following three vices, baseness, falsehood, and excess, are all categories of conduct that he must not consent to in others (*devoir ne pas consentir*). If Arthur is king, and the king does not lie, and the king has said that Enide *absolutely must* be honored, then the contradiction of this proposition is a falsehood to which it is Arthur's duty as king not to consent. Are you listening, lords? As for the positive obligations (*devoir faire*), Arthur must "preserve reason and justice," this because it befits the just monarch who upholds the law (*leal roi*). Here once again is an objectification of the self as Arthur slides from first-person reference to third – *il* doit: *he* must "maintain *the* law, truth, faith, and justice."

Up to this point in his speech, the verbal discourse has been carried along by an underlying inductive logic conveyed by syllogisms, of the type:

A I am the king.		A The king says X.
B The king must not lie.	*and*	B The king never lies.
C I must not lie.		C X is true.

In addition, Arthur moves from the concrete case to the universal, whereby the utterance of the case by the king is necessarily true, since the king must not utter falsehood (*mantir*); at the same time, he utters the proposition according to which the king must uphold Truth, along with Law, Faith, and Justice, as one of four universals. Moreover, if what the king says is right (*droiz*) is necessarily true, then his statement of what he says is *not* right (*n'est droiz*) is also necessarily true. What is not right – *n'est droiz* – moreover, is precisely this: *"n'est droiz* que nus de moi se plaigne" ("it is not right for anyone to have cause to complain of me"). Behind his intricate reasoning on the ethics of monarchy lies a far simpler message, which is that the king's position in this matter of who will be honored by the custom is necessarily right and true, while that of the barons necessarily is not. Furthermore, given the purport of the "demonstration," they have no cause for complaint.

As Arthur moves from duty to desire, *devoir* to *vouloir*, the barons now learn, not what Arthur as king absolutely *must* do, but what he really *desires*. Again Arthur first treats of volitional proscriptions (*ne pas vouloir*) before taking up positive desiderata (*vouloir*). He also progresses from the more contingent *voldroie* (would like) to the emphatic *voel* (want). "In no way" *would he want* to do "disloyalty" or "wrong" to "weak" or "strong," which, by implication, would involve failing to do what he has already said is "right" with regard to this case concerning the politically "weak," eccentric position of Erec and this winsome newcomer he has brought into their midst. Nor does he want *"the* custom" and practices maintained by his "lineage" to go unobserved. This is a matter of the utmost importance to the barons, as well, who are urged to consider the obverse hypothetical case: "It should (*devroit*) weigh heavily upon you if I were to impose upon you customs and laws other than those kept by my father the king." This appeal to a desire for the juridical continuity of customal law reflects a contemporaneous concern among the Plantagenets, as I have shown elsewhere.[56] Given the propensity of customal practices to "drift" or evolve away from their original coherence, depending upon memory and needs, it is all the more important for the monarch to replicate the legal practice of the ascendant.[57] Arthur *does not want* to subvert the law of the father by other laws. Moreover, the one thing he positively *wants* (*voel*) is to "keep and maintain" the *usage* of the king and emperor, his father, "at all costs" to himself. Thus do duty and desire, *devoir* and *vouloir*, coincide. Arthur fervently wants what in any case has to be, because it is right and true, because he says so, and because he is king. There is also ample evidence here that Arthur thinks this custom, which was "good enough" for his father, to be a "good enough custom" for the maintenance of law and order on this occasion.

Following this argument whose logic asserts the infallible judgment of the king in this dispute, it is remarkable that Arthur closes by returning to the *interrogative*, asking the assembly to express "toz voz talanz," to "voir dire," and, especially, to utter the *vérité* concerning the maiden who, though not of the household, "ought well and reasonably" ("doit bien et par reison") to receive the customal honor. All answer in perfect unison:

> "Par Deu, sire, ne par sa croiz,
> vos poëz bien jugier par droit
> que ceste la plus bele soit;
> an ceste a asez plus biauté
> qu'il n'a el soloil de clarté;
> beisier la poëz quitemant,
> tuit l'otroions comunemant." (vv. 1778–84)

"By God, sire, and by his cross, you may rightly judge that she is the most beautiful; in her is there more beauty than there is brightness in the sun; you may legitimately kiss her; we grant it unanimously."

In the accord reached by Arthur and his barons lies a fundamental ambiguity: was it really Enide's surpassing beauty, acknowledged by all, that made possible the enthusiastic agreement, or was it the persuasive force of Arthur's discourse, or was it both at once? The narrator has already told us that in Enide, Nature as God's handmaiden had realized her most nearly perfect specimen (vv. 411ff.), whence the possibility that she might serve as a symbol of the operations of divine and natural law and thus all the more appropriately as a basis for accord in this operation of human law.[58] Whatever its merits or lack thereof, the king's discourse adds an ethical imperative to that which all concur to be an empirical fact: the beauty of Enide. Fortunately, *all* agree that Enide is "la plus bele," for such agreement allows the custom to resolve itself in the traditional manner, regardless of the questionable efficacy of Arthur's oration.[59] In the euphoric outcome, the memory of the earlier deadlock, in which the court was poised on the brink of anarchy, fades away.

Happily, then, order is restored by the plenary presence and its discovery of an object of universal assent. Yet just suppose, momentarily, a possible world in which the object was *not* so beautiful; suppose, even, that Erec had come back with the Hideous Damsel. It is not a matter here of criticism rewriting fiction, but rather of seeing how much stress Arthur's intervention might withstand were he arguing on behalf of a lesser beauty, to a hostile audience. We have seen how Arthur heightens his oration with positive overtones in order to make its adamant, absolutist tenor less manifest and more palatable to the assembly: the frequent interrogative address helps to dissimulate the declarative decision and the logic that seeks to justify it as an *imperative*, which is the hidden grammatical mood of the entire speech. The logic of the absolute is made to seem contingent upon the common assent, the temporality of values is assimilated to the timeless, selfhood and presence are said to be valorized by a lineal and traditional past, while desire is elevated to duty. If this positive coloration helps to conceal an absolutist bias, it perhaps also reduces awareness of the extent to which Arthur's logic, despite its authoritative overtones of a demonstration based on necessity, is an instance of *logica probabilis* whose founding premises are based on opinions, whether his or those of conventional wisdom, as to what an ideal monarch should do and be.[60] If Arthur had been arguing on behalf of a less prepossessing creature – haggling over a hag, as it were – it is unlikely that the intrinsic qualities of his manipulative discourse would have been sufficiently persuasive to command the assent of the plenary presence. In the absence of a sufficiently alluring maiden, the verbal veils with which he seeks to shroud his fervent absolutism might well have seemed far more diaphanous.

The point of entertaining such a possibility is to suggest that the unanimity facilitated by Enide's surpassing beauty permits resolution of an immediate crisis while leaving the far more significant conflict wholly unacknowledged and unresolved. The short-term problem concerns procedure. The original terms of the custom prescribe that he who takes the stag bestow the kiss, as Gauvain had explained, while also warning Arthur that conflict might ensue: there are now 500 noble damsels, daughters of kings, and as many knights, each of whom will wish to maintain by single combat that his favorite is "la plus bele" (vv. 43ff.). In the self-interested wishes of these knights lies the potential for the custom's drift – perhaps toward something more akin to the nearby Custom of the Sparrowhawk which rewards precisely such chivalric interests.[61] The procedural matter at Arthur's court will be resolved in favor of the original terms of the custom; the deerslayer, and not the eventual winner of a chivalric contest, will perform the ritual kiss. Yet by making Arthur himself the deerslayer, Chrétien takes this opportunity to explore, by means of the customal issue, Arthur's political status. Not the knights, but Arthur, will have to "desresnier son droit" – uphold his right – not by swords, but by words, with which he argumentatively lays out the principles of his reign. In the outcome, Enide will serve to mediate the contradiction, but not to neutralize it.

What problematic, then, is dramatized in the underlying political situation of this discourse? In the first place, more than at any other moment in Chrétien's works, Arthur here fulfils the role of addressor, or *destinateur*. For his subjects he destines the usages, practices, and customs of the monarchy he has inherited. He is the *lawgiver* who acts as legatee of the juridical heritage of his forebears. He makes known to all that the ethic of his realm and its future transactions are to be modeled on the ethic and transactions of its past.[62] The project emphasizes continuity, and is essentially conservative in nature. On the other hand, the events leading up to Arthur's confrontation with his barons have dramatized the vulnerability of customs to drift, caused, in this instance, by the revisionary stratagems of those whose needs they no longer meet. This custom, which apparently had served the Arthurian – and, before it, the Pandragonian – plenary presence as a means of reaffirming a harmonious espousal of values symbolized by collective assent to the privilege of its victor, was on the verge of being appropriated and revised by the chivalric class to meet its own needs to exalt prowess and individual nobility.

"Li premiers vers" thus illustrates how a custom, as a legal procedure retained in collective memory, becomes vulnerable to revision as needs and objectives change. In consequence, the twofold ritual originally prescribed by the customs formula as a means of signifying communal accord risks being redesigned as a contest of prowess in order to identify the surpassing qualities of the chivalric individual. Thus does the myth of the royal founder come to the brink of foundering in the revisionist fiction of chivalry. The one kind of fiction upholds and seeks to project into the future the juridical paradigms of a venerable past; the other kind seeks to appropriate and modify the paradigms of a superannuated past in anticipation of an auspicious future in which their original intent no longer obtains. In a much later century, it was Auden who aptly captured this sort of attitude: "The words of a dead man are modified in the guts of the living."

It is clear enough, however, that for Arthur the words of the dead are a legacy to the living, that the law of the father will be his law. He reveres the institutions inherited from his paternal addressor and is eager, adamantly so, to maintain them during his own reign. His oration could thus be viewed as the vehicle by which he orally introduces this anterior order to the collective narratee which is his court, by addressing his father's mandate to the nobles in his realm.[63]

The double bind

Apart from its revelation of how profoundly the Arthurian present is informed by the Pandragonian past, perhaps the most revealing aspect of this discourse, as contextualized by "Li premiers vers," is its disclosure of the *double bind* which holds Arthur captive to two contradictory ideas of order. On the one hand, Arthur is bound by the constraints of hereditary monarchy to maintain the anterior order and its practices; on the other, he is compelled to seek baronial advice and consent. Together, these potentially antagonistic obligations stand to impose conflicting constraints on his exercise of power as he strives to uphold justice. The foregoing analysis of his discourse suggests that the paternal imperative compels Arthur to privilege one term in each of the aspectual oppositions to the detriment of the other. Whence his valorization of the declarative over the interrogative, the absolute over the contingent, the timeless over the temporal, past over present, ascendant over self, duty over desire. Yet at the same time, as a *primus inter pares*, a feudal monarch who is first among his peers and, like the beleaguered Charlemagne of the Oxford *Roland*, bound to seek and follow their counsel, Arthur also finds it necessary to privilege the other term in each of the oppositions.[64] Whence his show of attention to the uniqueness of the present situation, as well as his manifestly deferential attitude toward the contestatory mood of his barons. Whence also his repeated invitations to them to express *their* desire, and his solicitation of their consent. In this context his later recourse to baronial counsel in times of crisis (e.g., *Cligés*, vv. 1059ff.), even his tolerance of the disruptiveness of a Kay, are more readily understood.

The issue of completing the custom is what occupies the outer boundaries of "Li premiers vers" and becomes the principal tributary of its contents. Yet behind the customal issue looms the larger issue of how feudal monarchy may effectively enforce its hereditary mandates while accommodating the opposing mandates of its most powerful subjects. Adherence to custom obviates adherence to consensus; adherence to baronial consensus jeopardizes the integrity of custom. This scene evokes the twelfth-century paradox of the feudal king who owes his reign simultaneously to the principle of hereditary transmission and to the principle of ecclesiastical and seigneurial election, in accordance, moreover, with divine will.[65] In this respect, Chrétien comes closer to replicating problems confronting contemporaneous political institutions than do Geoffrey and Wace. His revisionary turn, away from Arthur as a dynamic, epico-heroic subject to Arthur as addressor torn between the priorities of two conflicting mandates, one past, one present, seems more attuned to the political complexity of monarchy as an institution of the second feudal age.

Given the pull in opposite directions exerted on this fictive king, toward the past and its paradigms of order as well as toward an idea of the present constructed on bases that may lie outside the confines of those paradigms or even subvert them, it is not surprising to find in Chrétien's Arthur a personage whose characteristics include stasis, passivity, even anguish. The frequent powerlessness and pathos of the waiting king, who does at times resemble the figure of *rex inutilis* among the monarchs of medieval history, may be ascribed, not merely to literary convention, but to the need to maintain a centripetal order modeled on *rex quondam*, while faced with the constant centrifugal propensities among his chivalric subjects. In this light, we may infer that a monarchy founded on custom and the active communal solidarity of the vassals, perhaps not problematic at its inception during the reign of Utherpandragon, has since become so because of a radical shift in the mentality of the court, whose warrior elite seek an independent status and identity. The ideal of the "Table Reonde" (*Erec*, v. 83) suggests a desire to maintain an egalitarian kind of solidarity, of vassals in resident service to the suzerain-monarch who seeks to harmonize this immediate social constellation with the practices of his lineal ascendancy – in essence, an ideal of stasis and order predicated on an *idealized past*.[66] It is above all else this anterior order which constitutes Arthur as an addressor and donor, whereby he destines this hereditary polity for his vassals and seeks within its functional formulas the bases of its sanctions. This is what makes him an ineffectual and seemingly indifferent addressor as regards the achievements of his knights in remote locales. For his primary juridical function as mandated by the past is to accord positive sanction to those juridical practices that preserve the old order and reaffirm its vitality in the present; hence too his desire for that plenary presence which reaffirms the viability of his order and provides a chivalric quorum with which ostensibly to ratify it anew.

These, then, are among the salient features of Arthur's anterior order, that is, the normative order of his reign as initially conceptualized by Chrétien de Troyes. Like the Arthur portrayed by Geoffrey and Wace, Chrétien's Arthur in his initial appearance suffers not from a vulnerability to dark forces lying far beyond his realm and beholden to some alien law, but from threatening circumstances emanating from within his own court. Unlike his two immediate predecessors, however, Chrétien does not identify these perils with the sudden manifestation of a treacherous villain. On the contrary, it is precisely this traditional option which he rejects in his recuperative rewriting of the Mordret episode in *Cligés*. The Arthur of earlier tradition owed his sudden loss of agency to one monumental reversal of fortune. In contrast, the opening crisis in Chrétien's Arthurian fictions, that in *Erec*, suggests that Arthur is subject to a chronic reduction of agency by virtue of his unswerving fidelity to the juridical foundations of the Pandragonian legacy. In short, Chrétien's transgression of the anterior Arthurian tradition, as dramatized in *Cligés*, enabled him to problematize, as his predecessors had not, Arthur's submission to the law of the father.

While "Li premiers vers" of *Erec* set the parameters of this adherence by making Uther's reign the paternal metaphor of Arthur's, its consequences remained to be explored in subsequent works. We have suggested that *Cligés* has already begun to hint at a certain instability in the Arthurian monarchy, but only in the three later works do the consequences of Arthur's juridical allegiance emerge in distressing detail. Along with *Erec et Enide*, these comprise a "tetralogy' that will frequently be referred to as Chrétien's "customal romances," in view of their extensive emphasis on the role of customs in elaborating the problematic of the Arthurian order. The next three chapters, dealing respectively with the *Charrete*, *Le Chevalier au lion*, and *Le Conte du graal*, will show how extensively the coherence of a variety of customs figures in the development of an heroic dynamic in each of these works. At the same time, it will be seen that the Arthurian anterior order set forth at the beginning of *Erec* also persists in principle on an intertextual basis, as an ideal *de jure* of the Arthurian monarchy. While adhering to a limited set of juridical protocols retained, like the Custom of the White Stag, in oral memory, the Arthurian court and neighboring communities are, we shall see, repeatedly subjected to the stratagems of malicious adversaries. They are simultaneously the foes of Chrétien's heroes and the exponents of eclectic, revisionary, *de facto* "laws" of strength and cunning arbitrarily modeled, moreover, on the very same customal procedures designed to prevent them. Examination of the later works in turn will enable us, in Chapter 5, to arrive at a fuller, more nuanced conceptualization of the intertextuality of crisis in Chrétien's Arthurian world.

2

Safely through the realm: customs in
Le Chevalier de la charrete

Chapter 1 identified a fundamental tension in Chrétien's Arthurian fictions, between a monarch dedicated to the maintenance of legal prerogatives established by the hereditary anterior order, and a chivalric elite eager to function independently of this tradition.[1] The present chapter and the two following will focus on how this tension is dramatized in terms of a juridical coherence based on customs. In the previous chapter, these mechanisms were seen to play a major role in determining the parameters of conflict at the very beginning of Chrétien's Arthurian series, where their importance was shown to be both structural and ideological.[2] Likewise in the three later romances – the contemporaneously composed *Charrete* and *Yvain*, as well as *Le Conte du graal* – customs play major roles essential to both structure and meaning in each work, again capturing the antagonism between the chivalric dynamic and the anterior order.[3]

A PRELIMINARY INVENTORY OF CHRETIEN'S LITERARY CUSTOMS

In his study of the "role" of customs in the works of Chrétien, Erich Köhler classified them according to a threefold typology, taking into account practices nominally identified as customs and those giving the appearance of being customs though not specifically identified as such:[4]

(1) "the 'customs' that King Arthur must observe": under this heading appear the Custom of the White Stag in *Erec* and Arthur's reception of prisoners who report the circumstances of their defeat, as does Yder in *Erec*, for example, or Anguingueron, Clamadeu, and Orgueilleus de la Lande in *Le Conte du graal*. Also included are Arthur's postponement of a meal until news of an adventure arrives (see, for example, *Le Conte du graal*, vv. 2818ff.), and the *don contraignant*, which can "paralyze" the court: "The principle of generosity, having become an automatic reflex, turns against the order it should protect" (p. 391).

(2) "the 'customs' whose abuse the hero ends, but which nonetheless continue to exist": here Köhler includes the Custom of the Sparrowhawk in *Erec*, in view of Yder's having been revealed as "unworthy" of the prize, and the Custom of the Perilous Fountain in *Yvain*, on the debatable assumption that Esclados was unfit for mastery of this practice because "not a servant of the Arthurian realm" (p. 392).

(3) "the 'customs' that are permanently abolished": while customs of the first two types are said to be "old," immemorial, and "invariable," those in this category are of a more recent, usually known origin, and arbitrarily enforced. They are: the "Joie de la Cort" in *Erec*; the Custom of "Pesme Avanture" in *Yvain*; the Custom of Gorre in the *Charrete*; and the "custom" of the Castle of Marvels in the *Conte du graal*. All are to be permanently ended by the hero.

In addition, Köhler notes that single combat is itself considered to be a "custom," as in this passage from *Erec*:

> Adonc estoit costume et us
> que dui chevalier a un poindre
> ne devoient a un seul poindre,
> et, s'il l'eüssent anvaï,
> vis fust qu'il l'eüssent traï.   (*Erec*, vv. 2822–6)

It was then custom and usage that two knights in a single confrontation should not go against one alone, and if they were to attack him, they would have been considered his betrayers.

Under the rubric of single combat as custom, one finds the judicial duel predicated on an oath, to determine guilt, as in the *Charrete*, or to adjudicate an inheritance, as in *Yvain*.

Köhler's study of the customs in Chrétien's romances, though a seminal investigation founded on a valid insight, was carried out only sporadically and at a level of abstraction at times exceedingly remote from the poems.[5] The following analyses, in contrast, often scrutinize the texture of episodes and sometimes linger over seemingly incidental details, in keeping with a conviction that the individual works merit and sustain such interrogation where the issue of customs is concerned. The present chapter and the next two will reveal that only a detailed analysis of each work can provide sufficient access to this highly significant – yet unduly neglected – aspect of Chrétien's romances.

THE CUSTOMS OF LOGRES AND OF GORRE

In *Lancelot, ou le chevalier de la charrete* two major customs can be identified. Each is introduced in the same manner, by a secondary character who, along with the narrator, describes the custom's canonic form. They differ considerably from one another, however, not only in terms of their content, their cognitive mechanisms and their narrative structure, but especially as to their land of origin. For this reason, they may conveniently be identified as the *Custom of Logres* and the *Custom of Gorre*.

The first mention of the Custom of Logres is made by a damsel who enlists Lancelot's protective conduct, she says, "par les us et par les costumes/qui furent ainz que nos ne fumes/el reaume de Logres mises" ("by the usages and customs established in the kingdom of Logres before our time," vv. 1299–1301). The narrator then describes this custom in detail:

> Les costumes et les franchises
> estoient tex, a cel termine,
> que dameisele ne meschine,
> se chevaliers la trovast sole,
> ne plus qu'il se tranchast la gole
> ne feïst se tote enor non,
> s'estre volsist de boen renon;
> et, s'il l'esforçast, a toz jorz
> an fust honiz an totes corz.
> Mes se ele conduit eüst
> uns autres, se tant li pleüst
> qu'a celui bataille en feïst
> et par armes la conqueïst,
> sa volenté an poïst faire
> sanz honte et sanz blasme retraire.   (vv. 1302–16)

At that time, the customs and privileges were such that if a knight were to find a damsel or a maiden alone, he would sooner slit his own throat than treat her in other than an honorable manner, if he cared for his own reputation. If he were to take her by force, he would be forever shamed in all courts. But supposing she were accompanied: if he desired her enough to challenge her escort and conquer her by arms, he would be free to do with her as he pleased, without incurring shame or blame.

This description of the custom reveals an extensive narrative dimension, with numerous possible functions, such as "encounter," "appropriation," "challenge," "combat," and so forth.[6] Equally remarkable is the dual temporal perspective established. On the one hand, there is emphasis on the fact that these practices took place long ago – they were here "before our time." Here the orally described Custom of Logres is a miniaturized juridical text which presupposes an indeterminate number of specific *past* enactments. Yet the damsel's recourse to it on this occasion also gives it a prospective value as a potential model for *future* circumstances.[7]

Because the terms of the custom are particularly harsh for an accompanied female if her escort is overwhelmed by a challenger, the martial quality of the defender is critical, as the damsel realizes:

> Por ce la pucele li dist
> que, se il l'osast ne volsist
> par ceste costume conduire
> que autres ne li poïst nuire,
> qu'ele s'en alast avoec lui.
> Et cil li dist: "Ja nus enui
> ne vos fera, ce vos otroi,
> que premiers ne le face moi.
> – Dons i voel ge, fet ele, aler."   (vv. 1317–25)

For this reason the maiden told him that if he were bold enough to escort her according to this custom so that others would not harm her, then she would go with him. And he said to her: "I guarantee you that anyone who would trouble you will first have to contend with me." "I wish to go with you then," she said.

The custom ostensibly protects the solitary traveler, though if she does choose an escort, it is essential to find one who can overwhelm all contenders.[8] With Lancelot, the maiden apparently feels secure, provided that he is familiar with the terms of the custom and willing, on the basis of a verbal contract, to comply with them.

Lancelot is also the narratee of the Custom of Gorre. A vavassor from Logres enumerates its provisions, with emphasis on the present moment:

> Maleoite soit tex costume
> et cil avoec, qui la maintiennent,
> que nul estrange ça ne vienent
> qu'a remenoir ne lor covaingne
> e que la terre nes detaigne;
> car qui se vialt antrer i puet,
> mes a remenoir li estuet. (vv. 2096–102)

"Cursed be such a custom and those who keep it, such that no foreigners may come here without having to stay and the land detain them. For whoever wishes to enter may do so, but he must remain."

Here continuity and contemporaneity are evident; all of the victims are apparently still alive. While the Custom of Logres has an archaic flavor, this one seems of more recent inception, though no less prospective:

> De vos meïsmes est or pes:
> vos n'en istroiz, ce cuit, ja més. (vv. 2103–4)

"For you, too, the die is cast: I do not believe you will ever get out of here either."

No choice remains to the hero: Lancelot himself is already a victim of this legal flycatcher. Unlike the Custom of Logres, this custom includes a mechanism that provides for its permanent abolition:

> Li vavasors li redit puis:
> "Comant? Cuidiez an vos issir?
> – Oïl, se Deu vient a pleisir;
> et g'en ferai mon pooir tot.
> – Donc an istroient sanz redot
> trestuit li autre quitemant;
> car puis que li uns lëaumant
> istra fors de ceste prison,
> tuit li autre, sanz mesprison,
> an porront issir sanz desfanse." (vv. 2106–15)

Then the vavassor said to him: "What? You believe you can get out of here?" "Yes, God willing, I'll do my best." "Then all of the others would leave without fear or constraint, for as soon as one legitimately leaves this prison, all of the others will be able to leave, blamelessly and with no impediments."

Departure is the liberating act, the sole condition for ending the arbitrary impingements upon individual freedom, provided that a single individual be equal to the task.

The two customs hold certain characteristics in common: a repeatable format; a narrative dimension; oral transmission; linkage of a future with a past; identification of an obligation; a preoccupation with individual privilege, and so on.[9] Each, however, also has its own unique mechanisms and modalities of existence. While the Custom of Logres projects an indeterminate series of juridical acts from the past into the future, with no limit to its validity foreseen, the Custom of Gorre identifies one future act that would invalidate all of the preceding ones falling under its jurisdiction, so as to effect its abolition.[10] This radical contrast is of the utmost importance to the poem as a whole, and the following analysis of its narrative organization will show that the conditions stipulated by each custom are programmatic for the circumstantial elaboration of this fiction in its entirety.

CUSTOMS AND STRUCTURE

From the very beginning of the *Charrete*, one may follow the progressive integration of each custom into the textuality of the poem. When Meleagant swaggers into Arthur's court, the Custom of Gorre has been gradually decimating the population of Logres for some time, according to the intruder who maintains it:

> Rois Artus, J'ai en ma prison,
> de ta terre et de ta meison,
> chevaliers, dames et puceles...   (vv. 51–3)

"King Arthur, in my prison I hold knights, ladies and maidens from your realm and your household."

This fact, however, is not represented here as the consequence of right of custom, but rather as the product of Meleagant's omnipotence, before which the King of Logres is declared to be powerless:

> mes ne t'an di pas les noveles
> por ce que jes te vuelle randre;
> einçois tel voel dire et aprandre
> que tu n'as force ne avoir
> par quoi tu les puisses avoir;
> et saches bien qu'ainsi morras
> que ja aidier ne lor porras."   (vv. 54–60)

"But I tell you this not because I wish to release them to you. On the contrary, I wish to inform you that you have not the might nor the means of getting them back, and know that you will die without having been able to help them."

Meleagant's version of the Custom of Gorre omits the stipulation, to be found in the vavassor's later formal description, concerning departure of a single inhabitant of Logres as a means of its abrogation. In the light of that later disclosure, it is evident that at Arthur's court Meleagant is reinterpreting the customal practice of his realm in order to suit his own interests.[11]

This does not mean, however, that Meleagant sets no conditions for invalidating the Custom of Gorre, as the rest of his challenge makes clear:

> "Rois, s'a ta cort chevalier a
> nes un an cui tu te fïasses
> que le reïne li osasses
> baillier por mener an ce bois
> aprés moi, la ou ge m'an vois,
> par un covant l'i atandrai
> que les prisons toz te randrai
> qui sont an prison an ma terre,
> se il la puet vers moi conquerre
> et tant face qu'il l'an ramaint." (vv. 70–9)

"King, if in your court you have even one reliable knight to whom you would dare entrust the queen, to be led into the woods where I'm headed, I promise to await him there and to return to you all who are imprisoned in my land, if he can but conquer her from me and bring her back here."

When the Custom of Gorre is later defined, it will become clear that Meleagant was attempting at Arthur's court to modify the mechanism of its resolution. Rather than adhere to the original conditions, stipulating a liberator's departure from Gorre (vv. 2106–15), his objective is to make liberation contingent upon the victory of an Arthurian knight. But his proposal is even more astonishing in the light of what we later learn of the Custom of Logres, because his desire to confront the queen's escort in a remote setting and not at court prefigures the basic scenario later identified with the Custom of Logres:

> Mes se ele conduit eüst
> uns autres, se tant li pleüst
> qu'a celui bataille an feïst
> et par armes la conqueïst,
> sa volenté an poïst faire
> sanz honte et sanz blasme retraire. (vv. 1311–16)

But supposing she were accompanied: if he desired her enough to challenge her escort and conquer her by arms, he would be free to do with her as he pleased, without incurring shame or blame.

This particular case, of course, concerns not just any "damsel or maiden" as in the later description of the Custom of Logres (v. 1304), but a married woman and one who is above all Arthur's queen. In order to resolve the Custom of Gorre definitively and in a personally profitable way, Meleagant wishes to replicate precisely the conditions specified by the Custom of Logres: because the queen will be in the safe-conduct of a knight, he may vie for her without dishonor.[12]

The stakes of the sylvan combat proposed by Meleagant are considerable: the prisoners *and* the queen, with honor. His victory would establish an important innovation with regard to the Custom of Gorre: with his right to the prisoners no longer predicated on a liberator's departure but on his own victory in a combat involving a pact or *covant* (v. 75), the custom would be relieved of all contingency, its eventual abolition no longer possible. His triumph would thus perpetuate his own realm's custom, while making his abduction of the queen an honorable feat by virtue of its conformity with the Custom of Logres.[13] On the other hand, a victory by the Arthurian escort would protect both the queen and the Custom of Logres, while also abolishing the destructive Custom of Gorre.

A juridical discourse thus problematizes the right of custom from the very beginning of the romance, even though the formal introduction of the two customs is deferred. Retrospective analysis of the opening scene in the light of the coherence of these two customs unmasks a willful manipulator of both and shows that the initial conflict is fundamentally a juridical one. This is compounded by the fact that, while Meleagant uses the Custom of Logres to the detriment of Arthur's realm, Kay resorts to the custom of the *don contraignant* in order to become the queen's escort, thus ensuring that the most inept defender will be entrusted with the response to the challenge.[14] In this monumental crisis, Arthur is thus doubly the victim of legal practices honored within his own realm. As in "Li premiers vers" of *Erec*, his adherence to custom places him in a disadvantageous position with regard to current circumstances. This time, however, the challenge comes, not from within the court, but from the realm's most dangerous adversary, who seeks to exploit the possibilities latent in Arthur's unflagging allegiance to customal procedures.

Born of the double imperative to eliminate the threat to the queen and free the prisoners in Gorre, Kay's immediate defeat and the long and tortuous journey of Lancelot are both products of a narrative logic constituted and overdetermined by a juridical logic already in place at the beginning of the work. And the customal coherence opening the romance also prolongs it, deferring any resolution of the juridical conflicts until the very end of the narrative trajectory.[15] The first deferral results from the fact that Meleagant's victory fails to modify the Custom of Gorre. His strategy will begin to unravel as soon as the readily undone Kay is seconded by an initially unidentified Arthurian knight. This champion is Lancelot, whose bizarre encounters repeatedly bring to prominence a customal type of discourse, each of whose elements must be examined in turn.

Prior to his arrival in Gorre, Lancelot's longest adventure features an "Immodest Damsel," a strategist who has her knights and domestics stage an attempted rape in order to provoke Lancelot's intervention on her behalf (vv. 935–2110).[16] This contrived situation featuring imperiled feminine honor and chivalric opponents again prefigures the canonic situation in the Custom of Logres, which is in fact formally described by the damsel immediately following this scene. Multiple tests of Lancelot's heroic mettle are apparent: he will successfully defend the damsel's honor against her "assailants" without subsequently yielding to her seductive charms during the night he agrees "par covant" to spend in her bed (vv. 932ff.).[17] Their journey together the next day brings them to a church where Lancelot easily lifts a tombstone movable only by the foreordained liberator of the prisoners (vv. 1874–1914). In sum, a threefold qualifying test, revealing extraordinary prowess in service to feminine honor, absolute fidelity to the queen, and a singular aptitude – indeed, an election – to abolish the Custom of Gorre.

Yet there is more. When this same damsel places herself in Lancelot's safe-conduct under the terms of the Custom of Logres, it is not surprising that a challenger looms out of the wilderness with the intention of carrying her away *precisely because* she is accompanied (vv. 1508–92). Escorted females, we recall, are fair game according to the custom's second "clause," and the challenger's claim specifically emphasizes that since she is accompanied no shame would attach to his leading her away (vv. 1576–9).[18] Yet while customal logic would have prescribed a decisive combat, this is thrice deferred. First the opponents select a more spacious area, the "pré aux jeux"; then the father of the challenger, recognizing the excessive volatility of his son, persuades him to observe this couple at length before provoking a confrontation (vv. 1649–1814); finally, Lancelot's awesome displacement of a tombstone persuades the son to abandon his designs on the damsel.

It is notable that, as at the beginning of the romance, this episode brings *both* customs simultaneously into play. The outcome of a situation to which the Custom of Logres seems pertinent is determined by the *merveille* of the tombstone which designates Lancelot as the eventual abrogator of the Custom of Gorre.[19] On the basis of a monk's explication of this marvel, the father identifies his son as the wrongful party before any recourse to combat. Whence an instance where normal observance of one custom is modified by an element pertaining to the other.

The focus now shifts increasingly to the Custom of Gorre. After arriving in this alien land, Lancelot learns of the custom's jurisdiction (vv. 2093–115), and the rumor soon spreads that he has come to exact the liberation (vv. 2289–303; 2413–421). Prior to arrival at the court of Bademagu located beyond the Sword Bridge, however, Lancelot encounters still another adventure reminiscent of the Custom of Logres. A chivalric "orgueilleux" shames Lancelot for riding in the cart, the "infamous" *charrete*, and declares his intention to behead him.[20] After Lancelot wins the ensuing combat, a maiden requests, as a *don*, that he behead this "disloyal" and "felonious traitor" (vv. 2566–924). Lancelot's additional combat, prompted by this woman's charge that his adversary had gravely dishonored her, is indicative that, in Gorre as in Logres, violations of the security and honor of females require an adjudicative standard. Significantly, moreover, this service rendered under circumstances evocative of an Arthurian customal model will ultimately make possible Lancelot's abolition of the Custom of Gorre at the very end of the romance. For the maiden is Meleagant's sister (vv. 6568ff.), and it is in gratitude for Lancelot's service to her on this earlier occasion that she will release him from her brother's tower in time for his decisive combat with Meleagant at Arthur's court.[21] "Ceci tuera cela": Lancelot's defense of the values guaranteed by the custom of Logres will utltimately make possible his abolition of a destructive custom upheld in Gorre.

As it nears the middle of the romance, at Bademagu's court, the story is fed by the two indecisive combats between Lancelot and Meleagant; by Lancelot's interviews with the queen before their night together; by the two quests undertaken to find Gauvain, a victim of the Underwater Bridge; and, especially, by the malevolent strategy that will hold Lancelot hostage in Gorre. Yet while the love at last passionately shared by Lancelot and the queen looms large throughout these episodes, the question of the two customs will not cease to motivate the flow of events.

Consider the circumstances surrounding the first of Lancelot's two skirmishes with Meleagant in Gorre. As soon as Lancelot has crossed the Sword Bridge, the captor first ponders the fate of the queen:

> D'ire, et de mautalant, color
> en a Meleaganz changiee;
> bien set c'or li ert chalongiee
> la reïne...   (vv. 3158–61)

In anger and wrath, Meleagant waxed crimson, for he knew he would be challenged for the queen.

Bademagu's paternal counsel also concerns the queen:

> Car t'acorde a lui et afeite,
> si li rant quite la reïne.   (vv. 3196–7)

> Fei lui tel enor an ta terre,
> que ce que il est venuz querre
> li done ainz qu'il le te demant.
> Car tu sez bien certainnemant
> qu'il quiert la reïne Ganievre.   (vv. 3203–7)

> Ce sez tu bien que hontes iert
> au chevalier, s'il ne conquiert
> vers toi la reïne an bataille.   (vv. 3237–9)

> Mien esciänt, il n'anquiert point
> por ce que l'an an pes li doint,
> einz la vialt par bataille l'avoir.   (vv. 3243–5)

"Work out an agreement and turn the queen over to him... Do him the honor of conceding what he seeks in your land before he asks you for it. For you know perfectly well that he is after Queen Guenevere... You are aware that this knight will be shamed if he does not conquer the queen from you in battle... In my judgment, he is not interested in getting her peacefully, but wants to reclaim her in battle."

There is no mention here of the famous Custom of Gorre, nor of the prisoners. Only the queen is a matter of concern, and jurisdiction of the Custom of Logres is clearly understood, for Lancelot is repeatedly seen as wanting to recover her in combat – "par bataille." The passage reveals that for Meleagant and Bademagu, no less than for Lancelot, the juridical problem raised at the outset remains unresolved. Lancelot wants to compensate for Kay's defeat – and shame – and the latter will later upbraid his companion for succeeding where he had failed (vv. 4007–12). The combat Lancelot eagerly desires is nontheless interrupted by Bademagu and Guenevere (vv. 3765–94) and rescheduled for a year hence at Arthur's court (vv. 3877–84). Suspension and deferral thus again postpone the juridical issues raised at the outset until the work's ultimate episode.[22]

A second combat will nonetheless occur in Gorre, after Lancelot's night with the queen. Meleagant, an inept interpreter of "signs" (vv. 4757, 4774), assumes that Kay betrayed his king in the queen's bed (vv. 4854ff.).[23] Lancelot will uphold the innocence of his compatriot, provided this be "par bataille," for inquest is an unsatisfactory procedure:

> – Ja ne vos an covient *pleidier*,
> fet Lanceloz, la ou je soie.
> Ja Deu ne place qu'an mescroie
> ne vos ne lui de tel afeire.
> Prez sui de la bataille feire... (vv. 4930–4)

"There is no point," says Lancelot, "in pleading your case wherever I might happen to be. God forbid that either you or he be misjudged in this matter. I am ready to do battle..."

Provided, of course, that this takes place according to proper legal procedure, which involves an oath:

> Et Lancelot dist: "Sire rois,
> je sai de quauses, et de lois,
> et de plez, et de jugemanz:
> ne doit estre sanz seiremanz
> bataille de tel mescreance." (vv. 4943–7)

And Lancelot said: "Your Highness, I am familiar with cases and laws, trials and verdicts: a battle over such a false charge must not take place unless there be an oath."

While taking advantage of the opportunity to conceal his own love affair, Lancelot willingly becomes God's agent for invalidating Meleagant's specious case against Kay.

   Whence a third juridical mechanism, the *judicium Dei*, whose various procedures included single combat under oath. While this instance of the traditional encounter again recalls the Custom of Logres in that two knights do battle over the honor of a woman, it also has an extensive historical dimension. Before the Fourth Lateran Council of 1215 and various royal edicts issued during the thirteenth century, it was not uncommonly a means of eliciting a "divine judgment" following accusatory and exculpatory utterances sworn over relics.[24] In the *Charrete*, the oaths of Meleagant and Lancelot bear exclusively on the guilt or innocence of Kay, an issue which, as God and the reader know, is trivial in comparison to the one which the oath neglects.[25] Mindful of more than the case at hand, Lancelot further vows to do away with his opponent if he gets the upper hand:

> "Mes ancor un autre an ferai
> del seiremanz, et jurerai,
> cui qu'il enuit ne cui qu'il poist,
> que se il hui venir me loist
> de Meleagant au desus,
> tant m'aïst Dex et neant plus
> et ces reliques qui sont ci,
> que ja de lui n'avrai merci." (vv.4977–84)

"Regardless of who approves or disapproves, I'll utter yet another oath, and swear that if today He lets me overwhelm Meleagant, so help me God only and these relics before me, I'll take no pity on him."

Thus would God have become the Accomplice of His accomplice at the end of this combat according to custom, had not Bademagu and Guenevere again decided to postpone all combats until the decisive confrontation at the Arthurian court. It is evident that deferred legal questions begin to weigh heavily upon the ultimate clash in Logres.

What, meanwhile, has become of the miserable prisoners? One finds no mention of them until after the interruption of the first combat between Lancelot and Meleagant, which is followed by widespread jubilation:

> A la pes toz li pueples cort,
> et devisent que a la cort
> le roi Artus iert la bataille,
> qui tient Bretaigne et Cornoaille:
> la devisent que ele soit,
> *s'estuet la reïne l'otroit*
> *et que Lanceloz l'acreant*
> *que, se cil le fet recreant,*
> *qu'ele avoec lui s'an revanra,*
> *ne ja nus ne la detanra.*
> *La reïne ensi le creante,*
> *et Lancelot vient a creante,*
> si les ont ensi acordez
> et departiz et desarmez.   (vv. 3885–98)

The news of peace draws a crowd, and there is talk that the battle will be at the court of King Arthur, lord of Britain and Cornwall. That is where it will be, they say, *provided the queen agrees, and Lancelot affirms, that if he is defeated by Meleagant, she will return undetained with him. The queen consents, and Lancelot as well.* Thus in agreement, the foes are separated and disarmed.

This provides further confirmation that the outcome of Meleagant's opening recourse to the Custom of Logres must await the closing episode. On these terms, the ultimate encounter will seal Guenevere's fate: while Lancelot's victory at Arthur's court would secure her definitive release and settle once and for all the issue raised by Meleagant in the opening scene, his defeat would return her to Meleagant for good. Yet there is no proclamation concerning the prisoners. Their joy evidently stems from an acute awareness of the conditions allowing their freedom according to the Custom of Gorre, and the narrator reiterates them at precisely this juncture:

> Tel costume el païs avoit,
> que, puis que li uns s'an issoit,
> que tuit li autre s'an issoient.
> Lancelot tuit beneïssoient...   (vv. 3899–902)

The custom of the realm was, that as soon as one captive were to leave this land, all would depart. They all blessed Lancelot.

Behind these details, one can infer the prisoners' assumptions: Lancelot entered

Gorre to claim the queen. Yet that matter has been postponed until later, in Logres, and so Lancelot will have to leave Gorre. Because the Custom of Gorre specifies that if one leaves, all leave, the prisoners joyfully assume that their liberation is at hand.[26] This *apparent* abolition of the Custom of Gorre thus stems from the decision to postpone resolution of the case pertaining to the Custom of Logres, which makes Lancelot's departure mandatory. Since the queen herself is at issue, the law of Logres is uppermost in the minds of the principals. It is precisely the change of venue back to Logres which inadvertently entails assumptions that the Custom of Gorre is abolished, assumptions which are, as it turns out, wholly premature.

Ensuing developments progressively undermine the clarity of a resolution which in fact is not one. First, Lancelot takes leave of Bademagu in order to search for Gauvain. His departure from the realm thus deferred, "cil qu'il avoit delivrez/et de prison deprisonez/li demandent que il feront" ("those whom he had delivered from prison ask him what they are to do," vv. 4087–9). Some will accompany Lancelot, while the others, including several maidens, ladies, and knights, will remain with the queen to await news of Gauvain, though all prefer immediate repatriation (vv. 4098ff.). The important thing here – the narrator emphasizes this – is that everyone *thinks* the prisoners have been liberated:

> Par tot est la novele dite
> que tote est la reïne quite
> et delivré tuit li prison,
> si s'an iront sanz mesprison
> quant ax pleira et boen lor iert.
> Li uns l'autre le voir an quiert,
> onques parole autre ne tindrent
> les gens quant tuit ansanble vindrent. (vv. 4107–14)

Everywhere the word is that the queen is free and all of the prisoners delivered, and that they will leave without impediment whenever they please. People ask one another about the truth of this matter and speak of nothing else when they gather.

Let them be patient a while longer, however, so that Lancelot and Guenevere can resolve their misunderstandings in time for their famous night together, followed by the indecisive judicial duel and Lancelot's second quest for Gauvain (vv. 5044ff.). Above all, let them assume during all of these episodes that the freedom of the prisoners is a foregone conclusion.[27]

What disappointment and dismay, then, during the renewed quest for Gauvain, when a dwarf, feigning participation in the search, leads Lancelot away:

> Et sa gent si grant duel en font
> de ce qu'il ne vient ne repeire
> qu'il ne sevent qu'il puissent feire.
> Tuit dïent que traïz les a
> li nains... (vv. 5086–90)

And his party is so deeply dismayed at his failure to return that they have no idea as to what to do. All agree that the dwarf has tricked them.

Little wonder that they feel betrayed, in fact, for if Lancelot does not precede them at the border, no one will leave. After hoisting Gauvain from torrential waters and informing him of their plight (vv. 5141ff.), they return to the court of Bademagu, with no prospect of departure.

Behind this distressing peripeteia one sees yet another of Meleagant's maneuvers, carried out by the dwarf.[28] As at the outset, Bademagu's son is prepared to manipulate the course of events to his own advantage. Consider his next tactic, which could appropriately be identified as a stratagem of "writing and deferral." The general melancholy reigning at Bademagu's court is dissipated by the arrival of a messenger bearing a letter (vv. 5241ff.). Its purported author is none other than Lancelot himself, who claims to have returned to Logres, where he is impatiently awaiting the return of his compatriots (vv. 5258ff.). Whence the general conviction that the Custom of Gorre has at last come to an end. One has left, so all will leave. With this letter, a new and positive relationship between the two realms seems imminent. The next day, King Bademagu himself leads the presumably emancipated band to the border, where in feudal solemnity they pledge the "services" of Arthur, the queen, Gauvain, and Kay. At this point, the divisive Custom of Gorre *seems* to have been set aside in favor of a peaceful and fruitful accord.

Why would Meleagant, who clearly instigated the ruse of the letter, provoke the bogus abolition of the custom which he had so strenuously sought to preserve? Clearly, he is playing off the queen and the prisoners while firmly retaining the needed trump: Lancelot. He will confine his adversary to the residence of his seneschal, then in a tower built exclusively to ensure his permanent captivity. Are these successive efforts – the artificial abrogation of the Custom of Gorre and the increasingly secure imprisonment of Lancelot – merely the products of a desire to confront at Arthur's court a champion inferior to Lancelot? Might we not perceive, once again, a manipulative stratagem designed to turn both customs to his advantage?

More is at stake here than a desire to avoid the personal shame that Lancelot's victory would impose. For this eventuality would also mean that all three issues pertaining to customs could be resolved against Meleagant. If Lancelot returns to Logres in time, Meleagant has everything to lose. By keeping him permanently in Gorre and defeating a lesser contender, he has everything to gain: the prisoners, the queen, and the unfinished judicial duel. In other words, given the repeated failures of the legal strategy that he deployed in the opening scene of the romance, he seeks nothing less than a *repetition* of the same scene at the end, with a view to obtaining the same twofold objective: the queen and the prisoners. Such a scenario would involve four basic elements: renewed defiance of King Arthur; confrontation with another inferior opponent, again in Lancelot's absence; repossession of the queen following the combat, legitimized, once again, by a verbal contract (vv. 3990ff.); and acquisition in perpetuity of the prisoners. In support of the latter objective would also be the assumption that, after having disappeared with the dwarf, Lancelot had never been able to accomplish the liberating act of leaving Gorre. In sum, Meleagant's initial stratagem of abusing one custom in order to perpetuate the abuse meted out by the other has inspired his efforts to replicate it more effectively in a second confrontation at Arthur's court.

To thwart the successful, disastrous replay of an initially abortive scheme, the story should have located, somewhere between beginning and end, an element capable of foreclosing on this circular movement. Lancelot did indeed locate such an element, we recall, one also entailing the repetition of a combative gesture. By beheading one adversary, the "orgueilleus," he has duly acquired the means of beheading another, Meleagant, whose grateful sister liberates the "liberator" so that he may return to Logres for the definitive combat. His adherence to the values upheld by the custom of Logres at the first beheading makes possible the abolition of the Custom of Gorre at the second, while at the same time defeating Meleagant's attempt to abuse the Custom of Logres and deciding the judicial duel. While obtaining freedom for queen and prisoners, so that all may henceforth proceed safely through the realm of Logres, the severed head also signifies closure of the juridical intrigue that determines the initial and terminal narrative boundaries of the romance.

MATIERE, SAN, AND THE MATTER OF CUSTOMS

There can be no doubt, then, that the two customs are tightly woven into the fabric of the *Charrete*.[29] Yet, after all, they are specifically mentioned only a few times within the ebb and flow of episodes that lead Lancelot to Guenevere and finally back to the Arthurian court, and scholars have argued in countless ways that it is the love intrigue that controls the meaning, or *san*, mentioned in the prologue (v. 26). Despite the ambiguity of its treatment, the sentimental and eventually scandalous behavior of queen and knight has remained, since the time of Gaston Paris, the primary topic of an often polarized criticism of "courtly love".[30] Compared to this major issue, the work's juridical coherence might appear to be of secondary importance.

In terms of the work as a whole, however, the episodes tributary primarily to the love intrigue are relatively few in number, while the relationship depicted between Lancelot and the queen bears almost no trace of its etiology and lacks any sort of closure.[31] The "narrative possibilities" of this couple whose past is unknowable are nowhere near exhaustion by the end of the narration, and the beheading of Meleagant in no way resolves the questions raised by their love, which remains as mysterious at the end of the romance as at its beginning. On the other hand, we have seen that customal discourse inaugurates, organizes, and terminates the narrative dimension of the entire work. The economy of the narrative trajectory in its entirety, and only in its entirety, provides the opening crisis with an effective solution. Following a lengthy series of delays and deferrals, the closing juridical coherence is coordinated with the opening problematic. It is thus the customal intrigue, not the love intrigue, which provides the narrative with closure.

Is the *Charrete* therefore an abortive project, a love story whose intrigue remains unfinished, its meaning impossible to determine? According to the testimony of a

narrator who speaks on behalf of Godefroi, Chrétien's designated assistant, this
seems doubtful:

> Seignor, *se j'avant an disoie,*
> *ce seroit oltre la matire,*
> por ce an definer m'atire:
> ci faut li romanz an travers.
> Godefroiz de Leigni, li clers,
> a parfinee LA CHARRETE;
> mes nus hom blasme ne l'an mete
> se sor Crestïen a ovré,
> car ça il fet par le boen gré
> Crestïen, qui le comança:
> tant en a fet lors an ça
> ou Lancelot fu anmurez,
> tant con li contes est durez.
> *Tant en a fet, n'i vialt plus metre*
> *ne moins, por le conte mal metre.*   (vv. 7098–112)

Lords, *if I were to say any more, I would exceed the matter,* and so will bring this to a close: here
ends the romance in full course. The clerk Godefroiz de Leigni finished the *Charrete*; let
none blame him for having put a hand to Chrétien's work, for he did it with the blessing of
Chrétien, who began it. He took up the story from where Lancelot was in captivity until its
end. *Having done that, he wishes to do no more, no less, for fear of harming the story.*

The intent here is apparent: if the love intrigue lacks closure, the matter on which
the *Charrete* is based is itself complete. At the end, the new narrator must therefore
forestall any possible disappointment on the part of the public. Ruled out is any
possibility that Godefroi, a less capable clerk, has not entirely finished his master's
work; he emphasizes that the project which at the outset proclaimed a perfect
harmony between "matter and meaning" (v. 26) has been fully realized.[32] If indeed
there is meaning in this matter that must not be exceeded, it must thus obtain in
more than just the scandalous love intrigue that remains unresolved at the end of
the work. Its rich, unexploited possibilities will indeed ensure Lancelot and
Guenevere a fictive future of long duration, beginning around the end of the
twelfth century. In the *Charrete*, meanwhile, it is the customal intrigue that
determines the economy of the narrative and provides closure.[33]

In furnishing Chrétien with the *matière* and *san* of the *Charrete* (v. 26), might the
Countess of Champagne have provided matter and a meaning involving not only
adulterous love but also a juridical issue, one determining the sacrosanct
boundaries of the *matière* and including the problematic of customs?[34] For obvious
reasons, pertaining to the irrecuperability of the historical transactions between
poet and patroness, the question will necessarily remain as unresolved as the love
intrigue itself, and our critical efforts to resolve it as inept, perhaps, as those of
Meleagant to decipher the enigma of the bloodstained sheets. The hypothesis
concerning a meaningful merger of love and customs is nonetheless strengthened
by the way in which the heroic dynamic is distributed between the two intrigues.
The featured performer in the customal intrigue is not Lancelot but Meleagant, the
malicious abuser of customs; he is the antagonistic instigator of the juridical

intrigue which he weaves and which, despite his clever machinations, puts an end to his days. As for Lancelot, he remains throughout the principal subject of the inconclusive love intrigue. In the end, moreover, it is his accumulation of a surplus of value in the love intrigue that helps enable him, rather than Gauvain, the exemplary exponent of the court, to bring the customal intrigue to a close.

This complementarity of narrativity and value recalls Haidu's demonstration, cited in the previous chapter, that in *Le Chevalier au lion* the resolution of the conflict with Laudine in the "sentimental intrigue" results from Yvain's progressive self-attribution of value through service to individuals and collectivities in the "chivalric intrigue."[35] In *Yvain*, love interest is ultimately the beneficiary of the hero's service to society, while in the *Charrete* society is enhanced by heroism in service to love. The analogy between the two works is only partial, however, especially where attribution of an ultimate sanction is concerned. Superficially, the Tournament of Noauz in the *Charrete* would seem to be functionally similar to Lunete's "geu de la verté" in *Yvain*, for both are manipulative stratagems culminating in a positive sanction of the hero. Laudine's sanction of Yvain is nonetheless more comprehensive: her oath that she will do everything she can to reconcile "the Knight of the Lion" with his lady stems from her recognition of this knight's surplus of value accumulated in the chivalric intrigue, and this sanction, deceptively exacted by her servant, necessitates her subsequent amatory sanction of Yvain when she discovers his true identity.[36] On the other hand, while the Tournament of Noauz enables the queen to signify her amatory sanction of Lancelot once she has, by means of a clever ruse, ascertained his identity, the surplus of value he wins in this tournament (one designed, moreover, to identify the most desirable chivalric mate) pertains only to the amatory sphere. In the balance of the work, there is no represented sanction of Lancelot's achievements within the customal intrigue. His status with regard to the values involved in the juridical sphere thus requires further scrutiny.

In order to obtain a more nuanced view of the relationship between love, customs, and the social dynamic, it is necessary to examine more closely Lancelot's relationship to the Arthurian order, particularly to the two conflicting images of Arthur as lawgiver revealed in the preceding chapter. While in "Li premiers vers" of *Erec* Arthur styles himself as the powerful hereditary upholder of paternal usages and customs, in his subsequent appearances he rarely mandates or sanctions the principal heroic achievements of his knights unless these pertain to the local security and integrity of his court. Lancelot's ultimate act of prowess clearly falls into the latter category. While abolishing a custom responsible for the enduring anguish and jeopardy of Arthur's realm, he also salvages the Arthurian Custom of Logres from the kind of manipulative abuse Meleagant sought to derive from it, to Arthur's personal and political detriment. Appropriately, then, the final lines of the narrative emphasize the Arthurian court's euphoria:

> Li rois et tuit cil qui i sont
> grant joie an demainnent et font.
> Lancelot desarment adonques
> cil qui plus lié an furent onques,
> si l'en ont mené a grant joie.   (vv. 7093–7)

The king and all present are exceedingly joyful. They who were never happier now disarm Lancelot and spirit him away in great joy.

This moment of communal rejoicing echoes the outcome of the "Joie de la Cort" in *Erec,* and Arthur, like King Evrain of Brandigant in the earlier romance, takes part in the festivities. Both works thus pay a degree of homage to the folktale paradigm of the grateful monarch whose realm is rescued by a superlative champion.[37]

Contrast overshadows resemblance, however. The ceremonial jubilation following Erec's victory at Brandigant fills over eighty verses (vv. 6275–358), as opposed to the above five sketchily evoking the scene at Arthur's court. One might well have expected a description exceeding in length and detail the earlier analogue, given the identity of this illustrious monarch and the magnitude of the crisis Lancelot has just resolved. Of course, much of this episode's energy has already been expended in ironizing the conventional love-interest in the aforementioned folktale type. It is not the king's daughter, nor even the hero's spouse, as in *Erec,* but the king's own *wife* who waits anxiously on the sidelines as the hero enters the lists. While his return inspires the barely dissimulated *frisson* of her covert joy (cf. vv. 6820ff.), her spouse more coolly "honors" Lancelot's arrival, candidly acknowledging that he has had not a clue as to the hero's whereabouts: "mes molt m'esbaïs/an quel terre, et an quel païs/vos avez si grant piece esté" ("but I was greatly perplexed as to what realm or land you were in for so long," vv. 6859–61). Adding that he has had him sought "high and low" during the entire year, Arthur says nothing about Lancelot's intervention in Gorre before his disappearance, about which heroism Gauvain, Kay, and the prisoners, if not the queen herself, must have informed him. His astonishing vagueness elicits from Lancelot a report of the latter's imprisonment, as well as of his release by Meleagant's sister – "une moie amie" (v. 6876) – and his intention to "repay" Meleagant for his treachery. In some respects, this encounter recalls the convention of Arthur as narratee of his knights' remote exploits. Yet because the king makes no response at all and never thereafter resumes the dialogue, there is no evidence that he rewards or sanctions the hero's involvement in resolving this continuing Arthurian crisis.[38]

While Lancelot's assumption of primary responsibility for resolving the crisis imposed by Meleagant involves neither an initial mandate nor any explicit ultimate sanction on the part of Arthur, the latter's deficiency as an addressor is matched by the eccentric status of his heroic benefactor. There are repeated reminders that Lancelot's mandates lie beyond the sphere of Arthur's concerns.[39] In his final accounting to Arthur, he is obsessed, not with the possibility of at last restoring security in Logres, but exclusively with unleashing his personally vindictive wrath (vv. 6882ff.).[40] At other times, his affective submission to the queen is attributed to the lordly domination of an exteriorized, imperious addressor, the god of Love:

> Li chevaliers n'a cuer que un
> et cil n'est mie ancor a lui,
> einz est comandez a autrui
> si qu'il nel puet aillors prester.

Tot le fet en un leu ester
Amors, qui toz les cuers justise.
Toz? Nel fet, fors cez qu'ele prise.
Et cil s'an redoit plus prisier
cui ele daigne justisier.
Amors le cuer celui prisoit
si que sor toz le justisoit
et li donoit si grant orguel
que de rien blasmer ne le vuel
s'il lait ce qu'Amors li desfant
et la ou ele vialt antant.   (vv. 1228–42)

The knight has but one heart, and it is no longer his own but has been commended to another so that he cannot lend it elsewhere. Love alone, which governs all hearts, consigns it to a single abode. All hearts? None, except those Love has captivated, and he whom Love deigns to control should value this fact all the more. *Love so treasured this knight's heart as to govern it in preference to all others* and endowed it with abundant pride. Thus I do not wish to blame him if he declines what Love forbids while adhering to that which Love allows.

Throughout his adventures, Lancelot's primary addressor is neither Arthur nor the order of Logres, but the law of Love, and despite his extensive involvement in the customal intrigue, it cannot be argued that he is as much a hero of the customal order as of the lofty order of *fin'amor*. [41] If he is not infrequently the agent of custom he is but an *involuntary* agent, as one who, being perennially in Love's service, on occasion finds himself inadvertently in the service of social institutions as well. While the episode in which he lifts the tombstone lends him the aura of an *élu* with regard to the task of liberating the prisoners in Gorre, as we have seen, it is nonetheless his self-absorbing obsession with the queen that compels him to the task. Here the tension between desire and the social order comprises one important, highly ironic vein in the global *san* of this romance. Herein lies the paradox of Lancelot: a lovelorn knight whose consciousness of a social mission is consequently truncated becomes, despite his most intimate, potentially scandalous concerns, society's benefactor precisely because of his effective exaltation.

The romance's overall meaning, however, is not confined exclusively to illustration of this aspect of the hero. For the ironic, almost myopic game of love and chance which – at least for the moment – restores order to an imperiled realm is far from optimistic as regards the problematic of monarchy and chivalry already broached in *Erec*. Like Erec, whose success in the Custom of the Sparrowhawk allows Arthur to resolve the crisis at hand, Lancelot will return with a solution to a far more ominous problem. Yet in neither case does the hero's intent to return involve a primary concern with the communal predicament: in the one instance it is a question of securing the queen's approbation of the knight's bride-elect, in the other of liberating the queen while exacting personal vengeance. In neither hero is there the embodiment of a personalized mediation between the feudal monarch victimized by his own juridical institutions and those elements within chivalry who would gainfully exploit them. By virtue of his acutely personal motives throughout, Lancelot himself serves instead to underline the persistent conflict between Arthur's centripetal ideal, consecrated to the impossible dynamic of ritualizing the present according to models from the past, and the centrifugal, future-oriented dynamic of chivalry.[42] That his love takes as its object the queen is all the more indicative of Lancelot's prominent agency within that dynamic, as well as of his relative indifference to the king's personal and political welfare.

The conflated intrigues of love and custom in the *Charrete*, as vehicles of a meaningful illustration of solidarity between the law of love and the restoration of civil order, confirm that as a motivating, ennobling force, love may indeed be conducive to beneficial heroic endeavours in the communal sphere. At the same time, however, a more disturbing component in the *san* of the *Charrete* has emerged in this chapter. It concerns a *defective reciprocity* between Arthur as monarch and Lancelot as his primary chivalric auxiliary. As a voluntary agent first of love, and then also of vengeance, Lancelot is motivated by values emanating in both cases from spheres independent of the monarch. In the first of these categories, moreover, the motivating influence of the god of Love determines an unacknowledged rivalry between the knight and his king, one which contrasts sharply with the characteristic solidarity of lawgiver and defender in folktales featuring heroic protection of an embattled monarchy. Yet once again, as in "Li premiers vers," the centripetal ideal is finally salvaged through the operations of an illustrious agent from within the chivalric sphere. Both Angrés and Meleagant are functionally akin to the Mordret of the anterior tradition, but neither in *Cligés* nor in the *Charrete* was Chrétien prepared, as were Geoffrey and Wace, to have his Arthurian order sundered by one unjust man.

In the *Charrete* it is a question, rather, of resorting to the latent opposition already productive of Chrétien's first Arthurian crisis, that in *Erec*, and of allowing it to erupt anew, in a more conflictual setting, with far more ominous consequences. Now the realm has become vulnerable from without as well as from within. Morever, a malicious villain has discovered that the skeleton key to the disruption of Arthur's anterior order may lie, not in the usurpation of a Mordret, but in the manipulation of Arthurian customal procedure. Thanks to the knight from Logres, the knight from Gorre never succeeds in opening the doorway to disaster. Yet this complex – and perplexing – hero of love and custom belongs to a type already intermittently broached by Chrétien in the personage of Erec, a hero who, if he is *of* the realm of Arthur, is not voluntarily *in* its service. By incarnating the centripetal chivalric principle of independence from the anterior order in the hero instead of within an undifferentiated contingent of knights and barons, Chrétien takes a significant, unsettling step toward individualizing the conflict between the centripetal dynamic and the anterior ideal.

As in a game of chess, the whole meaning of this literary enigma is tied up in the queen, the crucial piece.[43] Yet such meaning is wholly a matter of position and proximity, to black knight or to white, between white knight and white king. In this romance the white knight's move is decisive; in the meantime, to borrow a phrase from Eliot, Arthur sits "pressing lidless eyes and waiting for a knock upon the door."

3

Tenir terre: customs in *Le Chevalier au lion*

Customs, we have seen, are prominently involved in the exposition and resolution of one major Arthurian crisis in *Erec et Enide* and in *Le Chevalier de la charrete*. In each crisis two distinct, highly detailed customs come to the fore, one an Arthurian practice of long standing, the other apparently of more recent origin and maintained by a social entity geographically distant from Arthur's court. Despite this spatial disjunction, the two are brought into a crucial relationship. In *Erec*, this formula is confined to "Li premiers vers," where Arthur's inability to complete a re-enactment of the Custom of the White Stag because of the ominous procedural deadlock at court contrasts with Erec's successful engagement in the remote Custom of the Sparrowhawk; Erec's triumph in this chivalric and noble analogue of the monarch's hereditary obligation will ultimately provide a satisfactory basis for the latter's completion, as well as for resolution of this initial crisis. In the *Charrete*, on the other hand, the formula is extended to the global narrative dimensions of the work. The crisis erupts in the opening lines, as Meleagant boldly proposes a confrontation under the jurisdiction of the Custom of Logres in order to strengthen and perpetuate the jurisdiction of the Custom of Gorre; resolution of this crisis does not occur until the ultimate heroic function in the narrative trajectory is completed, when Lancelot decapitates the founder of the Custom of Gorre and the abuser of the Custom of Logres. In both works, then, when the formerly venerable status and canonic functioning of the Arthurian custom are in some way jeopardized, the remote, non-Arthurian custom becomes a significant factor in the crisis. The ensuing customal interlace, involving the hero in the sphere of the remote custom, ultimately culminates in restoration of the Arthurian custom's effectiveness as an adjudicative standard.

Yvain, ou le chevalier au lion also contains a variety of major and minor customs, and these bring to mind features of the earlier works. Like the *Charrete*, for instance, *Yvain* develops the full extent of its narrative line on the basis of an issue which involves customs. In both works, the juridical issue is conveyed through progressive stages that are closely associated with the dynamic development of the hero as this is shaped by what we have identified as a textuality of crisis. Once again, moreover, it will be seen that the hero's crisis in the midst of his enterprise is distinct, in terms of both structure and values, from the one disruptive crisis ultimately confronted by the Arthurian court. As in *Erec* and the *Charrete*, then, in *Yvain* we shall again find a lack of solidarity between the concerns of the hero and the king's promotion of the anterior order and its values.

The Custom of the Perilous Fountain

These tensions are indicative of a considerable degree of continuity among the first three works in the customal series. In *Yvain*, however, a new and persistent interest will be apparent, one that concerns the *kinds* of cases to which the customs pertain. While those in the *Charrete*, as we have seen, frequently address the rights and liberties of individuals, those in *Le Chevalier au lion* deal more consistently with the attribution or maintenance of rights of property, a concern summed up in the title of this chapter, "Tenir terre." Further, as regards the aforementioned *pairing* of customs in "Li premiers vers" and in the overall narrative dimension of the *Charrete*, the one Arthurian crisis in *Yvain* is neither located at the outset nor diffused throughout the entire work but confined to the penultimate episode, where a single custom is involved. Instead of organizing matter and meaning according to one predetermined customal format, Chrétien was obviously prepared to vary it in keeping with the exigencies of his *matière* and *san*. Yet, as in *Erec* and the *Charrete*, customs in *Yvain* again appear as discrete, formal loci whose intrinsic properties are replicated or otherwise recalled in larger sections of the whole. Cumulatively, this chapter's disclosures will suggest that no episode of *Yvain* remains untouched by their influence.

THE CUSTOM OF THE PERILOUS FOUNTAIN

Long before its identification with a custom, the perilous fountain is already quite familiar to Chrétien's listener or reader.[1] It first appears at the very outset, in Calogrenant's account of his shameful and abortive adventure seven years earlier (vv. 173–580).[2] On his way into the unknown, Yvain's hapless cousin passes through a variegated landscape in which a microcosm of feudal order borders on savage, uncultivated wilderness. Only moments after leaving the orderly and tranquil ambiance of an hospitable vavassor and his charming daughter, he is confronted by the awesome spectacle of wild bulls tearing each other limb from limb.[3] Among the lower animals, it is evident that only the strongest specimens prevail, and for a human to deal with them successfully superior strength is also necessary. This is the lesson of the Hideous Herdsman, a man whose craggy, shaggy countenance places him in a twilight zone between nature and culture, a "lord" who "governs" the forest's beasts by inspiring their fear of his overwhelming strength:

> car quant j'en puis une tenir,
> si l'estraing si par les deus corz,
> as poinz que j'ai et durs et forz,
> que les autres de peor tranblent
> et tot en viron moi s'asanblent,
> ausi con por merci crïer...　　　　　　　　(vv. 344–9)

"for when I can grab one by the horns and pin it down with my hard, strong hands, the others quake for fear and huddle around me, as if to beg for mercy."

Brutality, then, is the key to his elementary idea of order. Yet it is also he who describes, in remarkably poetic detail, a bubbling fountain flanked by a pine, as well as the destructive chaos wrought among flora and fauna when the fountain's water, poured over a stone, unleashes a tempest. Here, too, it is a matter of surviving a natural onslaught, and unless one "renders justice" to this phenomenon, one may not return unscathed. The herdsman never specifies what is entailed in the phrase "randre son droit" (v. 373); yet one might suppose that, from his primitive perspective, the "law" of might over right applies in yet another confrontation with the forces of nature.[4]

It therefore comes as no small surprise to learn, as Calogrenant unleashes the tempest, that he who would tamper with this natural marvel is subject to a penalty, according to the juridical conventions of a local feudal culture. When the chivalric guardian of the fountain suddenly appears and prepares to unhorse Calogrenant with a disabling blow, he harshly upbraids the intruder (vv. 491ff.): had he been "in the right," Calogrenant would have "defied" him, or at least have "sought a judgment" before initiating a "'war." This "evil" will be turned against its perpetrator, using the fallen timber as "evidence." The defender's formal "complaint" is "reasonable," he insists, for Calogrenant has "invaded" a land where neither wall, nor tower, nor fortress avails, and so he shall enjoy neither "truce" nor "peace." This volley of charges, featuring such juridically pregnant terms as *droiture*, *garanz*, and *plaindre*, assumes the tone of a formal legal indictment.

Where this mysterious fountain is concerned, much more is clearly involved in the concept of "randre le droit" than the herdsman had ever supposed. His prescription of an arbitrary personal investment of physical force against natural foes, in keeping with a primal law of *solitary* survival, here clashes with a more sophisticated law of *communal* security. Much later, when Yvain repeatedly unleashes the tempest in order to provoke his lady's acknowledgment of her need for his services, the helpless and exasperated natives describe the storm-making mechanism as a sort of curse:[5]

> Tel peor ont que il maudient
> lor ancessors, et trestuit dïent:
> "Maleoiz soit li premiers hom
> qui fist en cest païs meison,
> et cil qui cest chastel fonderent!
> Qu'an tot le monde ne troverent
> leu que l'an doie tant haïr
> c'uns seus hom le puet envaïr,
> et tormanter, et traveillier." (vv. 6537–45)

Their fear prompts them to berate their ancestors, and all say: "Cursed be he who first built a house in this land, and those who founded this castle! In all the world they could not have found a more hateful place, that only one man can so assail, and torment, and devastate."

The fountain's very presence in this unfortunate realm necessitates its defense against anyone who, for whatever reason, would unleash its destructive force. Sanctions are also mandatory for all who succeed in so doing, no matter how unaware of the illegality of such an encroachment. The past effectiveness of its defense is measured by the vavassor who informs a dejected Calogrenant, returning in embarrassed defeat from this encounter, that no violator before him

The Custom of the Perilous Fountain

has ever escaped death or captivity in the fountain's realm. Like it or not, then, defense has long remained an absolute necessity. Indeed, the attitudes of the herdsman and the defender reflect a similar concern. Whether for the solitary individual or the isolated group, "law and order" is a matter of local needs, of a necessity to "stand one's ground" – to *tenir terre* – against any impingement or incursion. And regardless of how one's defenses are maintained, whether with rustic brutality or with chivalric refinements, might is the guarantor of right, locally defined.[6]

The defender is consequently within his rights when he accosts an intruder in this vulnerable land. In this regard, the unsuspecting experimentation of a Calogrenant not only anticipates the whimsical curiosity of an Arthur who later visits the site as an intrigued "tourist": both are on an equal footing with the deliberate provocation of an Yvain who, as Calogrenant's cousin, will seek to replicate the adventure in order to exact vengeance for his kinsman's shame.[7] From the point of view of the society that maintains the custom, the disruption caused by the fountain is tantamount to the ravages of warfare (vv. 2082ff.), and he who activates the meteorological catastrophe is necessarily a lawbreaker before the standard of this local institution.[8] It is worthy of note at this point that the violators – Calogrenant, Yvain, and Kay – are all *Arthurian* challengers whose motives, whether a thirst for adventure, vengeance, or self-aggrandizing arrogance, preclude any concern for the security of this land and its inhabitants. It is precisely this domain's perennial susceptibility to the devastation caused by the fountain that prompts the frantic efforts to replace its defender after Yvain, a more fortunate intruder, has slain him.

The choice of an appropriate successor, not a matter to be taken lightly, does not depend solely on the desire of the defender's widow, Laudine, to appoint Yvain, once persuaded by a clever Lunete that the victor is the ideal candidate.[9] The servant advises her mistress to assemble her baronial council to assist her:

> Et au demain remanderoiz
> vos genz et si demanderoiz
> consoil del roi qui doit venir.
> Por la *costume* maintenir
> de vostre fontainne desfandre
> vos convendroit boen consoil prandre   (vv. 1847–52)

"And tomorrow you should convoke your vassals for advice concerning the king's arrival. It would be appropriate to take good counsel about maintenance of the *custom* of defending your fountain."

Here, for the first time, the mechanism of the fountain is designated as a *custom*. Again, as in the *Charrete*, formal identification of the customal procedure comes long after its coherence is initially manifested by the course of events. That it should be so designated in this romance at precisely this juncture is significant, for one identifying trait of a custom is its being perceived as obligatory within the collectivity that observes it.[10] Thus it is indispensable that administration of the fountain's defense involve the baronial council, and thus Laudine recognizes the need for a candidate whose prowess is exceptionally renowned in order to win the unanimous assent of the barons. Because none among them is equal to the responsibility of being an effective guardian, all will eagerly ratify her choice of a stalwart willing to relieve them of the unwanted peril (vv. 1857–70).

In the ensuing assembly, to underline the critical urgency of ratifying Laudine's candidate, her seneschal recalls the custom's history and the consequences of failing to maintain it. Implicit in this harangue is also the notion that, for want of an outsider to assume the defender's role, it would fall to Laudine herself:

> "Seignor, fet il, guerre nos sourt:
> n'est jorz que li rois ne s'atourt
> de quan qu'il se puet atorner
> por venir noz terres gaster.
> Ençois que la quinzainne past
> sera trestote alee a gast,
> se boen mainteneor n'i a.
> Qant ma dame se marïa,
> n'a mie ancor sis anz parclos,
> si le fist ele par voz los.
> Morz est ses sires, ce li poise.
> N'a or de terre c'une toise
> cil qui tot cest païs tenoit
> et qui molt bien i avenoit:
> c'est granz diax que po a vescu.
> Fame ne set porter escu
> ne ne set de lance ferir;
> molt amander, et ancherir,
> se puet de panre un boen seignor.
> Einz mes n'en ot mestier graignor;
> loez li tuit que seignor praingne,
> einz que la costume remaingne
> qui an cest chastel a esté
> plus de .lx. anz a passé."   (vv. 2082–106)

"Lords," he says, "war is upon us: the king is daily gathering his forces to devastate our lands. Before the end of a fortnight all will be laid waste, unless there is a proper defender. When my lady married less than six years ago, she did so by your leave. Her husband is dead, and this weighs heavily upon her. He who once held all of this country with such mastery now occupies but a small plot. The brevity of his life is a great pity. A woman cannot bear a shield or wield a lance; by marrying she can greatly improve her lot and increase her value. At present she has no greater need than this; counsel her to marry, then, before the custom kept in this castle sixty years and more goes unobserved."

The scene is reminiscent of the assembly of Arthur's barons in *Erec*, in that here again oratory brings unanimity. Here all kneel before Laudine while she, "as if despite herself," consents to do "that which she would have done even without their approval" (vv. 2107ff.). As with Arthur's elaborate efforts in "Li premiers vers" to secure a consensus for completion of the cynegetic custom, Laudine's outward behavior signifies her awareness that custom is neither automatic nor the product of one upholder's wishes, but rather a matter of collective consent. With the arrival of the Arthurian court ominously at hand, all agree that this custom, whose longevity surpasses tenfold the tenure of its previous "maintainer," must be maintained at all costs. It is a matter of preventing the *châtelaine*'s precariously placed property from being transformed into a waste land.

This scene marks the successful culmination of a series of three intrigues in which the custom has served repeatedly both as destination and as an objectifier of value. In Calogrenant's quest for adventure the fountain becomes, at the herdsman's behest, a likely substitute for a naïve valorization of *avanture* (v. 362). Then, following Calogrenant's defeat and concomitant shame, it constitutes Yvain's quest to avenge his cousin, and it is the homicidal outcome of this vengeful exaltation of familial value that leads to a third intrigue, engineered by Lunete, involving the valorization of Yvain as the fountain's defender. This proves to be a formidable task, but Laudine's acceptance of her spouse's slayer is in part conditioned by the custom's requirement of a knight of superlative prowess. Finally, as a chronic menace in their midst, the fountain inspires within the neighboring populace convergent attitudes concerning the custom. While Laudine valorizes her feudal obligation to uphold it, her barons sufficiently cherish their personal safety to ratify any likely candidate who would relieve them of the ordeal, whence, at last, unanimity. Thus in Yvain's initial progression, from the role of passive narratee who listens to his cousin's story, to that of instigator of a program of vengeance, and thence to the nominal role of guarantor of order in Laudine's domain, the custom consistently wields considerable power in organizing the value-structures that coordinate the successive intrigues.[11]

If the custom plays a major role in the objectification of value in personal, familial, and communal spheres, what valuation lies within the more immediate sphere of its enforcement? Let us look more closely at Lunete's persuasion of Laudine. Having promised in her first dialogue with Laudine that she will "prove" the existence of a potential husband superior to the one her mistress has just lost (vv. 1601–15), in their subsequent encounter she offers the following argument:

> – Par foi, vos poez bien entandre
> que je m'an vois par mi le voir,
> *et si vos pruef par estovoir*
> *que mialz valut cil qui conquist*
> *vostre seignor que il ne fist*:
> il le conquist et sel chaça
> par hardemant anjusque çà,
> et si l'enclost an sa meison.   (vv. 1706–13)

"By my faith, you can well understand that I am in the realm of truth *and prove to you by necessity that more worthy than your lord himself is he who conquered him*: he defeated and pursued him clear back here and imprisoned him in his own house."

Surprisingly, in adjudicating the most serious offense against the custom – the lethal, "*felonious* blow" (v. 866) dealt to the defender of the fountain by Yvain – Lunete here rules in favor of the custom's transgressor. Of course, her fondness for Yvain goes back to a favor he had once done for her at Arthur's court, as the reader has learned (vv. 1004ff.). Yet in her defense of the candidate she admires, she makes no effort to minimize the violence he inflicted on Esclados, and even approvingly evokes Yvain's relentless pursuit of his mortally wounded victim. Her rather thin "proof" of Yvain's superiority consists essentially of an assertion that the conqueror is worthier than the conquered: involved is an absolute valorization of physical strength, one that would admit of even the most brutal coercion. On close examination we find that to construct her specious argument Lunete appears to amplify her remarks on the basis of a single proposition, "In valor is value, in might right," in the manner of a rhetorical invention.[12] Contrary to her claim, this constitutes no demonstration founded on incontrovertible premises but a mere instance of *logica probabilis*.[13] Not necessity, but opinion, is the substance of her argument, and even Laudine will chide her for its irrationality ("desreison," v. 1714).

One cannot fault Lunete alone for harboring such a shallow view, however, for valuation of valor as a product of superior physical force is also the operative assumption behind the fountain custom. There, in fact, the principle that right is a function of might is institutionalized. Through the time-honored, conventional operation of the custom, the former exemplar of chivalric might as a universal has been supplanted by one who is mightier. Rather than modify the principle on the basis of other criteria, Lunete is suggesting, would it not be preferable to choose the individual more adequately representative of the universal?

During the first half of the romance, then, superior might is repeatedly valorized as a determinant of right, not only by the primitive herdsman, but also by the more "courtly" contingent, including Calogrenant, Yvain, Lunete, and Kay. Attributions of positive or negative qualifications – dominance, prowess, marriageability, shame, exclusion, and so on – are made solely on the basis of capacities or deficiencies in this area. Chief among these instances where might is venerated is the Custom of the Perilous Fountain, whose juridical ethos depends less on the ethical merits of consistent *principles* than on the relative brawn of conflicting *principals*:

> mes andui sont de si fier cuer
> que li uns por l'autre a nul fuer
> *de terre un pié ne guerpiroit*
> se jusqu'a mort ne l'enpiroit...   (vv. 851–4)

But both are of such fierce determination that, unless death intervene, neither would dream of *yielding the other a foot of land*.

As if it were the initial panel in the structural diptych created by *Le Chevalier au lion*, the spectacle of Yvain and Esclados locked in the heat of battle sums up in a single image the way in which the featured custom honoring the rightness of might also acknowledges the imperative to *tenir terre*.[14]

THE FOUNTAIN CUSTOM AND THE STRUCTURE OF *YVAIN*

The governing proposition of the fountain custom – "If might, then right" – is thus reflected in the texture of its fictionalization.[15] The development of Yvain through the first part of the romance, as evoked above, shows that *the principle is operative irrespective of the motives of its agent.* The fact that he marries Laudine with the approbation of all parties, thus replacing the victim by his killer, seems to bear out Lunete's assertion of the rightness of might. This view is never challenged in the first part of the story, which culminates in Yvain's excessively long period of wandering from one tournament to another, displaying his might and, presumably, his valor. In fact, up to the onset of Yvain's crisis, the romance effectively amplifies and illustrates this premise: it shows how Yvain, who is mightier than his cousin, repeats the latter's abortive adventure and brings it mightily to completion.[16] Not until the outbreak of the crisis, upon Laudine's repudiation of her perjured spouse, do the supposedly positive qualities of Yvain's might and valor come into question: toward what end is the exercise of might to be considered right? It was avenging Calogrenant's "shame" that had occupied Yvain through early episodes (v. 589: "g'irai vostre honte venger"), compounded by his preoccupation with avoiding Kay's ridicule should he present no evidence – no "anseignes veraies" (v. 899), or "true signs" – of his victory.[17] Even the beauty of a bereaved Laudine as her servants lower her husband's body into the ground does not diminish this obsession:

> que del cors qu'il voit qu'an enfuet
> li poise, quant avoir n'en puet
> aucune chose qu'il an port
> tesmoing qu'il l'a ocis et mort;
> s'il n'en a tesmoing et garant,
> que mostrer puisse a parlemant,
> donc iert il honiz en travers...   (vv. 1345–51)

For he is dismayed to see the body laid to rest, because he can take no part of it back as evidence that he killed it; if he has no evidence or proof to show to the assembly, he will be shamed to the quick...

The pertinence of the proposition is by no means restricted to the first part of the romance, however. Most of the second part is made up of episodes in which Yvain conquers further adversaries: Count Alier and his forces; a fire-breathing serpent; the gigantic Harpin; Lunete's three enemies; and the two monstrous, demonic "fils de netun." This series, in which Yvain is repeatedly measured against immeasurably stronger foes, features further reflections on the proposition; it yields the significant difference that Yvain's might is now directed to *altruistic* service rather than to the presumably satisfying objective of family vengeance. This reorientation is symbolized half way through the romance by Yvain's vigorous intervention on behalf of the lion to free it from a "felonious" serpent (vv. 3341–484).[18] Thereafter Yvain, as the "knight of the lion," and his leonine adjuvant acquired through rightful might will repeatedly prevail. Combining their energies into a formidable force, they will rescue others from bondages imposed by the malicious use of might. The resulting increment of value to the hero's emblematic name will finally effect his reconciliation with Laudine.[19] Only the monumental, indecisive combat between Yvain and Gauvain, to be taken up in the final section of this chapter, falls outside the pattern.

In short, the saturation of the romance with episodes that reflect in various ways the assumption "If might, then right" makes of this premise a dominant level of coherence. No episode fails to recall it in some significant way. The story's major bipartite sections coordinate first its negative then its positive illustration, the one *occasioning the crisis* because founded on a selfish and inadequate exemplification, the other *growing logically from the crisis*, as its altruistic rectification.[20] In addition, the premise shows a remarkable relationship to the customal level of coherence. As the operative assumption behind the fountain custom, it serves throughout as a principle to be tested and explored by a variety of episodes that shed further light on it while reflecting it prismatically. The larger implications of its prominence will be taken up in Chapter 5.

Despite the ethical equilibrium achieved by the bipartite sections, a sense of *openness* lingers at the end of *Yvain* as it does at the end of the *Charrete*. In both cases this is the result of a *sentimental intrigue* that to some degree signifies its own irresolution: here, the reconciliation of the couple during the final episode leaves something to be desired, its incompleteness on a deep, affective level obtaining in the artful manipulation by which Lunete precipitates the accord.[21] Once again, however, the logic initiated by the custom signifies narrative closure. From the outset, the overarching question of defending the fountain, whether explored in terms of its successive challengers or of its defensive agent, has remained a problematic issue. Yvain's definitive assumption of this role marks the work's closure, such that the narrator, not unlike his counterpart at the end of the *Charrete*, may declare:

> Del *Chevalier au lyeon* fine
> Crestïens son romans ensi;
> n'onques plus conter n'en oï
> ne ja plus n'en orroiz conter
> s'an n'i vialt mançonge ajoster. (vv. 6804–8)

Chrétien thus finishes his romance of the *Knight of the Lion*. I heard nothing further about it, nor will you, unless there is a wish to append thereto a lie.

Like the *matière* of the *Charrete*, that of *Yvain* has been maximally amplified, following out the customal intrigue to its logical conclusion; while frequently overdetermining narrative logic, logical possibilities generated from the custom ultimately achieve textual closure.

TENUOUS TERRITORIES: CUSTOMS AND THE IMPERILED FIEF

If we pursue the comparison with the *Charrete*, we find that the Custom of the Perilous Fountain is clearly akin to the second clause in the Custom of Logres, in that both make the determination of right consequent upon the prior determination of which of two adversaries will prevail by force. Yet each custom pertains to a different kind of case. While the Custom of Logres deals with *individual* rights, the Custom of the Fountain is exclusively concerned with the security of a feudal castellany – a fortification, its noble inhabitants and the surrounding community of

Customs and the imperiled fief

tenants in their service.[22] As suggested above, the primary function of the keeper of this custom could be summed up in the phrase *tenir terre*. This is how Laudine's seneschal expresses the irony of Esclados' fate:

> N'a or de *terre* c'une toise
> cil qui tot cest païs *tenoit*
> et qui molt bien i avenoit. . .   (vv. 2094–6)

"He who once held all of this country with such mastery now occupies but a small plot. . ."

If in terms of the love intrigue the first part of the romance turns on the irony of the widow's marriage to her husband's killer, in terms of the customal intrigue the irony of the pre-crisis phase stems from metamorphosis of the fountain's abuser into its communally designated defender. Abdication of the latter role is what entails the crisis. Appropriately, its onset is marked by Yvain's flight from a society where custom is observed into an uncultivated wilderness where the primary law is that of survival.[23] The teleology of the post-crisis development then centers on how this derelict defender, having relinquished his duty to defend the lady's domain, will finally recover the capacity and the unlimited privilege to *tenir terre*. The sentimental intrigue converges with the customal intrigue when it finally becomes possible for Yvain to "make peace" – *feire pes* (vv. 6513 *et passim*) – with Laudine, so that henceforth he will "tenir sa terre an pes."[24] It seems apposite, then, that in most of Yvain's post-crisis adventures, the ones that requalify him to *tenir terre* according to the custom, he is instrumental in restoring social order elsewhere, so that *others* may "tenir terre an pes."

The first of these follows Yvain's awakening and recovery of his rational faculties after his prolonged crisis; it is also the last of his adventures before he becomes "the Knight of the Lion." In its detail, it significantly recalls his previous failure as the defender of an imperiled domain while also foreshadowing his later recovery of this role. The Lady of Norison is in danger of losing her embattled lands to Count Alier. Having found Yvain unconscious in the forest, one of the *châtelaine*'s servants suggests that he might be of service in her struggle (vv. 2933ff.). The servant's argument is reminiscent of Lunete's persuasion of Laudine: in both cases, a noble lady has a critical need for a male to help her *tenir terre* against an aggressor. The account of Yvain's pursuit of Count Alier and his men, including the motif of equine dismemberment (vv. 3262ff.), evokes his earlier pursuit of Esclados. This recall is reinforced by contrastive parallels that further relate the two episodes. In this case Yvain only imprisons his adversary instead of killing him, and this time no ruse is needed to identify Yvain as a likely husband and lord, his prowess prompting the locals to wish "que il eüst lor dame prise/et fust la terre an sa justise" ("that he marry their lady and the land be his dominion," vv. 3249–50). The treaty with which Yvain ends the conflict stipulates to the count

> que toz jorz mes pes li tanra
> et que ses pertes li randra
> quan qu'ele an mosterra par prueves,
> et refera les meisons nueves
> que il avoit par terre mises.   (vv. 3305–9)

63

that henceforth he will be at peace with her, restore all losses that she declares on evidence, and rebuild new houses in place of those he had leveled.

The lady wishes to reward Yvain with herself and all of her possessions, but after restoring this waste land he departs, declining both matrimony and material rewards.

This episode marks Yvain's return to a functional level equivalent to that achieved prior to the crisis.[25] Yet there are differences. He has stepped into a role analogous to the one previously allocated to him as defender of the fountain, only this time no courtly visit is at issue but rather a forceful seizure of property, against which he acquits himself in exemplary fashion. Again he has been granted a right to "the lady and her land," but this time without recourse to murder or manipulation. In the sudden onset of his love for Laudine, he had lost control of his heart (v. 1364); in this case he acts vigorously with a "cuer de prodome" ("the heart of a valorous man," v. 3176). In subsequent adventures, he will progressively surpass this level of achievement, acquiring with the lion a surrogate identity and an unfailing helper in the pursuit of an even higher order of valor. His *deliverance* of the lion from the serpent will facilitate his role as "deliverer" in his next three exploits, all of which bring into play the coherence of customs.[26]

The first of these exploits pertains, once again, to the Custom of the Fountain. Laudine's seneschal and his two brothers have imprisoned Lunete on charges of treason, formally accusing her of beguiling Laudine into matrimony with a perjured defender.[27] This case, resulting from an alleged abuse of the Custom of the Fountain, will be decided by deviation from constraints imposed by the custom of single combat (*Erec*, vv. 2822ff.): Lunete has vowed that a single champion will defend her against *all three* of her adversaries. Her recourse to a combat involving such lopsided odds, stemming from her declared conviction that "God and right" (vv. 4326ff.) are on her side, is also predicated on the convention of judicial combat.[28] Yet deviation from the conventions of such engagements exists on both sides. The unjust magnitude of Yvain's threefold adversary is offset by the involvement of Yvain's noble companion. With the aid of the lion, God prevails, as does the *lex talionis* – "an eye for an eye" – the three "traitors" meet the fiery fate they had reserved for the accused:

> Et cil furent ars an la ré
> qui por li ardoir fu esprise;
> que ce est reisons de justise
> que cil qui autrui juge a tort
> doit de celui meïsmes mort
> morir que il li a jugiee.   (vv. 4564–9)

And they were burned on the very pyre that had been kindled to consume her; for it is reasonable and just that he who wrongly judges another should die by the same death he adjudged to the other.

Whence another juridical determination whose operative proposition is formulated in the hypothetical "if – then" manner of customs: "*If* the accuser misjudge, *then* he must die by the penalty prescribed for the accused." By putting an end to this suit brought against an inappropriate defendant, Yvain rectifies Lunete's wrongful suffering occasioned by his own abuse both of Laudine's love and of his obligation to uphold the Custom of the Fountain (vv. 3714ff.).

Intercalated into the middle of this episode redolent of customs comes the account of another victory by Yvain, that over Harpin de la Montagne (vv. 3764ff.). The hero arrives at a fortified castle to find a scene of devastation:

> mes fors des murs estoit esrese
> la place, qu'il n'i ot remese
> an estant borde ne meison.   (vv. 3773–5)

But outside the walls the place was a shambles, and neither hovel nor house remained standing.

This waste land is the work of Harpin, a giant who, failing in his suit for the hand of the lord's daughter, had razed the village and seized his six sons, killing two of them.[29] Yvain has arrived on the eve of the giant's deadline: if no defender dare meet him in combat on the morrow, or if the daughter is not surrendered to him, he will execute the four remaining sons (vv. 2850ff.). Although Harpin does respect the principle of single combat, in keeping with the chivalric custom, his preference for this procedure stems from the fact that his gigantic might would presumably ensure his victory over any chivalric challenger. In order to impose the combat, moreover, he has already resorted to extreme forms of coercion, including execution of two of Gauvain's nephews, threatening a cruel and infamous fate for his niece, and destruction of the adjacent town (vv. 3845ff.). Such atrocities foreclose on the custom's capacity to determine right. These circumstances mitigate the fact that Yvain, assuming the challenge in the absence of Gauvain, the family's kinsman (vv. 3910ff.), inadvertently contravenes the principle of single combat as the lion joins the fray. Together, however, knight and lion end Harpin's arbitrary abuse of this custom while at the same time enabling this noble family to reunite and *tenir terre*.

Yvain's third and final post-crisis struggle involving the lion earns him a stunning victory at the castle of Pesme-Avanture (vv. 5101ff.). As Yvain approaches the castle's outer walls, this "Worst Adventure" is anticipated by the locals' singularly unfriendly greeting. In fact, as an elderly woman explains, this warning is part of a custom:

> e par costume feire suelent
> autel a toz les sorvenanz,
> por ce que il n'aillent leanz.
> Et la costume est ça fors tex
> que nos n'osons a nos ostex
> herbergier, por rien qui aveigne,
> nul preudome qui de fors veigne.   (vv. 5146–52)

"and their custom is to behave thus toward all who arrive, to keep them from going inside. And the custom here is such that we dare not, under any circumstances, lodge in our quarters any valiant knight coming from afar."

This, however, is only accessory to the principal custom of the castle.[30] The interior features two radically incongruous settings that critics often tend to read as anticipations of economic and social conditions during the age of Marx and Proudhon: one, representing enforced labor, as if it were prefigurative of a page from Dickens, the other, portraying leisured nobility, as if it might have inspired a pastoral by Manet.[31] The idle serenity of father, mother, and reading maiden in the latter, however, no less than the abjection of three hundred silk weavers in the former, reflects medieval literary customal practice. Behind the extreme contrast lie two separate interpretations of the same custom, which merits examination in some detail.

The account by one of the captive females recalls the custom's inception. Long ago the king of their homeland, the Isle of Maidens, was journeying abroad when, like a "naïve fool," he fell into peril (vv. 5250ff.): in the castle of Pesme-Avanture, two demons, born of woman and a *netun* (v. 5267),[32] compelled the young monarch to face them both in combat. To avoid this fatal encounter, the king instituted a yearly tribute:

> et li rois qui grant peor ot
> s'an delivra si com il pot:
> si jura qu'il anvoieroit
> chascun an, tant con vis seroit,
> ceanz, de ses puceles, trante;
> si fust quites par ceste rante;
> et devisié fu a jurer
> et cist treüz devoit durer
> tant con li dui maufé durroient;
> e a ce jor que il seroient
> conquis et vaincu an bataille
> quites seroit de ceste taille
> et nos seriens delivrees...   (vv. 5273–85)

"and the king, who was terribly frightened, got out of it as best he could: he promised for as long as he would live to send thirty of his maidens here each year. He was acquitted by this forfeiture and was engaged to swear that this settlement would obtain for the lifetime of the two demons. On the day of their defeat in combat, he would be acquitted of this tax and we would be delivered..."

This practice is much more recent than the Custom of the Fountain, by approximately a half-century. For a decade, a generation of captives has entered this "workhouse" with a clear recollection of how the custom began.[33] In this regard the practice brings to mind its counterparts in the other three customal romances: the Joie de la Cort, the Custom of Gorre, the procession in the Grail Castle, and the "enchantment" in the Castle of Marvels are all practices whose inception can be recalled, and each involves a community awaiting the arrival of a chivalric champion to release it from its obligation to unwanted, debilitating constraints.[34] As with the Custom of Gorre, moreover, a periodic "payment" of prisoners is involved, and such terms as "rente" and "taille" are further evocative of historical customs involving a *taxe* or a *redevance*;[35] here it is the *châtelain* himself who has incurred indebtedness to an arbitrary overlord.[36] Of particular interest in

this case is the fact that the inception of the community's bondage was effected by
yet another abuse of the custom of single combat. Not only did the young king
negotiate the annual tribute to obviate a combat with the grotesque pair;
abrogation of this annual obligation remains contingent upon a lone knight's
victory over both monsters. Thus, the foundation as well as the perpetuation of the
harmful, unjust Custom of Pesme-Avanture both stem from the abuse of a second
custom. This brings to mind the customal stratagem of Meleagant at the beginning
of the *Charrete*, when he seeks to wrest from the Custom of Logres a means of
perpetuating the Custom of Gorre, and the inception of the Joie de la Cort, near the
end of *Erec*, where Maboagrain's lady abuses the custom of the *don contraignant* in
order to institute the virtual perenniality of a customal single combat. In every
case, one custom is (ab)used unscrupulously so as to ensure the durability and
longevity of another.

As in the enchanted orchard outside the walls of Brandigant in *Erec*, the heroic
intruder in *Yvain* finds that he is an unwelcome guest on the verge of a violent
demise. The hallmark of custom is its *obligatory* status,[37] and Yvain learns that this
condition pertains to him no less than to his unfortunate predecessors:

> Et ce nos fet anragier d'ire
> que maintes foiz morir veomes
> chevaliers juenes et prodomes
> qui as deus maufez se conbatent;
> l'ostel molt chieremant achatent,
> ausi con vos feroiz demain
> que trestot seul, de vostre main,
> vos covandra, voilliez ou non,
> conbatre, et perdre vostre non
> encontre les deus vis deables.   (vv. 5322–31)

"And it fills us with rage and sorrow that time and again we've seen knights young and
valient die in combat with the two demons. They pay dearly for their lodging, as will you
tomorrow when all alone, like it or not, you will have to take up arms and lose your good
name against these two living devils."

The damsel's profoundly disturbing account of the miserable conditions
imposed by the custom is soon followed by the lord of the castle's assessment from
a different perspective. He, too, emphasizes the custom's obligatory force:

> Por rien eschaper ne s'an puet
> nus chevaliers qui ceanz gise;
> ce est costume et rente asise...   (vv. 5495–7)

"No knight who stays here may leave for any reason; this is custom and fixed obligation..."

While the custom was imposed upon him, he nonetheless maintains it willingly:

> en cest chastel a establie
> une molt fiere deablie
> qu'il me covient a maintenir.
> Je vos ferai ja ci venir
> deus miens sergenz molt granz et forz;

> encontre aus deux, soit droit ou torz,
> vos convenra vos armes prendre. (vv. 5461–7)

"a ferocious demonic practice was established in this castle, and it behooves me to maintain it. I shall bring before you two of my armed footsoldiers; both are massive and mighty; rightly or wrongly you must take arms against them."

Because it offers the count his only hope of securing a worthy son-in-law and heir, he will award his winsome daughter *and* his entire estate to the victorious champion. Thus, as in Yvain's earlier engagement of the Custom of the Fountain and in his subsequent defeat of Count Alier, victory again entails bride-winning and the right to *tenir terre*. As for the count's adamant determination to continue observing the custom "rightly or wrongly," his attitude is reminiscent of Arthur's, both in "Li premiers vers" when he insists that the customs of his father will be kept "que que il ma'n doie avenir" ("regardless of the consequences," *Erec*, v. 1770) and at the beginning of the *Charrete* when his devotion to custom renders him powerless to counter its abuse. The count's discourse on the necessity of custom thus belongs within a larger context in Chrétien's romances, one which involves a critique of custom as an institution that privileges the inertia of traditions deemed obligatory regardless of how ill-suited they may be for dealing with current crises.[38]

It is apparent, then, that while both the abject laborers and their lord share essentially the same understanding of the custom's mechanism, each party has a different view of the stakes involved.[39] For the captive females, victory will ensure their liberation, while in the lord's account, his daughter and his estate are the only prizes. In the *Charrete*, we recall, the Custom of Gorre also conjoins the fate of the prisoners and the possession of a single woman, and there it raises the crucial question of agency: does Lancelot act exclusively out of his love for the queen, or is he mindful of the prisoners' liberation as well? We saw that, while both parties prematurely assume Lancelot has ended their captivity, the matter remains unresolved until the beheading of Meleagant. Here, however, after his victory with the help of the lion, Yvain's trenchant request resolves the ambiguity straightaway; politely declining the hand of the lord's daughter, he asks that the prisoners be released into his custody (vv. 5702ff.). The lord acquiesces in the request, but insists that daughter and dowry be accepted as well. Upon Yvain's repeated refusal, the lord declares arbitrarily that Yvain himself might not be allowed to leave:

> Ja mes, se je ne le comant
> et mes consauz ne le m'aporte,
> ne vos iert overte ma porte;
> einz remanroiz an ma prison... (vv. 5732–5)

"Without my counsel and command, my door will never be open to you; you would remain in my prison."

Although he soon yields because unwilling to force Yvain to oblige him, his thinking at this point recalls Meleagant's efforts to imprison the hero in order to take undue advantage of the custom's stipulations. These secondary resonances between the issues raised in Gorre and at Pesme-Avanture are suggestive not only of the two works' contemporaneous composition; they also reveal how extensively a custom remote from the Arthurian court is involved in the principal exploit of each hero.

The significance of Yvain's three "lion" adventures coheres on multiple levels. From one to another, there is an increase in the scope of his service. In the first, he struggles on behalf of an individual, Lunete; in the second, on behalf of a family, Gauvain's kin; in the third, on behalf of an entire community – the lord of the castle, his family, and 300 captives.[40] His moral growth, meanwhile, is progressively signified by contrastive analogy with developments in the first part of the work. As noted previously, Yvain's intervention of behalf of the Lady of Norison reconfigures his first "winning" of Laudine, substituting noble service for self-serving objectives. Having defended, symbolically as well as literally, "the lady and her land," Yvain then assumes the surrogate identity afforded by the companionship of the lion, upon which to build an incremental surplus of positive valorizations. Immediately after his rescue of Lunete, Laudine grants this "Knight of the Lion" an invitation to remain with her, on account of the "pris" he has earned pseudonymously (vv. 4578ff.); still incognito, he is now worthy of her renewed esteem. In the encounter with Harpin his voluntary substitution of himself for the absent Gauvain demonstrates his recovery of a knighthood equivalent to the Arthurian standard, in contrast with his flight in shame after the reading in Arthur's presence of Laudine's message of rejection. In the episode of Pesme-Avanture, his principal exploit, Yvain again wins the right to marriage and lordship, declining both out of fidelity to Laudine, and reveals in his liberation of the captive maidens an altruism greater than that of his previous adventures involving "the lady and her land."

With regard to customs, as we have just seen, all three episodes involve the hero in ending their abuse, while in addition each episode tests the governing proposition in the Custom of the Fountain – "If might, then right" – and each finds it to be inadequate as an absolute juridical determinant independent of an agent's motives. At the same time, all three manifest once more the other, feudal principle in the Fountain Custom: *tenir terre*. Yvain rids Laudine's land of its treacherous seneschal and thus helps her to *tenir terre* prior to his definitive return; he reunites Gauvain's sister's family and enables it to restore order to its manor: at Pesme-Avanture he rids the land of its demonic bondage. Through all of this, the lion is emblematic of strength nobly employed against grotesque and abusive violations of customal privileges and human rights.[41] In his so-called "lion adventures," then, Yvain is consistently a hero acting on behalf of castellanies destabilized by terrifying and arbitrary abusers of feudal proprietary privileges. Throughout this development, it is the customal intrigue, with its manifold problematic of right upheld by might, which receives pride of place.

CONTESTED SUCCESSION: CRISIS AT COURT

Readers of *Le Chevalier au lion* sometimes take it for granted that Yvain's principal heroic encounter is the one immediately preceding his ultimate return to Laudine.

Behind such a reading, perhaps, is the assumption that his progressive growth toward recovery of the right to *tenir terre* in Laudine's land, having thus far involved him in the defense of terrorized tenures, would logically culminate in a conflict over the rights of property, adjudicated, moreover, in the august ambiance of Arthur's court, following a spectacular combat between Yvain and Gauvain. While that episode's penultimate position and potentially climactic components might seem to favor such an assumption, a closer reading of the passage, which occupies nearly a sixth of the whole, will help to suggest that its place in the heroic dynamic is minimal compared with its importance as a further critique of the anterior order.

In Yvain's last exploit before his definitive return to Laudine and her custom, he engages in judicial combat with Gauvain in an attempt to resolve a disputed inheritance. Well before the two knights become involved, however, the matter has arisen as a quarrel between the two daughters of the Lord of Noire Espine. Upon the father's death, the elder sister laid claim to his lands, while the younger vowed to appeal for assistance at Arthur's court (vv. 4698ff.). Before the younger sister's arrival at court, however, her sibling has quietly engaged Gauvain to defend her claim in combat. Hence the young plaintiff finds no defender equal to her cause: since Gauvain was "otherwise engaged," "li miaudres li failloit" (v. 4758) – "she lacked the best" of the knights.

The unavailability of a suitable defender is expressed as the impossibility to "find counsel" (*conseil avoir*), and in view of the foregoing adventures, this casting of Chrétien's heroic knights as litigants is hardly astonishing. More striking is Arthur's attenuated role in compensating for the lack of defenders at his court. In response to the younger sibling's lament that she cannot find *consoil*, Arthur "counsels" the older sister to settle equitably with her sibling. To no avail. The older sister refuses because she has adequate representation; she is "seüre/del meillor chevalier del monde" ("backed by the world's best knight," v. 4758). Once again, might will ostensibly determine right: the older sister has recourse to the custom of judicial combat only because she believes she has engaged the mightiest defender. The best Arthur can do as mediator is persuade her to postpone the combat for forty days while her disadvantaged sister seeks a defender elsewhere.[42]

A decision in this case is thus deferred until after a quest for Harpin's now famous confounder, the anonymous knight "qui met sa poinne a conseillier/celes qui d'aïe ont mestier" ("who strives to assist ladies in distress," vv. 4811–12). The itinerary of this quest retraces Yvain's victorious campaigns against Harpin and Lunete's accusers and accompanies him through the ordeal at Pesme-Avanture. The case of the sisters of Noire Espine thus encompasses an interior reduplication, or *mise en abyme*, of Yvain's three qualifying trials as a public defender.[43] This long reflexive loop (vv. 4812–5100), and the intricate customal complex in the third and last adventure with the lion as companion at Pesme-Avanture, all generate a considerable degree of anticipation that the thorny conflict between siblings will culminate in an even greater litigious victory on Yvain's part.

Nothing of the kind. A bloody confrontation will bring the adversaries to the brink of mutual martyrdom before ending in a draw. Apart from public recognition, finally, that Yvain and "the Knight of the Lion" are one and the same, there is no spectacular heroic victory before the Arthurian assembly. The champions' mutual recognition and consequent double refusal of victory will refer resolution of the case to Arthur, not Yvain. The climactic moment in the series of progressively more formidable challenges Yvain surmounts had already occurred with his final victory, in the "Worst Adventure," which could plausibly have been followed directly by his return to the domain of the fountain.[44] What, then, is the point of this long penultimate episode, with its indecisive heroic struggle that follows a frantic quest for champions? It is certainly not simply a matter of dramatically asserting Yvain's heroic superiority to Gauvain, "the best knight in the world," nor of his rectifying yet another instance of social injustice.[45] Formulaic banality and pointless redundances are not characteristic of Chrétien's more subtle art. There is much here to suggest that he defies expectations of the hero's climactic *agon* in this episode by making the fury of the battle and even the sudden *anagnorisis* and *peripeteia* secondary to another probing study of *consuetudines* at Arthur's tribunal.

The semic vitality of the scene is nourished by many of the same customal themes that have prevailed in every one of the preceding post-crisis episodes. Again it is a question of *what*, legally, is to be decided. The principal objective is quite simple, as bluntly uttered by the instigator of the conflict, the older sister, who desires nothing so much as to "*tenir mon heritage an pes*" ("hold my inheritance in peace," v. 5899). This premise governs the preparatory quest for defenders before Pesme-Avanture as well as the long scene of litigation thereafter. The more important question, however, is *how*, by what legally binding mechanisms of enforcement, this conflict is to be decided, and in this regard the interpolated scene of monumentally successful heroic litigation at Pesme-Avanture, far from the Arthurian court, will contrast ironically with indecisiveness and confusion as Arthurian society strives to formulate a judgment. The Arthurian episode manifests once again the two governing principles of the Custom of the Fountain: first, "If might prevails, then right prevails," and secondly, attribution of the right to *tenir terre*. Against the background of an already extensive exploration of the problems inherent in these adjudicative functions, it studies in a leisurely but thoroughly disconcerting way the maladroit functioning of the Arthurian court as an institution for the determination and maintenance of right and justice.

To some degree, this process is summed up by the varied usage of the term *desresnier*, which appears repeatedly in the sisters' quarrel and ensuing quest for defenders. In response to the elder's proclamation of a lifelong claim to the land – "la terre a delivre" (v. 4705), free and clear – the younger sibling says she will address herself to Arthur's court in order to "desresnier sa terre" (v. 4710). There is no mention as yet of chivalric intervention; only after the elder has secured Gauvain's support does she propose that the younger find a knight to "desresnier son droit" (v. 4792). The second questing damsel asks Yvain to "desresnier" the younger sister's "querele" and her "heritage" (vv. 5070; 5080), and he agrees to "desresnier sa droiture" (v. 5100). Although defined by one editor of this work as meaning simply *défendre*, "to defend" (Roques), the term as exemplified above also suggests the notion of "contesting" an inheritance and of resolving a dispute, with or without chivalric support. It may also designate a charge or claim, a disputation concerning it, or a successful defense. Often it refers to a juridical procedure in which judgment involves acquisition of a right or exculpation. The latter could entail an exculpatory oath, with or without oath helpers, or "compurgators," or an ordeal or a combat predicated on an oath.[46] Elsewhere in Chrétien, Gauvain had warned Arthur in *Erec* that each of his knights, instead of observing the Custom of the White Stag in the traditional manner, would want to "desresnier" or uphold the supreme beauty of his own lady, while the more chivalric Custom of the Sparrowhawk prescribed that each contestant must "desresnier" through armed confrontation the superior beauty of his favorite (*Erec*, vv. 55; 575). Earlier in this romance, Laudine's imaginary *plet*, or legal interrogation of Yvain, led her to "se desresnier," or argue verbally to herself (v. 1759); among numerous later occurrences, the older sister argues prematurely that "Tot ai desresnié sanz bataille" ("I have won [my case] without recourse to combat," v. 5897), because the day of the deadline has arrived and her sister has not appeared.

According to the nuances suggested by these examples, judgment may be accomplished by verbal or martial means, or even by stipulating certain conditions that must be met, and this episode in fact explores a variety of ways in which to adjudicate the conflict between the two sisters. The first of these is an attempt to "desresnier sanz bataille," by arguing for a judgment by default:

> La dameisele qui tort a,
> vers sa seror, trop desapert,
> veanz toz, l'a a cort offert
> que par lui desresnier voldroit
> la querele ou ele n'a droit   (vv. 5878–82)

The damsel who all too clearly seeks to do wrongly by her sister avers in everyone's presence that she would like to have the court resolve this quarrel, in which she is not in the right.

Here the narrator leaves no doubt whatsoever as to where the injustice lies. Nor does the elder sister's deferential attitude toward the court betoken any willingness to place the decision in its hands. Her objective, rather, is to take full advantage of the deadline set by Arthur for the younger sister's procurement of a champion: she now argues that God's will prevents her sister's return, thus allowing her to win her case forthwith (vv. 5883ff.).[47] She is not "in the right," and it is clear from the context that even Arthur already knows that she is the wrongful party. Rather than acknowledge this openly and impose a judgment, however, he merely asserts his rights of deliberation and adjudication as befits his regal station. Thus he demurs, using the sort of kingly rhetoric he had deployed in "Li premiers vers":

> li dit: "Amie, a cort real
> doit en atendre, par ma foi,
> tant con la justise le roi
> siet et atant por droiturier.
> n'i a rien del corjon ploier,
> qu'ancor vendra trestot a tans
> vostre suer ci, si con je pans."   (vv. 5906–12)

He says to her: "Friend, in a royal court one must defer, by my faith, as long as the king's justice convenes and deliberates to determine rights. There is no need to crack the whip; your sister will get here in plenty of time, I do believe."

Circumstances do prove him to be correct, for the damsel and her defender ride into sight at that very moment. Yet it is also clear that, even though he has already identified the offender in this case, Arthur is not yet prepared to assert his right to supplant the invoked customal process of a single combat under oath in favor of a decision based on his own convictions. His inflated verbiage concerning the deliberative nature of the king's justice barely conceals his profile as the passive lawgiver, the "waiting king" adhering to a customal practice whose active principle is ostensibly vested in his knights.[48]

If not by default, the older sister demands that her claim be upheld, as she expects, "by battle" under oath. The disinherited plaintiff, although accompanied by a champion, leaves the way open to a negotiated, "courtly" settlement, to spare needless bloodshed. In vain: the Danube and the Saône will converge before her sister will decline the battle (vv. 5937ff.). They pass abruptly to the oath:

> – Dex e li droiz que je i ai,
> en cui je m'an fi, et fïai,
> en soit en aïde celui,
> e se lou deffende d'enui,
> qui par amors et par frainchise
> se poroffri de mon servise,
> si ne set il qui ge me sui,
> n'il ne me conoist, ne ge lui!" (vv. 5977–84)[49]

"I place and have placed my trust in God and my right in this affair. May both help and defend from harm the man who generously and freely offered to serve me, yet knows not who I am, nor I him."

In the broader context of the episode thus far this is an astonishing assertion. According to the conventions of a judicial duel, the critical factor in bringing about a victory is not the terrestrial struggle but the transcendental decision that overdetermines it: "God and right" will out, whatever the strength of their defender. The assertion of "not knowing or being known" by one's defender is therefore an impressive sign: one's faith is in God and one's right, and not simply in the martial might of an unknown champion. Yet both sisters have feverishly sought out and engaged the best and the most renowned of Arthur's knights, the elder making sure she is seconded by the "best knight in the world," the younger that she has the services of the renowned Knight of the Lion, whose reputation for providing chivalric counsel to damsels is widespread. These efforts are hardly in keeping with their publicly expressed faith that the custom will give access to a transcendental justice even if worldly might is less than superlative. There is also the insistence that this defender "generously and freely offered to serve me," as if it had been a matter of a merely spontaneous gesture on the defender's part, with little vigorous solicitation on the part of the beneficiary. Moreover, Gauvain's "not knowing" his employer has involved him in a wrongful cause. While Lancelot's oath prior to the *escondit* in the *Charrete* asserts a banal truth concealing a scandal, the sisters' scandalous oath barely dissimulates the untruth of the conditions whose existence it implies. The rhetoric built into the oath thus suggests an effort to emphasize the transcendental judgment which the procedure ostensibly elicits, while at the same time concealing any evidence of a complicated transaction among mere mortals that might diminish its apparently divine origins.

The narrator's skepticism concerning this enactment of the custom is far more forthright. Here the adversarial relationship of the sisters and their champions is transposed to the metaphorical plane and expressed in terms of psychomachian contradiction.[50] The two opponents, he points out, are chivalric intimates:

> Por voir, mes sire Gauvains ainme
> Yvain, et conpaignon le clainme
> et Yvains lui, ou que il soit. (vv. 5999–6001)

In truth, Sir Gauvain loves Yvain, and calls him "companion," and Yvain likewise, wherever he be.

Yet the contenders are anonymous: the identity of the champion being in principle a matter of indifference in an issue decided by God, Gauvain has had the privilege of remaining incognito, while Yvain brings only his surrogate identity into the arena. Thus the beloved name is severed from the inimical entity, so that Love and Hate strive within each contender:

> li anemi sont cil meïsme
> qui s'antr'ement d'amor saintime (vv. 6043–4)

> qu' Amors deffandre lor deüst,
> se ele les reconeüst
>
> (vv. 6049–50)

> Por ce est Amors avuglee
> et desconfite et desjuglee
> que cez qui tuit sont suen *par droit*
> ne reconuist, et si les voit.
> Et Haïne dire ne set
> por coi li uns d'ax l'autre het,
> ses vialt feire mesler *a tort*,
> si het li uns l'autre de mort. (vv. 6053–60)

The enemies are indeed they who share a saintly love... Love would prevent them, were he to recognize them... Thus is love blinded, defeated and deceived, for he does not recognize them who are his *by right*, and yet he sees them. And Hate knows not why one hates the other and *wrongly* wishes to set them at odds, the one hating the other mortally.

Hence the narrator's astonishment:

> Comant? Vialt donc Yvains ocirre
> mon seignor Gauvain son ami?
> Oïl, et il lui autresi. (vv. 6064–6)

What? Does Yvain thus wish to kill my lord Gauvain, his friend? Yes, and he to kill him, likewise.

More than a fondness for figures of paradox is apparent here: strict adherence to the custom has brought things to a perilous pass, and the narrator's allegorical excursus shows the margin for tragedy in this legal institution featuring chivalric violence. By devaluing the importance of personal identity in a process submitted to divine adjudication, the custom observed by the Arthurian order risks reducing the latter's ranks through homicide.

To avoid such an eventuality in this case, there is again anticipation that Arthur, under pressure from public opinion, may intervene (vv. 6143ff.). During a lull following an initial exhausting combat, the spectators murmur of a reconciliation between the sisters. The elder refuses; the younger would be receptive to the king's decree. The court presses Arthur for a decision:

> Mes l'ainz nee estoit si anrievre
> que nes la reïne Ganievre
> et cil qui savoient lor lois
> et li chevalier et li rois
> devers la mains nee se tienent;
> et tuit le roi proier an vienent
> que maugré l'ainz nee seror
> doint de la terre a la menor
> la tierce partie ou la quarte,
> et les deus chevaliers departe,
> que molt sont de grant vaselage
> et trop i avroit grant domage
> se li uns d'ax l'autre afoloit
> ne point de s'enor li toloit.   (vv. 6167–80)

But the elder was so obstinate that even queen Guenevere and those who knew their laws, and the knights, and the king favored the younger; and all came to beg the king, despite the older sister, to give a third or a quarter of the land to the younger and separate the knights. For both are exceedingly courageous, and it would be a great pity if one killed the other or took away any of his honor.

Again, as at the end of "Li premiers vers" and at the beginning of the *Charrete*, we find Arthur caught in a double bind, torn between strict adherence to custom and the will or need of the court. Again, custom prevails:

> Et li rois dit que de la pes
> ne s'antremetra il ja mes,
> que l'ainz nee suer n'en a cure
> tant par est male criature.   (vv. 6181–4)

And the king says that he will never make peace between them, for the older sister is such a wicked creature that she does not desire it.

The battle must continue, thanks to the king's deference to the wrongful party and his intractable devotion to customal procedure. The king's utterances and actions are revealing: what is shown here of indecision and a truncated sense of moral initiative is further underlined by his acquiescence as the knights "par martire enor achatent" ("buy honor through carnage," vv. 6192).[51]

As exhaustion again sets in and night falls, dark comedy provides an animated interlude. At last recognizing one another, the recumbent adversaries launch into a lengthy debate or "tançon" (vv. 6269ff.) in which each strives, not to claim victory but to award it to the other;[52] the scene becomes increasingly festive, the king and the barons augmenting the joyful commotion. When almost everyone seems to have forgotten that a solemn ordeal by combat is still officially in progress, however, Gauvain avers that had things gone only a bit further he would have died on account of the *tort* of the sister who sent him into battle (v. 6340). From within the judicial combat, then, a judgment comes, though ironically, in the form of a *verbal* judgment ... which Yvain generously refuses:

> mes bien sache li rois mes sire
> que je sui de ceste bataille
> oltrez et recreanz sanz faille.
> – Mes ge. – Mes ge," fet cil et cil.   (vv. 6348–51)

"But may the lord my king know that I am utterly defeated in this battle." "No, I am." "No, I am," says he and he.

This is the way the duel ends, not with a ban but with banter.

What prevails, then? God, by the traditional means? No. Heroic might? No. Royal proclamation? No. Majority rule? No. What prevails is *ruse*. Each knight having declared his own defeat, the king takes their pledges to abide by his determination of the matter, to their "honor" and his "everlasting glory" (vv. 6366ff.). He then voices a cleverly couched summons:

> "ou est, fet il, la dameisele
> qui sa seror a fors botée
> de sa terre, et deseritée
> par force et par male merci?   (vv. 6378–81)

"Where," he asks, "is the damsel who chased her sister off of her land and disinherited her by force and malice?"

Taken off guard, the older sister responds in haste, and in so doing unwittingly admits her guilt. By its manipulative characteristics, Arthur's ploy anticipates Lunete's *geu de la verté* in the next, and last, episode.[53] Both involve the deceptive solicitation of speech acts. Convinced by her servant that she is promising to reconcile the Knight of the Lion and his lady, Laudine in fact utters a pardon of Yvain, one that will allow him again to "hold the lady and her land in peace." Likewise, in an utterance that the older sister believes to be a simple reply, she in effect confesses her wrong.

Yvain, the most consummately executed of Chrétien's works, thus joins two other masterpieces of twelfth-century vernacular literature – the Oxford *Roland* and the *Jeu d'Adam* – in featuring stratagems of manipulation in the attribution of rights of property. Ganelon's treachery is conditioned by fears that if he were to die while on assignment in Saragossa, Charlemagne might award the patrimony, not to his own son Baudoin, a minor, but to his despised stepson Roland. Ganelon's manipulation of the Saracens' attack on the rearguard at Roncevaux thus serves to eliminate the latter. In the Anglo-Norman play, the Fall is represented as the result of manipulation leading to abrogation of a feudal contract and, as its consequence, to the first couple's eviction from Terrestrial Paradise.[54] In these examples the Court of the King of Heaven, the Court of Charlemagne, and the Court of King Arthur all witness a preoccupation with the noble privilege of property and the role of manipulation in its attribution or loss, a concern that may well reflect the contemporaneous instability of juridical procedures for effecting such transactions.

In the case of Arthur's arbitrary settlement of the issue at hand, he resorts to a second manipulative stratagem. He must now persuade the sister who has unwittingly acknowledged herself to be in the wrong to abide by his decision. The champions have yielded their power to him; that she is in the wrong is widely known. Now, he says, "A ce n'ai ge que demorer/des que la chose est sor moi mise" ("I have no wish to delay now that this matter has been thrust upon me," vv. 6406–7). Passive and dilatory until the eleventh hour, Arthur now moves in the direction of a decision, but with the less than deliberate speed of one who sees himself as a last resort, the reluctant heir of a responsibility to decide. Either you abide by my decision, he continues, or I shall proclaim my nephew the loser, to your greater loss. This is an idle threat, according to the narrator, inspiring fear to exact compliance. Yet when the elder sister yields, though against her inclinations, Arthur surprisingly favors her considerably in the judgment: rather than award tenure with equal authority to each sister, Arthur proclaims that the younger will *tenir terre* under the aegis of her elder sibling, as the latter's vassal (v. 6434). The terms of the settlement, which make Arthur himself their guarantor (v. 6430), stipulate that the plaintiff will receive a fraction – which is never specified in the accord (cf. v. 6175) – of the inheritance, and, in keeping with Arthur's wishes (vv. 6432ff.), she will hold it under the dominion of her older sister. The latter thus retains considerable feudal authority over her rival. It is in fact she, and not the king, who proclaims the details of the settlement, while Arthur remains passive even at the moment the judgment is made public. While this conferment of suzerainty upon an until recently tyrannical litigant who still shows signs of discontent is indeed disturbing, with its potential for the younger sister's eventual jeopardy, it is nonetheless commensurate with the immediate need of the court, as Arthur sees it, which is ever henceforth to have one with the matter.[5]

In a discussion of juridical aspects of this episode, Jonin maintains that the settlement reflects certain feudal customs.[56] The right of primogeniture characteristically gave the elder sibling all but a third or a quarter of the inheritance, the rest being parceled out to the younger sibling(s) who paid homage to the elder as the latter's vassal(s).[57] In Jonin's opinion, the judicial duel, the king's role as "supreme arbiter," and the terms of the younger sister's tenure as the vassal of her sister are all related to features of contemporaneous or earlier usage.[58] Yet he also wonders why, given the older sister's ruthlessness, Arthur preferred the solution of birthright when the model of peerage ("parage") was also precedented. As he interprets the latter, the fief would revert to the suzerain – in this case Arthur himself – while all siblings remained on an equal footing. Had Arthur chosen this option, the younger sister would not have been subejcted to the potential tyranny of her sibling. Rejecting any possibility that Arthur is portrayed in other than a favorable light throughout this episode, Jonin simply assumes that, since primogeniture was a more frequent practice during the late twelfth century than the older tendency to establish a peerage, Chrétien opted for the solution that would "satisfy the majority of his readers," a "concession" that would not in any case diminish his otherwise "powerful and original genius."[59]

Jonin is clearly uncomfortable with this view and by his own admission has difficulty reconciling it with his governing assumption that Chrétien would have portrayed Arthur only in a fully positive light here. Had his reading taken into account the wealth of detail, adduced above, which cumulatively discloses the king's considerable lack of legal acumen, he might have recognized that the settlement which Arthur finally arranges is fully complementary to the episode's generally negative appraisal of his judgment and bearing. It is quite appropriate to wonder why Arthur did not have recourse to a custom – one which finds many precedents in the annals of feudal inheritances[60] – that would protect the obviously vulnerable party while also augmenting the direct homage, not to mention the revenues, paid to the court. The reason is not to be found in a servile authorial desire to meet readers' expectations. Here as in many instances elsewhere, Chrétien depicts an Arthur who adopts the less satisfactory solution out of strict adherence to conventions prescribed by a custom deemed to be contemporaneously in force. If, as Jonin maintains, Chrétien is mindful of the developmental tendencies over a century or more of feudal customs pertaining to inheritance, his objective is, as elsewhere, to show by means of a specific fictive case the potential weaknesses of the practice and the risks incurred in its implementation. Thus, far from being a puzzling and unflattering anomaly in an otherwise sterling regal performance on this occasion, Arthur's dubious settlement harmonizes fully with the mordant critique of his policies (or, at times, lack thereof) elsewhere in this episode and more generally throughout the five works.

The episode's reflections on legal issues are thus especially numerous. The custom of judicial duel is represented as a potentially dubious, ineffective means of determining right. It is also implied that the governing premise of transcendental disclosure is no longer an article of faith for those who make use of it: uncertainty as to whether the custom operates under divine or human agency is apparent in the sisters' meticulous engagement of famed and formidable champions and in their inaccurate oath pertaining to them. Its inadequacy as a determinant of right is matched by its potential for decimating the ranks of chivalry to ensure its maintenance. While the episode identifies other potential means of adjudication, such as the use of evidence, the verdict of an assembly or a jury, or even a royal decree based exclusively on testimony of the litigants, they are supplanted by Arthur's deference to custom.[61] That submission, evident even when evidence and opinion make custom superfluous to the determination of right, reveals the king's willingness to risk both the perpetration of injustice and the loss of his most valued knights in order to honor tradition. As with Kay's clever recourse to the *don contraignant* at the beginning of the *Charrete*, Arthur respects this customal ritual for its formal mechanisms and not its consequences, even when the latter threaten peril or detriment to the realm.[62]

In sum, the Arthurian crisis in *Le Chevalier au lion* is unique with respect to the two previously examined crises in the customal series. Albeit precariously, both *Erec* and the *Charrete* involve the hero in resolving the juridical issues confronting the court, though with increasing emphasis on his involuntary agency in the operations of this process. In contrast, as the crisis involving litigious siblings evolves and deepens in *Yvain*, the focus shifts from indeterminate chivalric mediation to the role of the monarch himself in reaching a resolution. Whereas the crisis provoked by Meleagant had left Arthur virtually powerless throughout its successive phases, here he enjoys a considerable degree of agency in the conclusion of the disputed succession, a fact which alone has prompted some observers to see him in a positive light at this juncture, as a figure whose wisdom avails where chivalry had failed.[63] Yet such a reading overlooks the extremely negative depiction of Arthur's behavior throughout this episode: his ineffectual and dilatory bearing, as well as the partiality of his eventual judgment and his double recourse to manipulation in order to hasten the closure of this case all contribute to a portrait that is singularly unfavorable.

As in the two crises previously examined, much emphasis in *Yvain* is placed on the fact that Arthur's intractable allegiance to customal procedure, in keeping with the mandate of the anterior order, puts him at a disadvantage in dealing with present circumstances. More than in those cases, however, we now see in vivid detail how his devotion to custom as a determinant of right ironically prevents him from achieving the very objectives such fidelity was meant to achieve. At odds with his own awareness of inequity, as well as with public consensus and the empirical evidence of needless carnage, Arthur persists in his futile preoccupation with achieving a procrustean fit between customal procedure and the exigencies of the case at hand.

While adding new perspectives to the increasingly negative portrait of Arthur, *Le Chevalier au lion* again underlines the remoteness of the chivalric hero from the concerns of the anterior order and its sovereign enforcer. While this dichotomy was a matter of concern in *Erec* and the *Charrete*, it is developed in a new key, one which some might regard as the locus of a contradiction. While all of Yvain's exploits following his crisis demonstrate the viability of chivalric intervention in the resolution of cases pertaining to property rights, the failure of such initiative in the ensuing Arthurian crisis curiously appears to demonstrate precisely the opposite. Yet the contradiction is only apparent. In all of the previous episodes of the second part of the work, those that make up the heroic textuality of crisis, there is the suggestion that the absolute valorization of might as a juridical determinant neglects an essential ethical component. Recall the Custom of the Perilous Fountain: prior to his crisis, what Yvain lacks is unselfish motivation in the exercise of his superlative prowess, not only in his repeated performances both as challenger and as upholder of the custom, but in the subsequent round of tourneying that led him to dereliction of his personal and communal responsibilities. In this regard, the primary lesson of the recuperative trajectory that follows the hero's crisis is that *the ethical qualities of the agent* must figure in the exercise of might to uphold the rights of custom, and herein lies the essence of Yvain's qualitative transformation.[64]

A similar point regarding the ethics of agency is implicit in the crisis at Arthur's court. Since in the judicial duel knightly endeavor is necessarily an accessory to procedure, failure of this duel as a judicial determinant does not discredit chivalry as a potentially effective force in other such determinations. At issue, rather, is the questionable agency of the litigants who have recourse to it. Appropriately, the deficiency is particularly acute in the case of the older sister, whose *tort* is orally confirmed by her champion. This abuse of judicial combat is therefore on a par with the earlier abuses of custom by Laudine's senschal, by Harpin, and by the two demons at Pesme-Avanture, for in every instance might is selfishly exploitative of right. By contrast, there is a consistency of selfless motivation in all of the hero's earlier post-crisis engagements, and in the crisis at court it differs significantly from Arthur's compromising expediency in dealing with the last in a series of opportunists who would use customs toward abusive ends.

Despite the work's eventual discrimination between the hero's positive profile as an agent of proprietary right and justice and the king's ineptitude in such matters, at the end of the work there remains a sense that the opposition between the heroic sphere and that of the monarch is by no means absolute in this regard. As we saw, Arthur resorts to manipulation in order to make way for a property settlement which, while not equitable where the younger sister is concerned, is nevertheless effective in overcoming the elder's resistance to settling because she is favored in the settlement. Yvain likewise uses manipulation in order to prepare the terrain for a favorable settlement, by replaying a variant of his role in the first part of the work: once again, he makes a clandestine departure from court with the intention of activating the fountain (vv. 6507ff.). This time, however, it is not a matter of exacting vengeance for shame incurred by a kinsman, but rather of regaining the proprietor's love. Like Lancelot in the *Charrete*, his imperious taskmaster is Amor who, says the narrator, would bring about his demise if his lady were to grant him no mercy (vv. 6504ff.). Now activated exclusively by values emanating from the amatory sphere, he proceeds to transgress the very juridical values he had formerly upheld as he foments "war" at Laudine's fountain – "sa fontainne *guerroier*" (v. 6509) – resolving not to relent, regardless of the devastation, until by "force" and "necessity" she capitulates and "makes peace" with him (vv. 6512–13).

Joan Grimbert recently also commented on how machination typifies both Arthur and Lunete in the last two episodes, emphasizing the unsettling aspects of the accord between Yvain and Laudine as an end to the poem.[65] Among the disturbing elements in the ultimate scene, she also mentions Yvain's return to the fountain, for in her view it raises the question as to why Yvain, now worthy of his lady's pardon by virtue of his exploits as the Knight of the Lion, should need to resort to such destructive force.[66] The question is indeed apposite, and the text would seem to insist on the necessity of its being raised in the mind of the reader or listener. Having raised the issue, moreover, it emphasizes that Yvain is unhesitatingly prepared to become a *transgressor* of the custom provided it ensure his return to his lady's good graces. In addition, it shows us that, with the persuasive help of Lunete, he is thereafter eager to serve once again as the fountain's *defender* as a means of indefinitely retaining his lady's favor.

Thus, if the second part of the romance is an elaborate demonstration of Yvain's aptitude as a hero of proprietary rights and the commensuration of custom and justice, it finally discloses that, like Lancelot, he is ultimately the voluntary agent of Love and that this compelling force alone ultimately determines his double agency with regard to the featured custom. In other words, when it comes down to a choice between Love and Custom, Love prevails. So in the ultimate challenge Yvain yields to a less than absolute commitment to juridical priorities as ends in themselves, while also acquiring certain affinities with Arthur. While the king precipitates a settlement to the litigation at hand in order to restore communal serenity within the court's plenary presence, Yvain provokes the familiar crisis of the custom which lacks a defender in order to requite his desire for an amatory absence. In short, in the second part of the romance he effectively internalizes and acts upon the same efficacious principle that he had inadvertently discovered in the first part, which is that, regardless of however else he had initially understood his itinerary, the most direct access to his lady's heart is by way of her fountain.

Customs will remain in the foreground of the fiction in *Le Conte du graal*, a romance that also depicts one of the gravest crises confronted by Chrétien's Arthur. While that text renews the intertextual exploration of defective solidarity between the hero's values and those of the anterior order, it also indicates a discernibly different itinerary. We shall now turn to its double development of the heroic trajectory as we conclude our intrinsic examination of the romances in Chrétien's customal series.

4

Rexque futurus: the anterior order in
Le Conte du graal

Le Roman de Perceval ou le Conte du graal is unique among Chretien's romances in that
its conspicuously unfinished state has made the question of unity a matter of
concern among scholars. Some have minimized the importance of, or even omitted
from consideration, the adventures of Gauvain while focusing on those of
Perceval because in certain respects these give the appearance of being more fully
accomplished.[1] Yet arguments that the two intrigues lack unity, or even that they
were assembled by a later hand, comprise but a small minority as opposed to the
many studies that have brought to light a considerable variety of affinities between
the two strands.[2] This perception of a single, albeit unfinished, work reflecting one
unified project is reinforced by the importance of customs to both sections of the
poem. Indeed, among Chrétien's romances in the customal series, *Le Conte du graal*
contains the greatest variety of details pertaining to customs, and these are
distributed throughout the adventures of each hero. As in *Erec*, the *Charrete*, and
Yvain, localized evocations of customs are sometimes integrated into much larger
contexts, as amplified fictive explorations of their intrinsic properties and
potential. Although *Le Conte du graal* remained unfinished, it is sufficiently
elaborated to permit substantial insights about the customal dimension, as well as
extrapolations therefrom concerning the meaningful orientation of the whole.

This analysis will begin with the successive "overtures" to the romance,
considering the prologue and early presentation of Perceval as they anticipate and
deepen the grave Arthurian crisis in progress as the young aspirant to knighthood
arrives in the hall of the renowned monarch. We shall see how, in successive
phases, the opening brings into relief the troubled political and social background
of Arthur's reign following the death of Uther. A subsequent linear evaluation of
the customal dimension within the adventures of Perceval and Gauvain will
culminate in a contrastive assessment of their orientation. While it will be apparent
that Chrétien's last work provides further disturbing information concerning the
Arthurian ideal, we shall see at the same time that the itineraries of the two
protagonists bifurcate according to a design which reconstitutes the anterior order
while also suggesting the means of its displacement.

OVERTURES

Chrétien's previous Arthurian romances all open within the setting of a court, whether it be that of an emperor, as in *Cligés*, or of King Arthur himself, as in *Erec, Yvain*, and the *Charrete*. In the latter three, moreover, complications arising from a custom serve to activate narrative momentum from the very outset. Together, these precedents construct a "horizon of expectation" that in *Le Conte du graal* a customal overture set at Arthur's court will launch the narrative in some highly ingenious, dramatic fashion. While the characteristic "Arthurian overture" featuring customs does not appear in the opening lines of this work, it is by no means absent: it is simply deferred, until after the youth who will later identify himself as Perceval has encountered Arthur's knights, abruptly abandoned his disconsolate mother and disrupted the life of the Tent Maiden. The deferred "conventional" Arthurian opening thus coincides with Perceval's arrival at Arthur's court. It also coincides with the depiction of a crisis whose gravity exceeds in its destructive potential that of its analogues in the preceding works.

Seeking Arthur and learning that the king sits at Carduel, Perceval impatiently proceeds in the direction indicated and is soon accosted by a knight whose colorful panoply the youth vows to request from the king himself. Boldly informing the Vermilion Knight of his intentions, Perceval receives an extraordinary challenge:

> – Vallet, fait il, tu feras bien;
> Or va dont tost et si revien.
> Et tant diras al mauvais roi,
> *Que s'il ne velt tenir de moi*
> *Sa terre, que il le me rende,*
> Ou il envoit qui la desfende
> Vers moi qui di que ele est moie.　　　　　　(vv. 887–93)

"Young man," says he, "your petition is timely; go quickly, then, and hasten back. And tell that wretched king that if he doesn't wish to hold his land under my authority, then let him turn it entirely over to me, or else send someone to defend it against me, for I say that it is mine."

This litigious claim already suggests that the Arthurian realm is once again beset by a grave crisis, and what has transpired is in fact reminiscent of the crisis sparked by Meleagant in the *Charrete*. As before, an arrogant intruder has insulted the royal couple; it is again the queen who is particularly vulnerable, for the Vermilion Knight has seized Arthur's golden goblet and spilled the wine in her lap, causing her to flee to her chamber in wrathful anguish. The motif of insult to the queen links this passage with the other romances in the customal series, where it invariably occurs in the opening scene. Having eliminated any negative associations with the queen in his rewriting of Mordret's treason in *Cligés*, Chrétien consistently makes her the object, directly or indirectly, of harsh or aggressive treatment in all of his other depictions of opening conflicts at Arthur's court.[3]

Meleagant and the Vermilion Knight evoke different aspects of Mordret's treason: the former covets the queen, the latter attempts to appropriate the realm. Yet there is a remarkable similarity between the two challengers, for the

Vermilion Knight's strategy recalls that of Meleagant. The custom of single combat as an adjudicative mechanism venerated by the Arthurian court is now invoked, not to award possession of a female, as in the Custom of Logres and Meleagant's further perversion of it, but to award property.[4] At stake is no remote noble preserve, as in many episodes in *Le Chevalier au lion*, but Arthur's realm. It is now Arthur himself whose right to *tenir terre* is abruptly placed in jeopardy. The king's vow in *Erec* to adhere to the customs and usages of his father, regardless of the consequences, now seems ominous and darkly ironic, as the political security such adherence was assumed to guarantee threatens to legitimize its permanent undoing.

Nor does Arthur's entourage offer him support or consolation at this critical juncture. Although celebrating his recent defeat of Rion, "king of the islands," Arthur is also dismayed that the most opportunistic of his knights have departed, not for adventure, but to seek greater courtly comforts at other castles.[5] The rest are indifferent to his plight, seemingly oblivious of the challenge and insult that have just been delivered:

> Et li rois Artus ert assis
> Au chief de la table pensis,
> Et tuit li chevalier rioient
> Et li uns as autres gaboient
> Fors il, qui pensis fu et mus. (vv. 907–11)

A pensive King Arthur was seated at the head of the table, and all of the knights were laughing and boasting one to another, except the king himself, who was thoughtful and silent.

In view of crises in the earlier romances, the knights' attitude comes as no surprise. They had disdained the traditional, collective meaning of the White Stag Custom, listened indolently to a story of how one of their number unwittingly violated the security of a remote community protected by custom, and even looked on passively as a custom was maliciously invoked to lay claim to the queen. Things had somehow always worked themselves out. Why should this incident be any different?

Indeed, like the other crises, this one is also resolved so as to preclude catastrophe. Its resolution, however, is due only to the ingenuous ambition and forthright materialism of the newcomer. Dismayed by the pathetic spectacle of an ineffectual, so-called "king who makes knights" and egged on by Kay's sarcastic insistence that he is entitled to what he most desires, Perceval dons the vermilion panoply after unceremoniously slaying its bearer who had threatened to subvert "le droit le roi" ("the king's right," v. 1088). While this foreclosure on an attempted appropriation of the Arthurian domain earns Perceval the king's abiding gratitude, it is evident that, like Erec and Lancelot before him, he is initially the purposeful agent of his *own* designs and only involuntarily – indeed, quite unwittingly – the sole defender of the Arthurian realm on this occasion. Like *Erec*, *Yvain*, and the *Charrete*, *Le Conte du graal* depicts a dichotomy of values, between the heroic subject and the regal custodian of the anterior order. Surfacing early in the work, as in *Erec*, this tension assumes a considerably greater, more disquieting intensity: the conventional Arthurian opening involving conflict or crisis has taken on a new, far more alarming aspect, suggestive of a society hovering on the brink of an abyss.

This opening, moreover, no longer enjoys pride of place as it had in previous poems in the series: it is preceded by another "opening" in which the hero vows to journey to the renowned Arthurian court in the hope of obtaining knighthood there. This initial presentation of the future hero requires examination in some detail, so as to weigh its considerable significance with regard to the particular qualities of Perceval as well as of the court which magnetizes him from afar. Hearing the approach of horsemen as he hunts in the forest, he hesitates between making the sign of the cross, in conformity with his mother's earlier advice against devils, and dispatching the strongest among them with a spear (vv. 113ff.). Instead, he concludes that these radiant beings are not devils but angels and falls to the ground in adoration. Learning that neither demons nor angels but *knights* are what confront him, the youth admits his ignorance of either the term or its referent; finding them "more beautiful than God," he plies their spokesman with questions about the name and function of their trappings. Thus initially, the widow's son, who misreads the phenomenal world beyond his immediate ken and responds inappropriately using a ritual based on his rudimentary religious training, is an eager apprentice in his first encounter with Arthurian chivalry. His defective understanding of the institutions represented by the knights is summed up by his informant, who patiently observes that the youth "ne set pas totes les lois" ("does not know all the laws," v. 236).[6]

Initiation into the institutional coherence of the Arthurian order begins with the fateful utterance of a signifier: "*Chevaliers* sui" ("I am a knight," v. 175). The utter strangeness of the term begins to diminish as the youth solicits definitions of the synecdoches of knighthood – lance, shield, coat of mail – and inquires into origins: "Fustes vos ensi nez?" ("Were you born that way?" v. 282). Giving birth is within the maternal sphere, to which the chivalric sphere has long been alien: the boy's mother will swoon upon her son's first mention of the word "knight" (v. 403), and before his departure she will also, in a final clinging, nurturing gesture, "swaddle" her son in supple Welsh garments (vv. 496ff.). But it is nonetheless *her* familial narrative that enables the nascent hero to find an idealized image of himself – and of his future apart from her – antiticpated within the story of his family and its misfortunes, and it is from *her* successive predications of the term "knight" that an explicit social context gradually emerges:

1. "Chevaliers estre deüssiez" ("You were to have been a knight"), though she admits having tried to keep him ignorant of knighthood (vv. 407ff.)
2. "N'ot chevalier de si haut pris, / Tant redouté ne tant cremu, / Biax fix, come vostre peres fu / En toutes les illes de mer." ("There was no knight more valorous, more feared or dreaded in all of the seaward islands, dear son, than your father," vv. 416ff.)
3. "je suis de chevaliers nee, / Des meillors de ceste contree" ("I am born of knights, the best of this land," vv. 423ff.)

4. "vostre dui frere,/Au los et au conseil lor pere/Alerent a deus cors roiaus/Por avoir armes et chevaux." ("Your two brothers, upon the advice of their father, went to two royal courts to get arms and horses," vv. 459ff.)

As it turns out, knighthood involves lineage, father, mother, family, even oneself. But it also involves death:

5. "Les angles dont la gent se plaignent,/Qui ocïent quanqu'il ataignent" ("the angels folk decry, who kill all they touch," vv. 399ff.) His brothers "A armes furent mort andui" ("both died by arms," v. 475), and "Del doel del fil morut li pere" ("The father died grieving over the loss of his sons," v. 481.)

In the discourse of the mother, the son discovers his own infantile image: "Petis estiez e alaitans" ("You were but a nurseling then," v. 457). Yet he also encounters images of the absent father: the father maimed in his manhood – "Vostre peres, si nel savez,/Fu parmi la jambe navrez,/Si que il mehaigna del cors." ("You know not that your father was wounded between the legs and became infirm," vv. 435ff.) – and the dead father.[7] Above all, he finds *the trace of his father's mandate* that the son seek out the court of the king, the lawgiver and custodian of chivalric privilege. The knight in the forest had told Perceval, "ensi peüst ja nus hom nestre" ("No man can be born thus," v. 284): the chivalric subject is *made*, not born, constituted by the language, emblems, name, and law of the father of knights: "tot cest harnois me dona/Li rois Artus qui m'adouba." ("King Arthur who dubbed me gave me this entire panoply," vv. 289ff.) With the desire of the father comes the subject forever alienated, by the language of chivalry, from the anterior self.[8] The mother's narration delineates the romance's once and future story: "Au roi d'Eschavalon ala/Li aisnez . . . Et li autres, qui puis fu nez,/Fu au roi Ban de Gomorret." ("To the King of Escavalon went the elder, . . . and the other, born thereafter, to King Ban of Gomorret," vv. 464 ff.) And now, too, her only remaining son will depart: "Molt m'en iroie volentiers/Au roi qui fait les chevaliers." ("Gladly would I go to the king who makes knights," vv. 493ff.) Here is ample evidence of the process of individuation at its inception. Out of this specular encounter an itinerary is born, and the son, filled with visions of a splendid chivalric destiny, will make his way back into the anterior order.

The more profound, ultimately more consequential message in the mother's lesson, while it apparently falls on deaf ears and does not diminish the youth's determination to depart, reminds us of Arthur's own anterior order, as the mother describes it:

> Apovri et deshireté
> Et escillié furent a tort
> Li gentil home aprés la mort
> Uterpandragon qui rois fu
> Et peres le bon roi Artu.
> Les terres furent escillies
> Et les povres gens avillies,
> Si s'en fuï qui fuïr pot.   (vv. 442–9)

"After the death of Utherpendragon who was king and father of the good King Arthur, the nobility was unjustly impoverished, deprived of its legacies and driven into exile. Lands were laid waste and poor people made wretched. Those who were able fled."

Some unspecified social catastrophe subverted virtue and justice while evil prevailed on every side.[9] The results were to be of long duration, and the mother's penury and seclusion are but the first of many indications throughout the romance that conditions have not improved. Whatever its specific nature, the calamity divided the seemingly prosperous and peaceful golden age of Uther from the precarious, imperiled tenure of his son, marked at its inception by rampant injustice and the proliferation of evil. The mother dwells on these circumstances in philosophical terms:

> "S'est bien en pluisors lius veü
> Que les mescheances avienent
> As preudomes qui se mai[n]tienent
> En grant honor et en proëce.
> Malvestiez, honte ne pereche
> Ne dechiet pas, qu'ele ne puet,
> Mais les buens dechaoir estuet."   (vv. 428–34)

"It has often happened that misfortunes befall worthy men upholding high honor and prowess. Wickedness, shame and indolence cannot but flourish, while the good must decline."

The lad's mother here adheres to the proposition that "li meillor sont decheü" ("the best have fallen," v. 427), one which was also echoed in medieval historiographical reflections on the eschatological intensification of evil in the world. In its fully elaborated form, pessimism concerning the present combines with a conviction of the necessity of decline prior to an inevitable apocalyptic retribution and redress.[10] The mother's abbreviated variant is amplified from her own experience. She discloses that the youth's father was maimed and infirm and had lost the land and wealth he had acquired as a *preudom* before being borne, accompanied by his family, into the Waste Forest to finish his days in poverty. As the father was maimed, and for the same obscure reasons, so is the Arthurian order deeply flawed. Little wonder, then, that in the opening of *Erec* Arthur is adamant about maintaining the customs and usages of his father "que que il m'an doie avenir" ("regardless of the consequences," *Erec*, v. 1770). His tenacity is remarkably similar to that of the widow's son, who vows to find Arthur "cui qu'il em poist" ("regardless of who might object," v. 495). In both cases, the image of the dead father as lawgiver motivates the effort to obey his supposed mandate and to recover the anterior orders from which both king and nascent hero have been separated.

The plot of the double search for the father by two individuals who meet and, establishing a relationship based on reciprocity, provide mutual compensation for a paternal lack can make good fiction, as James Joyce has shown in his *Ulysses*. The logic of the underlying pattern reflected in all of Chrétien's Arthurian fictions could in fact have accommodated such a scheme, had the author so desired. In the case at hand, the monarch could have conferred the order of chivalry upon the youth and thus have fulfilled the latter's desire to honor the mandate of the noble father, while the new knight might then have enabled the monarch to reign peacefully thereafter in accordance with the mandate of the royal father. This, in fact, would have been the ideal story for Arthur to relive time and again with all of the youthful aspirants who came to his court. It is the ideal plot for a "maker of knights" who relies on the latter to protect his patrimony and its customs.

This, of course, is *not* the way Chrétien developed the story-type in any of his works. Whether it be part of the main story as in *Cligés* or antecedent to it as in *Erec*, *Yvain*, and the *Charrete*, the Arthurian court is always *initially* the magnet that attracts the candidate for chivalry to its midst.[11] Once the coveted status has been conferred, however, as we have seen in considering Arthur as lawgiver in Chapter 1, the heroic knight's ultimately far-flung objectives lie well beyond the sphere of the Arthurian court. It invariably becomes clear in retrospect that Arthur is but the initial encounter on the way to many others. Yet it is also increasingly apparent from one work to the next that this early encounter is always invested with special significance, not only with regard to the hero's departure for exploits that take him far afield but also, especially, as regards what is revealed about the problematic nature of the court itself.

While these two openings lend particular emphasis to this point in *Le Conte du graal*, a third, the prologue, also identifies the court as a highly significant locus. At the request of Count Philip of Flanders, we learn, Chrétien has undertaken "to versify the greatest story ever told in a royal court" (vv. 62ff.). If the initial situation in this romance differs from its predecessors in that it begins in a remote rural setting with a carefree youth who has never heard of knights, kings, or courts, the court is nonetheless represented in the prologue as the story's ideal public. While the prologue to *Erec* revealed that the story, or *conte*, upon which it was based had characteristically been narrated in corrupted versions "before kings and counts" (vv. 19ff.), the prologue to *Le Conte du graal* alters the reader's perception of the source from which it was derived. King and count are no longer individualized narratees of the same story: the royal court is now the addressee and collective narratee of a *conte* contained in the *written* book supplied to Chrétien by Count Philip. Now Chrétien serves not only as translator and as versifier but especially as facilitator of the court's literary communication in the form of a narrative characteristically destined for the royal court.[12] This exordial nuance is worth bearing in mind as one analyzes the poem. In its identification of the source as being ideally suited to a royal court, the prologue hints that this romance not only depicts contrastively the adventures of two remarkable heroes in terms of the virtues of prowess and charity highlighted in the exordium. It also adapts the perfect narrative for a specific institution. The prologue thus joins the two fictive openings in suggesting that the potential significance of the court as institution, no less than that of the "developing individual," must receive serious consideration.[13] Yet in terms of this exordial suggestion of the court's importance, there is considerable irony in the unconventional opening scene that evokes the flawed order of the Arthurian court, to be followed in the familiar Arthurian opening with the depiction of a court on the brink of foreclosure. It is represented as being such a dismal community that even the heretofore naïve hero is bitterly disenchanted.

Why does so much of the work's initial energy go into decentering and disfiguring the Arthurian court? We have in fact seen that the court was, albeit temporarily, decentered in an earlier work. As suggested in Chapter 1, *Cligés* effects the "swerving away" from antecedent Arthurian tradition as Alexander's journey to Arthur's court merges into Chrétien's rewriting of Mordret's treason. The Greek hero had helped to rescue the canonical story from its traditional closure, leaving Chrétien free to develop Arthurian fiction in new ways. Yet while the Arthurian court in *Cligés* is somewhat decentered, it is scarcely disfigured, and the preceding chapters have shown that the court's disfigurement becomes an increasingly important objective within the customal series. In this broader context, the successive overtures to Chrétien's final work are suggestive of an attempt to synthesize earlier representations of the Arthurian order and its chivalric luminaries. Its graduated opening thus involves a rewriting of the opening of *Cligés*, so that once again an ambitious youth seeking Arthurian knighthood arrives at the celebrated court and is soon instrumental in extricating it from a crisis that threatens its very survival. But now repetition of the pattern furnishes a disturbing contrast, between a court once capable of surviving unscathed the kind of crisis that announced its end in the works of Geoffrey and Wace, and the same court in its crepuscular phase, presided by a debilitated monarch amidst an assembly largely indifferent to his tribulations. Whence an enticing hypothesis: having once rewritten in *Cligés* the traditional "beginning of the end" of Arthurian society in order to give it a reprieve in his own romances, Chrétien rewrote it again in *Le Conte du graal*, to provide what was to have been his own version of the beginning of the end of Arthur's reign.

In such a synthesis we might expect to find prominently featured that vast problematic of customs already elaborated in the three previous customal works. Indeed, the series culminates with extended attention to customs in the related but contrastive itineraries of *two* heroes, one of whom is none other than the old monarch's cherished nephew, Gauvain. The work's overall significance unfolds from the twin trajectories of Perceval and Gauvain, rather than from within the court *per se*; yet it is precisely against the background of an imperiled Arthurian court, its values and its history, that the experiences of both heroes achieve their maximum significance. Within the conceptual frame variously constructed by the work's successive "overtures," the dual development of a textuality of crisis in *Le Conte du graal* will relate significantly to the opening problematic of the court.

The widow's anguished explanation identifies a twofold blight that has endured since the complete overthrow of justice at the beginning of Arthur's reign:

> Les *terres* furent escillies
> Et les *povres gens* avillies (vv. 447–8)

"*Lands* were laid waste and *poor people* made wretched."

The ensuing scourge had entailed widespread destruction and seizure of property as well as a decline in personal well-being and safety. As has recently been observed, "the impassioned lament of Perceval's mother, identifying the disruption of political and social order as the source of suffering for the ruined nobility as well as for the weak and dispossessed, is programmatic for the narrative."[14] It is "programmatic" also with regard to the kinds of customs that highlight political and social disruption throughout *Le Conte du graal*. Blancheflor's beseiged fortress, the Grail Castle, and the castle occupied by the kin of Arthur and Gauvain are all locales that suffer as a result of the original upheaval or its later effects. At such locations, as well as in numerous wilderness settings, both heroes encounter *individuals* victimized by arbitrary impingements upon their personal security. In addition, whether as king or nobleman, the recurrent figure of the maimed leader simultaneously represents both the personal and the material dimensions of economic, social and political injustice, configuring the impotent and disabled patriarch whose lands are devastated.[15] It will be recalled that these are precisely the two types of social problems addressed by the customs depicted in the *Charrete* and *Yvain*. The Customs of Logres and Gorre both involve the rights of individuals, the latter custom serving as an arbitrary yet formal mechanism for their abuse, the former attempting to delineate conditions that protect them. In contrast, the Custom of the Fountain as well as most of *Yvain*'s later customal adventures concern privileges of acquiring or holding property, ultimately making this hero a guarantor of the right to *tenir terre*. These two "middle" works in the customal series are thus complementary studies in customs, each romance exploring one of the two types of injustice identified by the widow in the Waste Forest. *Le Conte du graal* deals extensively with both types: it will be seen that the customs organizing and structuring the adventures of both Perceval and Gauvain comprise a detailed fictive study of collective as well as individual rights and the practices that ostensibly uphold them.

CUSTOMS AND THE INITIATION OF PERCEVAL

The story of Perceval, first given widespread prominence by Chrétien de Troyes, has been rewritten and analyzed over the centuries in myriad ways, often independently of the adventures of Gauvain. For some, especially those following upon the heels of Chrétien, it was a question of continuation and completion, while for others it has meant adaptive translation; a change of medium – opera, painting, cinema; retelling the story in modern dress; even recourse to theology, anthropology, or psychoanalysis to account for the story's prestige among the seminal narratives of western civilization. Chrétien's own incomplete version has long enjoyed a lively and controversial critical reception involving a broad array of topics: the mature narrative art of its author; the nature of his sources; the story's incomparable blend of irony, humor, and mystery; its seemingly profound ethical import; its apparent initiatory dimension; its possibly arcane meanings, especially as regards the bewildering ceremony in the remote castle and the symbolism of its relics.[16] The list goes on. Paradoxically, however, apart from providing a rich and intensive program of reading and reflection on the periphery of a relatively brief tale, this abundant tradition of commentary often serves to render the story overly familiar and thus less "visible," even as it seeks to illuminate its obscurities. The cumulative opacity of the story's reception, especially of those portions pertaining to Perceval, necessitates a certain degree of defamiliarization in any attempt to see it anew.

The customal dimension of this romance, however, has somehow escaped the familiarizing processes of criticism. While it is not uncommon for critics to assert, at length or in passing, that a major component in Perceval's individuation concerns his initiation into chivalry,[17] and then ultimately his transcendence of this order as he affectively internalizes the precepts of Christianity during the episode beginning on a Good Friday,[18] the extensive role of customs in this cognitive and spiritual itinerary has yet to be taken fully into account. Rereading Chrétien's story of Perceval from an intertextual customal perspective discloses that his development involves not simply a gradual apprenticeship in broad, idealized twelfth-century categories of human experience – prowess, love, Christian charity – but a much more specific kind of enculturation, one in which customs signify the continuity as well as the vulnerability of an Arthurian social order.

The initial presentation of Perceval, we have seen, emphasizes his ignorance of feudal institutions: "He does not know all the laws." The knight's comment suggests that, rather than being unaware of a specific *body* of laws, Perceval lacks conventional wisdom concerning social practices, usages, and customs in the broadest sense of the term. The knight's elementary explanations and his mother's account of a lineal and social past begin to fill this void. Her farewell contains more specific, prescriptive social "laws" pertaining to his conduct abroad: serve and honor ladies and maidens; know one's companion by name; keep company with virtuous men and counsel them wisely; frequent churches and pray for divine guidance in honorable paths (vv. 527ff.). As in Perceval's earlier encounter with the knights, this scene prepares a second illustration of how he zealously yet inappropriately implements knowledge and advice regarding social behavior.[19] When in the following episode he accosts the Tent Maiden (thinking her temporary abode to be a church), steals a few kisses and takes her ring, he believes himself to be in strict conformity with his mother's teachings concerning religious edifices and liberties allowed by damsels (cf. vv. 544ff. and 656ff.). His frequent misapplication of the "laws" of conventional wisdom persists through his encounter with King Arthur, where the latter's lack of ceremonious hospitality stemming from the crisis at hand is surpassed only by Perceval's own unconscious rudeness. Not until after his new mentor, Gornemant de Goorz, has counseled him at length concerning martial and courtly conduct will his behavior begin to conform to the normative "laws" of feudal society.

Even before the inception of his formal training, however, Perceval had been instrumental in preserving the precarious integrity of one feudal order, becoming its champion by upholding Arthur's right to retain his kingdom against the outrageous claims of the Vermilion Knight. Here, however unwittingly, he is a defender of the king's right to *tenir terre*. While as yet ignorant of the formalities of knightly strife, he remains equally unaware that he has uninceremoniously defeated an attempt to abuse the conventions of adjudicative combat. Yet by thwarting manipulative use of a custom against the very court that maintains it, Perceval simultaneously preserves the realm and protects, at least momentarily, its juridical foundations. That he is not thereupon inducted into the order of chivalry is a further indication of the court's decline, concerning which Gornemant's own comments on Arthur are suggestive. When Perceval tells him that the king has made him a knight, he exclaims:

> – Chevalier! Se Dex bien me doint,
> Ne quidoie c'or en cest point
> De tel chose li sovenist;
> D'el quidoie qu'il li tenist
> Ore que de chevaliers faire. (vv. 1371-5)

"A knight! By heaven, I didn't think he was mindful of such things at this point. I thought he was busy with matters other than making knights."

To compensate for the youth's obvious deficiencies, Gornemant trains him in the martial arts, while also correcting his rustic manners and supplementing the mother's truncated instruction.[20] Significantly, the detail of a specific custom is singled out in the formal ceremony of induction:

> La costume soloit tex estre
> que cil qui faisoit chevalier
> Li devoit l'esperon cauchier. (vv. 1626-8)

According to custom, he who made the knight had to fasten his spur.

Gornemant admonishes Perceval to forego further citation of his mother's counsel and to cite instead the teachings of his mentor, "Li vavasors .../Qui vostre esperon vos caucha" ("the vavassor ... who affixed your spur." vv. 1686-7). In short, Perceval is henceforth to predicate his behavior on the authority and counsel of the keeper of the chivalric custom.[21]

Perceval's progressive development in his successive heroic tests is signified in terms of his success or failure to remedy situations where injustice holds sway. The circumstances in which he finds Blancheflor and her land recall Count Alier's siege of Norison in *Yvain*.[22] Here the situation is even more critical: the besieged niece of Gornemant is *avillie*, unwillingly earmarked as the conquest of Clamadeu, while her lands have been laid waste – *escillies* – by his seneschal, and because she is on the verge of losing her clear title to them, she prefers to die rather than be *deshiretee*. In his rescue, Perceval rectifies the kinds of vices his mother had singled out as being widespread after Uther's death.[23] In addition, willingly meeting the seneschal in combat, he becomes for the first time in his career a *voluntary* agent in resolving a conflict. In a far more conventional manner than at Arthur's court, the custom of single combat here *adjudicates the right of property*, as is apparent from what Perceval tells Blancheflor: "Ainz avrai tote vostre terre/Em pais mise, se j'onques puis" ("Rather will I bring peace to your land, if I possibly can," vv. 2098-9). Also at stake is *the lady herself*, for Enguigeron seeks to win her for Clamadeu; in the opposing camp, Perceval has secured her love as a *guerredon*, or recompense for victory, despite her reluctance to engage him in a sentimental "contract" – *covant* or *loi* – endangering his life (vv. 2103ff.). The freedom of Blancheflor's vassals also hangs in the balance. The conflict thus assumes overtones of a judicial duel (vv. 2146ff.) to determine the fate of the lady, her land, and her imprisoned retainers. Its subtle resonances with the customs of Logres, of the Fountain, and of Gorre serve to intensify the juridical dimension of the episode, while bringing into focus the image of Perceval as at once an upholder of individual liberty and a defender of contested property.[24]

Yet victory over the seneschal does not end the siege; a futile ruse lures Perceval into a further *mêlée* with twenty knights – in violation of the principle of single combat – before he meets and defeats Clamadeu. An Arthurian custom is then evoked and applied to both of Perceval's defeated opponents. Fearful because of past offenses, both are unwilling to surrender to Blancheflor or Gornemant, but both agree to submit themselves to the custody of Arthur in conformity with the obligation:

> Costume estoit a cel termine,
> Sel trovon escrit en la letre,
> Que chevaliers se devoit metre
> En prison atot son atour,
> Si come il partoit de l'estour,
> Come il avoit conquis esté,
> Qu'il n'i eüst ja rien osté
> Ne rien nule n'i eüst mise.   (vv. 2722–9)

At that time the custom was, as we find it written in the source, that a knight should proceed to prison equipped as when he left the combat, fully accoutred, just as he had been conquered, doffing or donning nothing.

The prisoners' arrival, furthermore, coincides with the observance of Arthur's custom of not dining before news of his knights is told (vv. 2820ff.).[25] Meanwhile the narrator celebrates Perceval's qualification as "cil qui avoit desraisnie/Vers lui la terre et la pucele" ("he who had won for himself the land and the maiden," vv. 2910–11).[26] The land is now his *toute quite* – unencumbered – but he will return and *tenir terre*, he says, only after he has learned what became of his mother.

After Perceval's two successive rescues of imperiled communities, first inadvertently at Arthur's court in Carduel then by choice at Biaurepaire, the reader's expectations of a third triumph of yet greater import are countered by Perceval's failure at the Grail Castle. This episode belongs to a particular category of customs within the *intertextual* dimension of the customal series.[27] The four romances in this series reveal regularities in the linear placement of two types of custom. The first, within the Arthurian court, features a conflict involving a custom that soon becomes pertinent to the hero's subsequent exploits. While this type of opening, recurring at the very outset of *Erec*, *Yvain*, and the *Charrete*, is deferred in the case of Perceval, it remains the scene of his first complete adventure. The adventures of Gauvain also begin at Arthur's court, as we shall see, with Guingambresil's challenge to a later judicial combat in Escavalon. Yet while the Arthurian court is invariably the point of departure of a customal intrigue, initiated by what we may thus designate as "the Custom *in* the Arthurian Opening," that intrigue invariably culminates in a decisive triumph at a remote location where a second major custom – one that we may identify as "the Custom *at* the Remote Locus" – comprises the supreme test of the hero. In *Erec et Enide*, this ordeal is located in the enchanted garden where Maboagrain, enslaved in order to fulfil the *don contraignant* exacted by his lady, has killed *seriatim* a large number of knights in single combat. Its analogue in *Le Chevalier au lion* is the Pesme-Avanture where, as we saw, the custom of a tribute is enforced by the daunting condition of combat against overwhelming odds. In the *Charrete*, the Custom of Gorre holds the queen and a host of Arthur's subjects hostage until an arbitrary condition for liberation can be met. In *Le Conte du graal*, Perceval's adventure of the Grail Castle, like that of Gauvain at the Castle at La Roche de Canguin, to be discussed later, belong to this category.

All the adventures in this series share similar characteristics. Chief among them is the locale's apparent subjection to inexplicable, often supernatural forces: the garden of Maboagrain is sealed off by a wall of air; two demonically engendered monsters preside at Pesme-Avanture; easy entry into Gorre, long before the ordeal of the two bridges, contrasts with the oddly binding constraints regarding departure;[28] the Grail King has been sustained for twelve years by the contents of the vessel, while the perilous Bed of Marvels at La Roche de Canguin deters unwanted visitors. In each situation, the conditions of normal existence have been suspended while some onerous obligation drains the vitality of the community beset by this blight. Maboagrain's bizarre ritual weighs heavily upon Brandigant and its king; 300 silk-weavers live in weary and hopeless abjection in their enslavement to an artisanal chore; Gorre teems with hostages from Logres; and the two castles in *Le Conte du graal*, in a kind of suspended animation, have long awaited their respective deliverers. Finally, emerging as the site of the hero's supreme encounter, this Remote Locus hints that a covert addressor had presided over his itinerary: in surmounting the ultimate challenge, the hero may achieve the ultimate qualification for lordship or crown. The "Joie de la Cort" immediately precedes the closing episode depicting Erec's coronation; Pesme-Avanture is Yvain's last *decisive* battle before he rejoins Laudine.[29] Lancelot's indeterminate future at the end of the *Charrete*, as part of the open love intrigue, falls outside the pattern. In *Le Conte du graal* the pattern is modified: Perceval and Gauvain both accede to the Remote Locus prior to their respective crises, so that for both the decisive resolution of the adventure is deferred until their intended *return*, when Perceval would ask the salutary questions and Gauvain would presumably engage in a monumental combat with Guiromelant.[30]

This intertextual comparison of episodes of the Remote Locus clarifies the significance of the Grail Castle to Perceval's pre-crisis itinerary. As in the case of the other remote sites, the qualities associating it with custom – obligatory force, longevity of practice, communal assent to the conditions of the obligation, and so on – are augmented by a further semantic category pertaining to the *destiny* of the one individual who masters it as if by election. Of these five episodes of heroic mastery, however, this is the only one in which the requisite feat involves no monumental physical struggle against an adversary. The pragmatic and brutal "statement" of physical force with lance and sword, which became the most dazzling exploit of Erec, Yvain, and Lancelot and promises to be so for Gauvain as well, is replaced by the significance, soon to be disclosed, of unanswered questions.[31]

In his first encounter with the Remote Locus, however, Perceval is totally unaware, as he had been at Arthur's court, of the significance of his actions, though now the consequences are disastrous. As Gornemant had retrospectively provided a degree of *positive* cognitive sanction for Perceval's rescue of the Arthurian court, so does the hero's cousin fulfil a similar, though *negative*, function following his failure at the Grail Castle. When Perceval intuits his own name, "Perchevax li Galois" (v. 3575), she renames him "Perchevax li chaitis" (v. 3582) – "the unfortunate" – because, she tells him, his sin in abandoning his mother had later prevented him from asking the necessary questions.[32] The consequences of this failure concern the loss of undisclosed benefits to both Perceval and his host:

> Que tant eüsses amendé
> Le buen roi qui est mehaigniez
> Que toz eüst regaaigniez
> Ses membres et *terre tenist*,
> Et si grans biens t'en avenist! (vv. 3586–90)

"For you would so completely have restored the good king who is lame that he would straightaway have regained the use of his legs and governed his land, and great good would have befallen you."

Here Perceval first learns of his mother's death; yet while he has been unaware of its occurrence, from the moment he left home his mother has obviously been "dead" for him in more than a literal sense, for it was her counsel to ask the name of one's host and give aid to *preudomes* (vv. 557ff.). In his host at the Grail Castle he found a lame *preudome* unable to *tenir terre*, and the fact that this venerable man had been wounded between the thighs in battle sparked no recall in Perceval of his mother's description of his father's last days, nor of the injustices to person and property that she said had befallen others like him since the days of Uther.[33] Chivalric precepts prevailed: his strict allegiance to Gornemant's caution about loquacity (v. 1648) further prevented him from succeeding in circumstances involving spontaneous empathy and compassion rather than consummate mastery of chivalric and courtly skills. Without the motivating influence of obvious enticements – akin to either the Vermilion Knight's panoply or the love of Blancheflor – Perceval's conventional chivalric heroism was utterly useless.

Provision of a negative sanction for Perceval's only unredeemed failure prior to his personal crisis is not the only function of this scene. His cousin, like the Tent Maiden, is a victim of the Orgueilleus de la Lande, and the declaration of her misfortune is followed by the sequel to the Tent Maiden episode, which must be examined in some detail with regard to customs.

Perceval, it will be recalled, had on his first journey to Arthur's court accosted the Tent Maiden in a manner evocative of rape. Awakened by the clatter of his horse, the terrified maiden attempted both verbally and physically to resist his advances:

"Vallet, fait ele, tien ta voie.
Fui! que mes amis ne te voie.
– Ains vos baiserai, par mon chief,
Fait li vallés, cui qu'il soit grief,
Que ma mere le m'ensaigna.
– Je voir ne te baiserai ja,
Fait la pucele, que je puisse.
Fui! que mes amis ne te truisse;
Que s'il te trove, tu es mors.
Li vallés avoit les bras fors,
Si l'embracha molt nichement,
Car il nel sot faire autrement.
Mist le soz lui tote estendue,
Et cele s'est molt desfendue
Et gandilla quanqu'ele pot;
Mais desfense mestier n'i ot,
Que li vallés en un randon
Le baisa, volsist ele ou non,
Set fois, si com li contes dit.   (vv. 691–709)

"Young man," says she, "be gone. Away, before my lover sees you!" "But I'll kiss you first,
I will," says the youth, "no matter who objects, because my mother instructed me about
such things." "Never will I kiss you," said the maiden, "if I can help it. Leave, before my
lover finds you here; for if he does, you're dead!" The lad's arms were powerful, and he
kissed her very clumsily, because he knew no other way to do it. He stretched her out
beneath him, and she defended herself and tried her best to wriggle free. To no avail, for in
that struggle the young man kissed her, against her wishes, seven times, the story says.

This unconventional encounter replicates a conventional conflict, that of knight
and shepherdess, in the lyric *pastourelle*.[34] Perceval's model here, however, is not
the lyric poetry of the day: it is his mother's counsel. The correct maternal advice to
follow, in order to calm the terrified maiden, was obviously that concerning the
protection of females in distress. Instead, Perceval follows her admonition to enter
churches and her permission concerning kissing damsels and accepting rings
without proceeding to the "le sorplus" (v. 548). Thus obedient, he refrains from
more extensive violations.

In Perceval's conduct on this occasion, we find that the episode assumes major
significance with regard to customs. Although he stops short of raping the Tent
Maiden, he subdues her physically and seizes her emerald ring *a force* (v. 720), and
this conduct constitutes an infraction of the Custom of Logres. In the second part
of *Le Conte du graal*, where Gauvain's adventures deal extensively with this custom,
he will cite it:

Neporquant bien savoies tu
Qu'en la terre le roi Artu
Sont puceles asseürees;
Li rois lor a trives donees,
Si les garde, si les conduit.   (vv. 7121–5)

"You nonetheless knew very well that in the realm of King Arthur maidens are protected.
The king has given them safe-conduct and thus ensures their passage."

Customs and the initiation of Perceval

The custom is described at length in the *Charrete* (vv. 1302ff.), and we have seen in Chapter 2 that it is seminal to the amplification and meaning of that romance. Its first stipulation concerns knights who, if they forcefully accost solitary damsels or maidens or act toward them in other than an honorable fashion, incur shame in all courts. The punishment for such offenses varies in a rather arbitrary manner: Meleagant's sister requests that Lancelot behead her offender (vv. 2800ff.), while Lancelot's beheading of Meleagant thwarts the latter's efforts to acquire a clear title to the queen under the terms of the custom. Gauvain, as we shall see, chooses a penalty more in keeping with the notion of shame, obliging an offender to eat with the dogs. In Perceval's visit, too, the infraction has grave consequences.

These begin after Perceval's departure, with the return of the damsel's jealous companion, the Orgueilleus de la Lande. We are prepared for this irascibility: she had twice warned Perceval to leave before his return and predicted that, if he took her ring, she would be abused and he would die (vv. 731ff.). Disbelieving her precise account of what has occurred during his absence, the enraged Orgueilleus denies her a change of attire and feed for her palfrey until he can behead Perceval. When the two reappear after Perceval has left the Grail Castle and bidden farewell to his cousin, a long odyssey has obviously taken its toll: maiden and palfrey are both a sorry sight. The maiden again warns Perceval to flee:

> Mais fuiez tant come il vos loist;
> Que li Orgueilleus de la Lande,
> Qui nule chose ne demande
> Se bataille non et mellee
> Ne sorviegne a ceste assemblee;
> Qui s'il nos trovoit chi alués,
> Certes, il vos ocirroit lués.
> Tant li poise, quant nus m'areste,
> Que nus n'en puet porter la teste,
> Qui en parole me retiegne,
> Poroec que il a tans i viegne.   (vv. 3816–26)

"But flee while you may, before the Orgueilleus de la Lande arrives. He wants nothing so much as a battle, and if he found us right here, he would kill you straightaway. He's enraged when anyone stops me in order to talk; they're as good as beheaded if he comes back in time."

The insane knight, venting his rage on numerous victims encountered during their wanderings, was in fact the one responsible for the beheading of the knight over whom Perceval's cousin was weeping (v. 3422ff.). He now challenges Perceval:

> Crïant en haut: "Mar i estas,
> Tu qui lez la pucele vas.
> Saches que ta fins est venue
> Por che que tu l'as retenue
> Et arestee un tot sol pas."   (vv. 3835–9)

Crying out: "Woe be unto you who go alongside the maiden. Your end is at hand for having detained her a single step of the way."

97

Before engaging combat, however, he insists on narrating again Perceval's visit to the tent, appropriated from the maiden's account and turned into his own tormented fiction: Perceval had forced himself upon her, and she had yielded "le sorplus" because, according to his misogynistic assumption, a woman "velt qu'en a force li face" ("wants to be taken by force," v. 3875). Whence his repeated enactment of revenge on innocent victims, "Tant que je venisse au desore/De celui qui l'ot esforcie,/Et mort et la teste trenchie." ("Until I could overcome the one who forced her, and behead him," vv. 3896–8.)

Like the Meleagant who misconstrues the evidence of bloody linen, the Orgueilleus bases his vindictive actions on a misreading of signs – *ensaignes* (v. 788) – making defective inference the accessory of the sword.[35] And while Perceval is only inadvertently a violator of the Custom of Logres, the Orgueilleus is clearly its conscious abuser. In the rather odd combination of elements of the custom as described in the *Charrete* (vv. 1302ff.), two distinct hypothetical cases are involved, each entailing a radically different kind of sanction. The knight who forcibly dishonors the unaccompanied female incurs the permanent stigma of shame in all courts; if he takes her by victory in single combat, no reprobation obtains. Two laws are thus disclosed, one identifying what is proscribed, the other what is permissible.[36] The first clause, that invoked by Gauvain later in *Le Conte du graal*, offers the itinerant woman security; the second shifts the issue from public to private sanction consequent upon chivalric victory: the stronger of two knights may with impunity claim the female. While Perceval in his encounter with the Tent Maiden is an unconscious violator of the first clause, the Orgueilleus seeks to justify his homicidal revenge on the basis of the second clause. He will commit homicide upon those who dare to approach "his" female, but only in situations in which "his" female is "accosted," regardless of how innocently, so as to adhere to the conditions of the second clause. His method, it appears, has consisted in leaving the maiden in a conspicuous place and lying in wait until some knight dared to "go alongside" her in conversation, whereupon he would emerge and utter his challenge, narrate the story of his grievance, and engage the battle. Eventually, he seems to have supposed, this strategy would lead him – as indeed it does – to the original offender. Like Meleagant at the beginning of the *Charrete*, the Orgueilleus has elaborated a manipulative and transgressive possible world from the latent potential of the custom.

Whence another episode in Chrétien's continuing study of customs and the criminal mind, as the Orgueilleus joins ranks with Meleagant, Harpin, the two "fils de netun," the Vermilion Knight, and others who arbitrarily distort the jurisdictional boundaries of customal discourse so as to serve selfish and destructive ends. The Orgueilleus thinks that, without "blame" or "shame," he may repeatedly reconquer "his" female in combat, even though misconstruing the nature of others' advances and the justifiability of homicide. Ironically, the Orgueilleus seeks to use the umbrella of the custom to mete out the kind of abuse to a female that it was originally designed to prevent.

Through his victory over the Orgueilleus, Perceval expiates his earlier unwitting abuse of the first clause in the Custom of Logres by defeating a far more pernicious abuser of the second. He also honors Gornemant's counsel never to kill an adversary. The brilliance of this victory, however, is somewhat diminished by a symbolic detail that brings together two earlier phases of his itinerary. While a guest at the Grail Castle, Perceval had received a magnificent sword bearing an inscription that the weapon was destined to break in a single peril known only to its forger (vv. 3130ff.); he had then been warned by his cousin that the sword would fail him in a great battle and could be repaired only by its maker, Triboët (vv. 3654ff.). In his combat with the Orgeuilleus, Perceval strikes such a fierce blow "Qu'il a en deus pieces rompu/Le bon brant al Roi Pescheor" ("that he broke in two the good sword of the Fisher King," vv. 3926 *f* and *g*) and in order to achieve victory he is thus obliged to use the sword that had belonged to the Vermilion Knight. The episode may well foreshadow a qualitative change in Perceval's heroic status: in the finished work he would likely have found his way to Triboët to have the other weapon repaired (cf. v. 3670), to learn that his early transgression of the Custom of Logres had perhaps made him an unworthy user of the Fisher King's sword, an instrument symbolizing his election to a higher calling.[37] Despite this detail, however, the episode here culminates in a generally positive image of Perceval as the redeemer of Arthurian customs, as he uses the weapon captured from an abuser of one custom to defeat the abuser of another.

In sum, Perceval's non-grail adventures between his abrupt departure for Arthur's court in search of knighthood and his reintroduction into it on a snowy morning two weeks later establish him as an upholder of personal and property rights against abuses of customs designed to guarantee them. By this juncture he has begun to rectify the two types of injustice singled out by his mother, even though he has yet to recall the most important aspects of her counsel. Yet his failure at the Grail Castle reveals that he is prepared to deal with such injustices in only one manner, that represented by the standard of achievement still upheld in word, if not always in deed, by the Arthurian court. Accordingly, the sight of blood drops on the snow inspires only a reverie in the courtly register, recalling the beauty of Blancheflor; it provokes no associations with the enigmatic bleeding lance concerning which he had failed to inquire at the Grail Castle.[38] As the courtly Gauvain brings him back into the Arthurian fold, the court's recognition of his superior mastery of knighthood fulfils earlier prophecies to mark the end of this first, heroic cycle.[39] Immediately thereafter he hears the strident cries of the Hideous Damsel, and his own crisis begins in earnest.

The long appraisal of Perceval's failure by the Hideous Damsel extends the negative assessment concerning the Grail Castle adventure already adumbrated by Perceval's cousin, providing more details about its disastrous consequences:

> A mal eür tu [te] teüsses,
> Que se tu demandé l'eüsses,
> Li riches rois, qui or s'esmaie,
> Fust ja toz garis de sa plaie
> *Et si tenist sa terre en pais,*[40]
> Dont il ne tendra point jamais.   (vv. 4669–74)

"Woe that you spoke not, for had you asked, the powerful king who now agonizes would already be healed of his wound and would govern in peace the land that he will never control."

Had Perceval inquired about the indices of martial carnage and spiritual sustenance, the Fisher King would even now be back in control. The venerable leader will instead remain an invalid, his social functions unperformed. As a result, misfortunes are to proliferate on every side; as in the contemporaneous metaphor assimilating the body politic to a human figure, the deficiency of the head weakens the other members.[41] Warfare will continue to claim the *paterfamilias*; sons will die in battle; daughters will be orphaned, widows deprived of legitimate inheritances, lands ravaged by the mighty and the lawless (vv. 4669ff.). The panorama of social disorder in the Hideous Damsel's harangue is clearly reminiscent of what Perceval had ignored in his mother's disclosures. The repressed has returned, in a ghastly incarnation.[42] The devastations his mother had attributed to the past and present are now projected into the future: terror and tribulation will continue to mar the age of Arthur.

Out of obedience to what he had assumed to be the paternal mandate reflected in the maternal discourse, which was to seek knighthood at the hand of a monarch, Perceval has come to this critical pass. Now, as the mother's implicit mandate is reiterated by this grotesque scold, he suddenly alters his course in the direction of the Grail Castle (v. 4727). Rather than fulfilling the paternal mandate to seek the order of chivalry beyond the maternal sphere, it had been a matter of finding and restoring the image of the incapacitated father represented *within* the discourse of the mother. He thus vows to launch out into the future in order to make his way back into that aspect of his past that had eluded him as he had elided it.

CUSTOMS AND THE INDICTMENT OF GAUVAIN

All of this occurs amidst a new and seemingly auspicious Arthurian "opening," for in the Hideous Damsel's public declamation are multiple calls to adventure (vv. 4685ff.). Perceval's solemn resolve is all but forgotten in the flurry of fifty knights who vow to vie for fame and glory in formidable lands. Appearances are deceptive, however. Little more than a fortnight earlier, Arthur had been dejected because of the opportunists who had left the court; now their ranks will diminish again. In addition, the two adventures announced by the Hideous Damsel have unpleasant antecedents. Her description of Chastel Orgueilleus is particularly suggestive:

> El chastel chevaliers de pris
> A cinc cens et soissante et sis
> Et sachiez qu'il n'i a celui
> Qui n'ait s'amie aveques leu,
> Gentil feme, cortoise et bele.   (vv. 4691–5)

"At the castle are 566 renowned knights, not one of whom hasn't his beloved with him, each a noble, courtly and beautiful lady."

Customs and the indictment of Gauvin

These lines cannot fail to evoke Gauvain's description in the opening of *Erec* of Arthur's own court as he is about to reactivate the White Stag Custom:

> ancor a il ceanz .vc.
> dameiseles de hauz paraiges,
> filles de rois, gentes et sages;
> n'i a nule qui n'ait ami
> chevalier vaillant et hardi. (vv. 50–4)

"there are 500 ladies of high birth here, noble and wise daughters of kings, not one of whom hasn't her suitor, each a brave and valiant knight."

We now find that the Arthurian court, formerly the fashionable place for gatherings of young knights eager to impress their elegant and noble ladies, has clearly been decentered: what once gave it its beauty and animation has moved elsewhere. Equally resonant is the "main event" at Montesclaire:

> "Mais qui voldroit le pris avoir
> De tot le mont, je quit savoir
> Le liu et le piece de terre
> Ou l'en le porroit mix conquerre,
> Se il estoit qui l'ossast faire.
> Au pui qui est soz Montesclaire
> A une damoisele assise;
> Molt grant honor aroit conquise
> Qui le siege en porroit oster
> Et la pucele delivrer,
> Et s'avroit toutes les loënges,
> Et l'Espee as Estranges Renges ... " (vv. 4701–12)

"He who would garner the world's esteem: I think I know the place where he might best win it, if he dare. On a summit under Montesclaire a damsel is besieged. He who could raise the siege and deliver the maiden would have won great honor, all praise, and the Sword of the Strange Hangings."

This formal "event" is evocative not of the Lady of Norison and Blancheflor as besieged women, but again of "Li premiers vers" of *Erec*:

> "Qui l'esprevier voldra avoir,
> avoir li covandra amie
> bele et saige sanz vilenie;
> s'il i a chevalier si os
> qui vuelle le pris et le los
> de la plus bele desresnier,
> s'amie fera l'esprevier
> devant toz a la perche prandre,
> s'autres ne li ose desfandre.
> Iceste costume maintienent
> et por ce chascun an i vienent." (vv. 570–80)

"He who would garner the sparrowhawk must have a virtuous female companion, beautiful and wise. If a knight be so bold as to uphold her supreme beauty, he will have her take the sparrowhawk from its perch, before everyone, if no one dares to prevent it. This custom is maintained and all come to see it."

Like the Custom of the Sparrowhawk, the event at Montesclaire is a *contest*; but unlike its relatively tame and pleasant precursor, this contest turns a siege into a chivalric game in which to win honor, worldly renown, and a special prize.

What purpose is served here by evoking precisely the two moments at which customs become crucial in the opening segment of Chrétien's first Arthurian romance? Arthur's decision to re-enact the custom of the stag has generated his first major crisis. Having taken the stag himself, we recall, he had moved to bestow the traditional kiss but was opposed by his knights, each of whom wanted to "desresnier" (v.55) in combat the supreme beauty of his own favorite. The old custom, having apparently served as a symbolic renewal of unanimity in Uther's time, allowed for no such chivalric determination of privilege. Elsewhere, however, Erec had been able to "desresnier" in combat Enide's supreme beauty in the Custom of the Sparrowhawk, observed by nobility apart from a royal court. Two versions of the contest of "La plus bele," one royal, the other chivalric, thus allow a compromise: Arthur's barons will ratify his choice of Enide, won in a remote demonstration of chivalric privilege.[43] Yet while resolved, that crisis disclosed a dangerously centrifugal majority at court, suggesting that other crises might arise whenever the king's perennial need for the plenary presence to uphold Uther's customal legacy is threatened by his knights' desire for adventure and personal status. As we now see that this desire compels them to go wherever they can gainfully ply their trade, these echoes of the twin customs in *Erec* emphasize the intertextual dimension of the Arthurian court's propensity to disband in disarray, its collective integrity disrupted. With regard to the chivalric opportunists at court, the cynicism of the Hideous Damsel is all too apparent. She seems to know precisely what vainglorious and lucrative enticements, casually mentioned as she makes her exit, might best reveal how her chastisements, understood by Perceval, were to his companions, in the words of the Prologue, but seeds sown in worthless soil.[44]

The previous ironies in this Arthurian opening are brought into sharper focus by the indictment of Gauvain. Before that paragon of chivalry can leave for Montesclaire, Guingambresil accuses him of treason for murdering his lord (vv. 4247ff.). Their judicial combat is set for forty days hence, in the presence of the King of Escavalon, the victim's son.[45] As litigious issues accumulate along the way and, thanks to repeated deferrals, ultimately hang in the balance when the fragment ends, Gauvain's itinerary, like Perceval's, leads him through a series of adventures in which customs play a significant role.

Before arriving in Escavalon, Gauvain is delayed at Tintagel, where the local lord, Tibaut, has organized a tournament. Aware of the gravity of his mission, Gauvain at first avoids the contest, but his two shields, seven squires, and as many horses inspire erroneous speculations: have *two* Arthurian knights arrived (v. 4923)? On the other hand, because of his horses and his abstinence from the jousts, some insist that he is a merchant or a trader, masquerading as a knight in order to evade payment of "les costumes et les paages" ("the customs and tolls," v. 5085). Tibaut's older daughter warns her father about the "fraudulent" newcomer:

Customs and the indictment of Gauvin

> Escus et lances fait porter
> Et chevax en destre mener,
> Et einsi les costumes emble
> Por che que chevaliers resamble,
> [Si se fait franc en ceste guise
> Quant il va en marceandise.]   (vv. 5223–8)

"He has shields and lances borne along with him and horses in tow, and thus evades the customs by resembling a knight; he gets off scot free in that get-up when he goes a-selling."

Here non-noble, urban types of custom, new in the works of Chrétien though by no means uncommon in late twelfth-century Champagne, are the basis for a tense interlude.[46] Tibaut is on the verge of having the newcomer seized as a delinquent merchant when Gauvain candidly explains his odd convoy and true purpose. Apart from the obvious humor in the spectators' erroneous inference, the incident's incorrect suggestion of Gauvain as a petty abuser of bourgeois pecuniary customs will retrospectively take on a gentle kind of irony when he is later portrayed as an upholder of weightier customs pertaining to justice and order.

The other major aspect of the episode, involving a quarrel between the two daughters of Tibaut, develops within the more familiar register of Chrétien's literary customs. The older sister's champion is Melians de Lis, for whom the tournament affords an opportunity to "earn" her love (vv. 4864ff.), while she boasts to the onlookers that he is *le plus beau* – the fairest in the fray (v. 5036). She strikes her younger sister for referring to a stranger who is "more handsome and masterful," and still smarting from this blow, the sibling engages Gauvain to "uphold her right" against her older sister. Her sleeves being far too short to make a proper banner for her champion, the doting father fashions a massive replica for the occasion, which flutters in the wind as Gauvain triumphs in the lists. Again customs in the previous romances are called to mind. Gauvain and Melians undertake to "desresnier" by combat which of them is "le plus beau," in a masculine variant of the game of "la plus bele," while the motif of adjudicative combat on behalf of feuding sisters also recalls the near-mortal encounter between Yvain and Gauvain in *Le Chevalier au lion*. Here, however, the shallowness of the issue trivializes the juridical procedure and emanates from the frivolous kind of courtly narcissism to which Gauvain is seldom immune.[47]

Susceptibility to distraction is again in evidence when Gauvain finally arrives in Escavalon. Unrecognized upon arrival, he is soon locked in a passionate embrace with the daughter of his alleged victim. News of his presence reaches the townspeople, however, and they seek to take justice into their own hands, attempting to kill him after prematurely branding the transgression of which he is accused as a proven fact (v. 5918).[48] Subversion of due process according to the custom of judicial combat is averted by Guingambresil's explanation of the terms of the engagement agreed upon at Arthur's court. This ostensibly decisive duel, however, is deferred for a year, so that Gauvain may, under oath, quest for "the lance that bleeds at its point," identified here as the instrument of the destruction of Arthur's kingdom:

The anterior order in *Le Conte du graal*

Et s'est escrit qu'il ert une hore
Que toz li roiames de Logres,
Qui jadis fu la terre as ogres,
Sera destruis par cele lance.   (vv. 6168–71)

"And it is written that the hour will come when the entire Kingdom of Logres, which was long ago the land of ogres, will be destroyed by this lance."

If, as anticipated, he fails to find it, Gauvain pledges to return to imprisonment in Escavalon.

Deferral of this judicial combat leads Gauvain into a second cycle of adventures, but only after the account, examined later on, of Perceval's arrival at the abode of his hermit uncle on a Good Friday. The lance is not at issue in Gauvain's remaining adventures, which emphasize two distinct aspects of customs. One, pertaining to the Remote Locus, will be examined in the next section; the other, once again, concerns the Custom of Logres. The most extensive and intricate segment of Gauvain's later adventures progressively introduces two secondary stories that reflect backward into an indeterminate past involving the Custom of Logres. It is this doubly retrospective fiction, gradually unveiled before and after his arrival at the Remote Locus, that creates the perplexing, enigmatic quality often attributed to the Gauvain section of the romance by modern readers.[49]

The first part of the segment precedes Gauvain's arrival at the castle of his kinsmen and involves two successive encounters that seem to have little or no mutual pertinence. In the first of these, he happens upon a damsel weeping over the body of a knight who, unlike the headless *ami* of Perceval's cousin, is badly wounded but alive.[50]

After Gauvain has revived him, the grateful beneficiary counsels avoidance of the *borne* of Galloway, a perilous passage from which only he, "mortally wounded" by the ferocious guardian, has ever returned.[51] Typically, while promising assistance to the damsel if her companion should expire, Gauvain determines to inspect this peril. Farther along, he encounters a solitary female who admires herself in a mirror. She warns him away as he approaches, saying that she knows of his intention to spirit her away on his horse, as knights are wont to do; if only he will fetch her palfrey, however, she will accompany him until grief, shame, and misfortune befall him. As he complies, bystanders warn him that this wicked female has caused the beheading of many a knight. The damsel, preening herself again before her mirror, forbids him to touch her or her possessions with his "sullied" hands. Together they return to the wounded knight. Once again Gauvain revives him, now with an herbal remedy, and the knight expresses his wish to go to confession. Gauvain fetches him a squire's pack horse nearby, but his gesture results in an altercation over the nag, after which the discourteous squire threatens Gauvain with loss of the hand and arm he had raised against him. The convalescing knight suddenly recognizes Gauvain: no longer either near death or grateful to Gauvain, he takes the latter's horse and cavorts about, leaving the nag to the amused hero. This is no innocent prank, however. The ungrateful knight is Greoreas, who appropriates the horse as his revenge for having once been forced

104

by Gauvain to eat with the dogs. Gauvain will recover his horse, after defeating the nephew of Greoreas whom the latter had sent to behead him. By this time the second damsel, his malevolent companion, has disappeared.[52]

In this bizarre passage, the primary conflict arises from a past transgression of the Custom of Logres. As previously noted, Gauvain had evoked the custom to justify his unusual punishment of Greoreas because "in the realm of King Arthur maidens are protected. The king has given them safe-conduct" (vv. 7121ff.). Public shame accrues to all violators, as indeed it had to Greoreas, and Gauvain insists that his strange penalty had fulfilled "loial justise,/Qui est establie et assise/Par toute la terre le roi." ("Licit justice which is established and maintained throughout the king's realm," vv. 7129–31) Gauvain's victory over the vindictive nephew of Greoreas suggests the legitimacy of his claim that he had been within his rights to humiliate the violator of the custom. Yet a number of questions raised by this segment are not resolved by recognition of its reflection of the Custom of Logres. One wonders, for example, about the interlacing of these two encounters: what does the story of Greoreas have to do with the malicious female? Why, furthermore, does this alluring creature recoil from Gauvain's innocent touch? Why is she eager to accompany him, but only to witness his misfortunes and even – if the warnings are correct – his beheading?

The enigma is to be resolved gradually and only in the sequel, elaborated after Gauvain's sojourn at the remote abode of his matrilineal kin. From within this castle, Gauvain sees the malicious maiden again, riding along the opposite bank of the river in the company of a knight with a battered shield. Despite the reluctance of the elderly queen, who discloses that the maiden's companion has killed many knights in the vicinity of the castle, Gauvain secures temporary leave to meet the couple. As he approaches them, the temptress recognizes him, and the knight vows to deny him the satisfaction of having negotiated the Galloway passage. Gauvain defeats him, however, turning him over to the castle's venerable ferryman, and at the maiden's behest he obligingly undertakes to do that which, she reports, her companion had done for her countless times before. Consternation reigns among observers within the castle as she leads him to a torrential crossing, the redoubtable Guez Perilleus (v. 8495). Remembering that he who crosses this chasm would win "tot le pris del monde" (v. 8510) – we recall that "world renown" was also one of the alluring prizes at Montesclaire – Gauvain leaps his horse vigorously into the air and, falling short of the mark, plummets into the torrent.[53] As horse and rider clamber onto the opposite bank, he finds a handsome knight who assures him that he has indeed won all worldly esteem as the first to cross the ford, despite the maiden's malicious attempt to see him drown.

The story told by the obliging informant details the turbulent background of the deviant maiden. She is the Orgueilleuse de Nogres. In vain had he, Guiromelant, once loved her; never kissing her "se force ne li fis" ("except by force," v. 8565), he had finally claimed her by homicide:

> Et un suen ami li toli
> Qu'ele soloit mener od li,

> Si l'ocis et li em menai
> Et del servir molt me penai. (vv. 8569–72)

"And I deprived her of the suitor she customarily traveled with; I killed him, took her away and tried my best to please her."

Outraged by this murder and abduction, she left him at the earliest opportunity, taking up with the knight whom Gauvain has just defeated, the Orgueilleus del Passage a l'Estroite Voie – the guardian of the Galloway passage.

Like the story of Greoreas, Guiromelant's confession is measurable according to the standards prescribed by the Custom of Logres. Greoreas had accosted a *solitary* female, thus violating the custom's first clause, as did Perceval when he constrained the Tent Maiden; hence the prescribed sanction of shame in the punishment imposed by Gauvain. Guiromelant's homicide falls under the jurisdiction of the second clause, where the accompanied female is fair game for the challenger; he specifies, in fact, that he seized her from her customary *escort*, "Qu'ele *soloit mener od li*." Thus, like the successive beheadings committed by the Orgueilleus de la Lande during his staged combats, Guiromelant's homicide occurred within the confines of the permissible according to the terms of the custom's second clause, and in the excesses of both lies a critique of the atrocities implicitly permitted to knights vying for possession of a female according to the custom.

Perceval's victory over the Orgueilleus de la Lande constituted a demonstration of the latter's wrongful excess. Gauvain takes no similar action against Guiromelant; in fact, it is the latter who initiates litigious action against Gauvain, by arranging a judicial combat in the presence of Arthur seven days hence. The motive is a double vengeance, Guiromelant alleging the murder of his father by the father of Gauvain, and of his cousin by Gauvain himself. This notwithstanding, Guiromelant is now the suitor of an unwilling Clarissant, Gauvain's own sister and potentially the next victim of his "forcible affection." Was Gauvain to have defeated Guiromelant before the court, as Lancelot had defeated Meleagant, and then to have submitted him, as Perceval had submitted the Orgueilleus, to the custody of Arthur, according to the custom regarding prisoners? The romance breaks off before the confrontation takes place.

Guiromelant's self-reflexive story, like that of the Orgueilleus de la Lande, reveals its etiology in the rage born of the offender's affective frustration. For quite different reasons, this quality is also dominant in the moving story told by the Orgueilleuse, the victim of Guiromelant's seizure. Having agreed to meet Guiromelant at the appointed time, Gauvain easily leaps his horse back across the raging water and discovers that the previously treacherous Orgueilleuse is now suddenly mollified and eager for his pardon. She proceeds to tell him why she has been vindictive "Vers toz les chevaliers del mont/Qui avec als menee m'ont" ("toward every knight in the world who took me away with him," vv. 8929–30). Not unexpectedly, Guiromelant was at the root of the trauma:

> Cil chevaliers cui Diex maldie,
> Qui dela oltre a toi parla,

S'amor en moi mal emploia,
Qu'il m'ama et je haï lui;
Car il me fist molt grant anui,
Qu'il m'ocist, ne celerai mie,
Celui a cui j'estoie amie.   (vv. 8932–8)

"That knight who spoke to you over there, may God curse him, abused me with his love, for he loved me when I hated him. He brought me profound anguish, I'll not hide it, when he killed the one I loved."

The brutal loss of her beloved inspired a profound desire for revenge:

Mais de mon premerain ami,
Quant mors le desevra de mi,
Ai si longuement esté fole
Et de si estolte parole
Et si vilaine et si musarde
C'onques ne me prenoie garde
Cui j'alaisse contralïant...   (vv. 8947–53)

"But after death separated my first love from me, I was for such a long time insane, harsh of tongue, wicked and foolish, that I cared not a whit whom I vexed..."

Her desire to punish "every knight in the world" for the offense of only one also concealed a death wish:

Ainsi le faisoie a escïant
Por che que trover en volsisse
Un si irieus que jel fesisse
A moi ire[stre] et correcier
Por moi trestote depechier,
Que piech'a volsisse estre ocise.   (vv. 8954–9)

"... but did so deliberately in the hope of finding someone so irascible that he would become enraged with me and put an end to me, because for a long time I had wanted to die."

Now unburdened of the long story of her suffering, she begs Gauvain to render this justice upon her, so that other maidens, hearing her story, would not dare to say shameful things to any knight. He declines, and they ride together in the direction of the castle.

While the Orgueilleuse is clearly a victim of the kind of abuse proscribed by the Custom of Logres, it is apparent that the method of her vengeance had also taken its cue from conventions identified by this custom. Her unsentimental, sinister partnership with the Orgueilleus who guarded the Galloway passage, eagerly awaiting his chivalric victims; her minimal attire and ceaseless preening before a mirror when a knight would approach her, as did Gauvain; her reiterated revulsion at the prospect of his hands coming into contact with her flesh or her garments; her insistence on being *accompanied* by her knights she had lured into her company; the relish with which she foretold their doom; the warnings about her responsibility for the beheading of countless knights – all of these curious details are retrospectively accounted for by her confession. It would appear that, in order to exact her revenge, the Orgueilleuse had characteristically *staged* a highly seductive situation, suggesting, as to Gauvain, that she was normally prepared to be accosted and carried away by a knight, "as is their wont" (vv. 6706ff.). Her previous victims provoked to abduction by this scenario, all having fallen in the category of the knight "who took me away with him," soon encountered her henchman, the second Orgueilleus, and so met their doom. Gauvain, an upholder of the king's decree regarding solitary females, eluded that trap; hence her offer to accompany him (vv. 6711ff.).[54] Cumulatively, this evidence suggests that she sought to lure potential abusers of the first clause of the Custom of Logres into a malicious and deadly game replicating the conditions specified by the second.[55] Thus, in retrospect, the curious juxtaposition of Gauvain's successive encounters with Greoreas and with the Orgueilleuse is clarified through the negative involvement of both with the Custom of Logres. Was Greoreas lured to the perilous passage by the Orgueilleuse, or did he happen there by chance? Whatever the case, there is some poetic justice in the fact that Greoreas, a former abuser of the Custom of Logres, should have been wounded by the violent and normally merciless guardian of the passage, whom the Orgueilleuse had used to "avenge" her own suffering at the hands of an abuser under the custom's second clause.

As far as the two heroes of this romance are concerned, the two "Orgueilleus" segments both depict their effective handling of deviant behavior stemming from abuse of the Custom of Logres. Neither Lancelot's beheading of Meleagant nor Gauvain's earlier humiliation of Greoreas furnishes a model for the kind of rehabilitation that both Perceval and Gauvain put into effect. The Orgueilleus de la Lande benefits from Perceval's application of the Arthurian custom of sending prisoners into the clement custody of the king, while the repentant Orgueilleuse willingly goes with Gauvain to the Roche de Canguin, where she finds a favorable welcome. Here the transgressor's reintegration into society is not effected by coercion: the hero's role is rather to hear the abuser's story and thus to understand the abuse. In both cases, as we have seen, a victim of customal abuse had become in turn an abuser, dramatizing the self-perpetuating tendencies of violence and injustice. Punishing the offender by inflicting the same offense that constituted the crime would only prolong the cycle; genuine rehabilitation is shown to stem, rather, from the hero's service as the offender's empathetic narratee.[56] In the case of the Orgueilleuse, moreover, understanding of the suffering inflicted by Guiromelant ultimately overshadows the magnitude of her destructive retaliation: in Gauvain's eyes she is "bele" after her confession (v. 8964), and he declines to render the punitive justice that she herself requests.[57]

THE ANTERIOR ORDER RECONFIGURED

The two series of episodes pertaining to the Custom of Logres place Perceval and Gauvain on a comparable footing.[58] Both are upholders of the Custom of Logres, and in their respective dealings with offenders, both abolish practices that threaten the security of individuals within the realm. In the depiction of the Custom at the Remote Locus, however, the significant *contrasts* between the two heroes eventually outweigh the features they hold in common. While neither concludes the second, definitive visit to this site before the work breaks off, each hero's return is anticipated in enough detail to permit revealing comparisons, and from these to foresee contrastive destinations at the end of the two heroic itineraries.

Perceval's failure at the Grail Castle and its subsequent negative assessments by his cousin and the Hideous Damsel lead eventually to his move away from the conduct and concerns of an exemplary Arthurian knight. To some extent, this is implied in the contrast between his sober vow to rediscover the Grail Castle and the other knights' haste to undertake more worldly pursuits. Given Perceval's earnest determination on that occasion, it is somewhat surprising that when the narrative returns to his adventures, five years have elapsed with no significant progress toward the Grail Castle. This time it is the narrator who, on the authority of his source, delivers the negative sanction:

> Perchevax, ce nos dist l'estoire,
> Ot si perdue la miemoire
> Que de Dieu ne li sovient mais.
> Cinc fois passa avriels et mais,
> Ce sont cinc an trestot entier,
> Ains que il entrast en mostier,
> Ne Dieu ne sa crois n'aora. (vv. 6217–23)

The story says that Perceval's memory had lapsed so much that he no longer remembered God. April and May passed five times, five full years elapsed during which he neither entered a church nor adored God or his cross.

The void in Perceval's memory is only partial: he has neglected neither the chivalric counsel of his mentor, Gornemant, nor the implied injunctions of his cousin and the Hideous Damsel concerning the need to return to the Grail Castle and ask the requisite questions. Forgotten, rather, were the lessons of his mother concerning the necessity to frequent churches and to ponder, at "masses and matins," the sacrificial meaning of the life of Christ (...)67ff.).

It is this forgotten mandate that returns when he encounters three knights and ten ladies, all clad in the garb of penitents.[59] They explain the commemorative significance of Good Friday and admonish him to take the path that leads to the hermit, to make this confession.[60] The lesson of penance concludes with a further injuction specifically regarding knights, who on this day should bear arms neither in combat nor in quest (vv. 6299ff.). Whence a change of direction in Perceval's itinerary: as he tearfully makes his way to the hermit for spiritual counsel, he lays aside his armor and "repairs to God" (v. 6314). The first words of his confession constitute a wholesale indictment of his past five years:

> "Sire, fait il, bien a cinc ans
> Que je ne soi ou je me fui,
> Ne Dieu n'amai ne Dieu ne crui,
> N'onques puis ne fis se mal non." (vv. 6364–7)

"Sir," he said, "I have wandered for at least five years, neither believing in God nor loving him, and have done nought but evil things."

This negative appraisal bears directly on what by the narrator's standards were positive exploits in conventional chivalric terms:

> Tot einsi cinc ans demora,
> Ne por che ne laissa il mie
> A requerre chevalerie;
> Et les estranges aventures,
> Les felenesses et les dures,
> Aloit querant, et s'en trova
> Tant que molt bien s'i esprova. (vv. 6224–30)

Thus did he remain five years, yet he never abstained from chivalric pursuits. He went in search of extraordinary adventures, cruel and harsh, and found them, such that he acquitted himself in fine form.

The achievements, moreover, had been scrupulously reported according to the conventions of Arthur's court:

> Soissante chevaliers de pris
> A la cort le roi Artu pris
> Dedens cinc ans i envoia. (vv. 6233–5)

Within five years, he took sixty worthy knights as prisoners and sent them to the court of King Arthur.

On an average of one captive per month, Perceval had faithfully continued to fulfil the Arthurian custom regarding prisoners, just as he had done in sending Clamadeu, his seneschal, and the Orgueilleus to Arthur. Yet in his wooden and routine observation of this custom, translatable as a mere matter of statistics, he had continued to supplement the plenary presence, paying tribute to the father of knights while forgetting the Father of mankind.

Now the lesson of the hermit identifies Perceval's missed destination, the one already specified by his cousin and the Hideous Damsel, as a site of eucharistic communion, like that long ago idealized by his mother in her definition of a "church":

> Une maison bele et saintisme
> Ou il a cors sains et tresors.
> Si i sacrefion le cors
> Jhesucrist, le prophete sainte... (vv. 578–81)

"a beautiful and most holy house containing sacred relics and treasures. There we sacrifice the body of Jesus Christ, the holy prophet..."

His mother was the sister, not only of this hermit, but also of the king served by the grail, he whose subsistence the ascetic describes in ethereal terms:

> D'une sole oiste le sert on,
> Que l'en en cel graal li porte;
> Sa vie sostient et conforte,
> Tant sainte chose est li graals.
> Et il, qui est esperitax
> Qu'a sa vie plus ne covient

> Fors l'oiste qui el graal vient,
> Douze ans i a esté issi
> Que for[s] de la chambre n'issi
> Ou le graal veïs entrer.   (v. 6422–31)

"He is served a single host, carried to him in the grail. So holy is the grail that it sustains and comforts him, and he so spiritual that the host in the grail is all that his life requires. For twelve years he has remained thus, never leaving the room where you saw the grail go in."

The ritual in the Grail Castle, then, is in service to a static transcendence. Moreover, the Grail King is the maimed Fisher King's father, and now upon the image of the maimed father in Perceval's mother's discourse is superimposed the image of the incapacitated son in the discourse of the hermit.[61] The pathetic image of temporal fathers and sons maimed by the lance of chivalry is redeemed by the mystery of the Eucharist celebrating the identity of the spiritual Father and of a Son sacrificially afflicted by a lance on Good Friday.

Thus whatever its terrestrial nature, for Perceval the Remote Locus ultimately involves a transcending of time and space, those dimensions in which his mechanically repetitive observation of the Arthurian custom of taking prisoners has been enacted. That persistence has brought him no nearer to his goal, and he renounces it, appropriately enough, on the very day that commemorates the *liberation* of time-bound prisoners in Christ's Harrowing of Hell (vv. 6284ff.). His Remote Locus is the point at which several previously heard discourses finally blend into a single coherence, so that at last he may fulfil his mother's mandate to seek the spiritual Father instead of the father of chivalry, and in so doing learn from the hermit how his neglect of that admonition had related to earlier castigations for his initial failure to ask the questions at the Grail Castle. The very nature of that failure was already indicative of what he now fully realizes for the first time: that the essence of his quest is not primarily a tangible object or a special place, but above all a *cognitive discovery*.[62] The answer to the question "Who is served by the grail?" is supplied by the hermit, eliciting recognition of how a flawed temporal order was – and can be – redeemed:

> Issi Perchevax *reconnut*
> Que Diex el vendredi rechut
> Mort et si fu crucefiiez.
> A le Pasque communiiez
> Fu Perchevax molt dignement.   (vv. 6509–13)

Thus did Perceval *recognize* that on Friday God received death and was crucified. At Easter Perceval communed most worthily.

Significantly, the Grail Castle is the only Custom at the Remote Locus whose ritually reiterative aspect does not require abolition and where no physical violence or bloodshed is involved in the heroic act. In contrast with the din of chivalric combat in the earlier analogues of the custom, Perceval's projected return to the Fisher King's castle is to a locus marked by tranquility and ambient silence, anticipating a scene that would have been dramatic and moving in its sublimity. This contrast with the other depictions of the Custom at the Remote Locus suggests, through the customal level of coherence, a higher plane of human achievement, one that would have set Perceval radically apart from Chrétien's other heroes.[63] As Perceval's principal test, questioning entails cognitive access to knowledge of a higher order. While it obviously cannot be known precisely how Perceval's inquiry was to have been salutary to the Fisher King, restoring his realm and enabling him to *tenir terre*, the episode at the hermitage is highly indicative. It suggests that the solution to this enigma lies at the end of Perceval's journey from total ignorance of laws to mastery of a set of orally transmitted customs that serve as laws (though at best precariously), and thence to "la nouvele loi escrist" – "the new written law" – which Christ gave to his followers as a new mandate (vv. 6255ff.), under whose jurisdiction Perceval's later itinerary was to unfold.

As his initiation at the hermitage culminates in the eucharistic ceremony, he becomes a co-participant, with the hermit and the Grail King, in the rite which is observed also at the Grail Castle. His heroic endeavors are henceforth inscribed into a context whose significance is determined by two associated factors, lineage and transcendence. The noble lineage of Perceval's mother – than which there was none nobler in her time (v. 425) – had not escaped the massive social catastrophe that occurred after the death of Uther, as evidenced further by the disrupted reign of her nephew, the Fisher King. Yet through the spiritual kinship provided by the grail, this lineage is set apart from its coevals.

One is reminded here of how John of Salisbury, lamenting that political iniquity "banishes charity," evoked a society without princely rule. In such a society, kingdoms, says John, "would be as peaceful ... and would enjoy as undisturbed repose as the separate families in a well-ordered state, or as different persons in the same family; or perhaps, which is even more credible, there would be no kingdoms at all, since it is clear from the ancient histories that in the beginning these were founded by iniquity."[64] chivalric – and not princely – iniquity has repeatedly "banished charity" from its domain while marring Arthur's reign, apparently from its inception. In the scattered and ruined noble families of *Le Conte du graal* might one recognize the precursors of a utopian design, one in which the negative anarchic principle of courtly chivalry was to be set aside, perhaps replaced by the philosophic anarchism of a Christian communism, not unlike the realm evoked by John of Salisbury?[65] The unfinished text can only imply, but never confirm, such a conceptualization, but it does not allow us to conclude, along with Köhler, that with Perceval Chrétien was preparing to disclose an "eschatological mission" for chivalry.[66] Nor does the later orientation of Perceval seem to anticipate the "imminent end" of Arthurian society, as Köhler maintains.[67]

The unfinished text does prompt one to ask if it would eventually have contrasted the problematic Arthurian monarchy with a new concept of order signified by one noble family's quasi-ascetic retreat from a flawed and decadent courtly world. If this were so, then perhaps the penitent knights and ladies encountered by Perceval on Good Friday, or the sacred mysteries whispered to Perceval in the hermit's prayer, might be viewed as foreshadowings of an earthly society under the sole rule of God, His law, and Charity, about which the prologue is so explicit in its praise. Confronted with that enigmatic Fisher King awaiting the chivalric guest who will finally restore his realm and heal his infirmity, the text invites its reader to ask the essential question that Perceval failed to ask during his sojourn at the Grail Castle: "Who is served by the grail?" To this question it also supplies the answer, in the figure of the king who, unlike Arthur, no longer awaits an elusive plenary presence but is served and sustained in perpetuity, not by any knight, but by the consecrated wafer in the grail; a king whose exile is a kingdom unto itself, and who, like the exemplary citizen of Augustine's City of God on earth, is but "a stranger and a pilgrim in this world" (*De Civitate Dei*, Book XVIII, 51).

There is another question that Perceval had failed to ask: 'Why does the lance bleed?'[68] The answer to that question may well lie *beyond* the sphere of his election to restore the temporal functions of his own family's realm.[69] For Gauvain's adventures reveal that Perceval's "family of the grail" is merely the temporary custodian of the lance, whose fortunes may lie far afield.[70] It is Gauvain who, in Escavalon, swears to seek the lance: "Vos jüerrez que de la lance/Querre ferez vostre puissance." ("You will swear to seek the lance within your capabilities," vv. 6187-8). The symmetry of royal lineages is particularly suggestive here: one line of the narrative tells of Perceval's eucharistic initiation evocative of the rite that sustains the invisible Grail King, whose incapacitated son awaits Perceval's rescue of his realm from the temporal effects of the ongoing catastrophe; the other, meanwhile, speaks of Gauvain's alleged murder of the old King of Escavalon and of his son who awaits Gauvain's return with the lance that, it is said, will destroy Logres and thus, presumably, bring the catastrophe to a sinister climax. Like the inverted symmetries in a romanesque tympanum depicting the Apocalypse, the two story-lines seem at times to unfold in diametrical opposition, one haloed in the effulgent aura of the grail, the other obscured under the shadow of the lance.[71]

Between these two kingdoms of father and son, the dual intrigue of *Le Conte du graal* suspends the fate of a third, the order of Uther and Arthur, as it, too, awaits its champion. In the final lines of the fragment, while a faltering Arthur, bereft of Gauvain, sits anxiously at Orkeney amidst a mute assembly of barons, the city teems with a rabble of the gangrenous and the infirm. The scene marks a considerable decline compared to its already disturbing counterpart early in the romance. This deformed and wretched contingent asks anxiously what counselor the king can rely on to deal with the affairs of the kingdom. From other pathetic and disconsolate bystanders, all lamenting the absence of Gauvain, comes the alarming reply:

> "Vos deüssiez estre en effroi
> Et esmaié et esperdu,
> Quant nous celui avons perdu
> Qui toz por Dieu nos sostenoit
> Et dont toz li biens nos venoit
> Par amour et par charité." (vv. 9206-11)

"You should be beside yourselves with fear and dread now that we have lost him who in God's name always championed us, from whom all good things came to us through love and charity."

113

The reign of Uther had known justice and prosperity by the sword of chivalry. Will that of his son, fallen prey to iniquity and decadence, die by the lance? In a fit of grief over the absence of his nephew, Arthur falls into a swoon as his subjects rush forward to sustain him, and the text lapses into an endless silence, its question unanswered.

Can this be the end for which Chrétien, in *Cligés*, had rewritten "the beginning of the end" as portrayed by Geoffrey and Wace? Unless they depict the eschatological end of time, apocalyptic symmetries are seldom perfect. In Gauvain's encounter with the Remote Locus, the definitive closure of the Arthurian era anticipated in the prophecy concerning the lance is reopened on to new and somewhat more auspicious vistas, through a series of comparative perspectives that relate the Grail Castle and the Roche de Canguin in significantly contrasting ways.

As in the case of the Grail Castle, *questions* are of major importance at the Roche de Canguin. Here they help Gauvain to unlock its secrets. Whereas Perceval, excessively deferential to his mentor's counsel, refrained from verbalizing his curiosity, Gauvain makes inquiries of the ferryman about the castle soon after he arrives: "Who is lord of the land and the castle?" "Who defends them?" The ferryman cannot answer the first question, but speaks of 500 bowmen who defend it, as well as of two queens, mother and daughter, who long ago brought their family treasure to this fortified manor. Only after his crisis, described in Chapter 1, does Gauvain begin to obtain substantial facts about the locus of which he has become the reluctant master. Like Perceval, he had failed to inquire about something crucial, as he learns from his encounter with Guiromelant:

> "Mais de la roïne kenue
> Me dites se vos le veïstes
> Et se vos point li enquesistes
> Qui ele est et dont ele vint.
> – Onques, fait il, ne m'en sovint,
> Mais je le vi et s'i parlai." (vv. 8726–31)

"But tell me if you saw the gray-haired queen, and if you asked her who she is and whence she came?" "I never thought to do so," he said, "though I saw and talked to her."

The query neglected by both heroes would have revealed the *identity* of the most elderly and venerable figure in the castle.[72] Here the matriarch is Queen Ygerne, the widow of Uther, after whose burial she had retreated to the palace accompanied by her daughter, wife of King Lot and mother of Gauvain and of Clarissant, born after their arrival (vv. 8740 ff.).[73] In certain respects, Guiromelant is the courtly analogue of the ascetic hermit: both inform the hero, after his initial visit incognito to the Remote Locus, that a community led by members of his matrilineal family is to be his collective beneficiary.

In point of fact, Gauvain is the abolisher of *two* destructive customs at the Remote Locus. Within sight of the castle walls, as we saw, he puts an end to the stratagem operated by the Orgueilleuse and her accomplice, the Orgueilleus del Passage. Within the castle itself, moreover, he surmounts the deadly mechanism designed to deter intruders. Unlike the ritualized custom of the Grail Castle, marked by the *merveilleux chrétien*, that within the Roche de Canguin involves the *féerique*, in a potentially mortal encounter with a formidable foe.[74] In this respect, it is more akin to previous ordeals of the Remote Locus – at Brandigant, Pesme-Avanture, and in Gorre. As in those cases, no previous contender has surmounted the challenge, though here combat with a visible foe is replaced by submission to an invisible force. The "enchantment" of the Perilous Bed, with its slings and arrows and ferocious lion – reminiscent of a trial encountered by Lancelot (*Charrete*, vv. 459ff.) – is part of the "merveille" engineered by the "cleric learned in astronomy" whom Ygerne had brought with her. This prototype of Merlin, the "Enchanter" of later Arthurian fiction, had established the mysteriously automated onslaught as an adjudicative test, which will immediately dispatch any knight save the one who is not covetous, avaricious, cowardly, traitorous, or a perjuror (vv. 7548 ff.).[75] Gauvain slays the lion and all enchantments cease; still unrecognized, he is acknowledged to be "le meillor de toz les preudomes" ("the greatest of honorable men," v. 7935); and treated by young and old as the long-awaited lord of the manor.

Thus, although his kin never recognize him before the abrupt end of the text, Gauvain is far more quickly and extensively integrated into the leadership of his matrilineal family than is Perceval in his first sojourn at the Grail Castle.[76] Moreover, just as Gauvain's adventure in Escavalon contains at least one possible answer to Perceval's unasked question concerning the lance, his sojourn at the Roche de Canguin provides a more *positive* image of precisely that which was the most negative in the Hideous Damsel's appraisal of Perceval's failure. Whereas she had uttered a litany of unfulfilled functions in the Fisher King's realm, resulting from Perceval's omission, Gauvain's relative inquisitiveness will soon lead to fulfilment of at least some of the duties accruing to the lordship of the manor. The castle's occupants include more than 500 servants, young and old; disinherited widows; orphaned maidens. All await the one perfect moral and physical specimen of knighthood:

> "Cil porroit le chastel tenir;
> cil rendroit [as dames] lor terres
> Et feroit pais des morteus guerres,
> Les puceles marïeroit
> Et les vallés adouberoit
> Et osteroit sanz nul relais
> Les enchantemens del palais."   (vv. 7598–604)

"He would be able to take over the castle; he would restore lands to widows; change mortal warfare to peace; marry off maidens; dub the squires; and without delay end the enchantments at the palace."

As in previous investments of the Remote Locus, abolition of the custom entails rescue of the community under its dominance from the effects of impaired leadership: Evrains, Bademagus, and the Fisher King could not reign effectively, while the count at Pesme-Avanture could neither *tenir terre* nor see that his daughter was married to a respectable suitor. Unlike previous counterparts, however, it is now the hero himself who is destined to assume the lordship of the manor, under the tutelage of the queen mother Ygerne. Inasmuch as his new subjects include the widow of Uther as well as Arthur's mother and sister, his unexpected investiture assumes overtones of a supernaturally elective lordship whose projected culmination would have been an association to the throne of Logres.[77] Between the contradictory father–son kingdoms of the Grail Castle and Escavalon, the embattled and faltering legacy of Uther and Arthur would now seem to be earmarked for Gauvain, the tested and approved *preudome*, lord of the Roche de Canguin, as well as the redeemer anxiously awaited at Orkeney by an evanescent Arthur and his deeply troubled subjects.

Yet if from a matrilineal point of view Gauvain could be viewed as a resplendent suzerain and a monarch-elect, his patrilineal heritage looms on his horizon as a murky uncertainty. Gauvain himself and his late father, King Lot, make up the fourth royal father–son combination of the romance. Auspicious indeed would be Gauvain's accession to the Arthurian legacy, whose court now convenes in Orkeney, the seat of Lot's kingdom, if he were to reign in the realm of his father and in that of his maternal uncle as well. In the path to his creation of such an augmented dynasty, however, stands Guiromelant, whom he has yet to face according to the custom of judicial combat if he is to clear both himself and his father of the charges of murder leveled by his adversary. This uncertainty is compounded by that of his alleged murder of the King of Escavalon; these issues leave much unresolved at the end of the narrative.

Thus, if Gauvain *appears* to have come much closer than Perceval to a mastery of the realm in his encounter at the Remote Locus, the *ethical* status of his projected achievement seems far more indeterminate. Are there any hints as to the likely outcome? Long after this text has ceased to speak, it sustains the hermeneutic imperative with its prophecies. Of course, the prediction concerning the destruction of Logres and the retribution of the lance was uttered by an anonymous vavassor in Escavalon, citing an unidentified text whose authority is indeterminate.[78] Nonetheless, as the examples of the prophetic fool and the smiling maiden attest, no prophecy in *Le Conte du graal* should be taken lightly.[79] The last of these, it may be recalled, concerns Gauvain directly: the discourteous squire from whom Gauvain seized a pack horse for Greoreas had predicted that Gauvain would lose the hand and arm that had struck the lad a staggering blow (vv. 7036–40). Fulfilment of the fool's prophecy had resulted in Kay's broken clavicle; does a similar fate await Gauvain? The future of his arm, as that of Logres, are among the text's unanswered questions.

Has the untimely death of the narrative left posterity with an unsigned will, an undecidable crux? Despite its premature demise, this text develops, in highly significant detail, a *reconfiguration of the anterior order*. Our last glimpse of Gauvain comes, appropriately, immediately before the last remaining scene, the one in which Arthur sinks unconscious to the floor. While the Arthurian court now seems to have lapsed into a state of permanent crisis, its plenary presence reduced to a helpless contingent, there is no hint of impending doom at the Roche de Canguin. On the contrary, Gauvain is welcomed as a savior by his joyful subjects.

The anterior order reconfigured

In what was to be his last depiction of the Remote Locus, Chrétien took his cue from the first in that series of heroic victories over a destructive custom. The Roche de Canguin is the scene of a rewritten "Joie de la Cort." Like Erec, Gauvain entered a rural setting next to the castle that had long borne witness to an atrocious form of carnage. Like Erec, he had put an end to the beheading trap set by a scheming damsel whose charms had lured a long succession of knights to their deaths at the hands of the chivalric executioner with whom she collaborated. Like Erec's defeat of Maboagrain, Gauvain's unprecedented victory and clement treatment of the cutom's misguided keepers brings joy to the adjacent court. As Erec's restoration of the functions of King Evrains had symbolically qualified him to assume his late father's throne, so Gauvain's regal accession seems imminent. In Escavalon, he had acquitted himself capably against an angry mob using Escalibor, Arthur's sword (v. 5902). Now he sends his messenger to summon the Arthurian court to witness his battle with Guiromelant seven days hence outside the castle walls.

In his last depicted act at the Roche de Canguin, Gauvain presides over a most high and solemn ceremony. In emulation of the king who made 400 new knights before Erec's coronation (*Erec*, vv. 6597ff.), Gauvain confers the order of chivalry on the throng of squires in his hall:

> Par matin mesire Gavains
> Chauça a chascun a ses mains
> L'esperon destre et çaint l'espee
> Et si lor dona la colee.
> Lors ot tel conpaignie viax
> De cinc cens chevaliers noviax.   (vv. 9183–8)

That morning lord Gauvain affixed the right spur and buckled the sword of each one with his own hands and gave them all the accolade. Thus did he create a fellowship of at least 500 new knights.

It is now Gauvain who is the keeper of the initiatory Custom of the Spur that Arthur could not observe when the widow's son from the Waste Forest had entered his hall. Within the shadow of Arthur, Gauvain now assumes the primary function of the king who makes knights. The future of the glorious realm of Uther, *rex quondam*, now crystallizes around the ambiguous figure of Arthur's nephew, *rexque futurus*. Will Gauvain reign and restore order to the lands of Lot and Arthur, or will the last two prophecies prevail, making Gauvain in his turn the maimed patriarch of a wasted land?

We shall never know. Yet in what remains of this unfinished masterpiece, there is a strong sense that Chrétien did not delete the Arthurian Armageddon of Geoffrey and Wace only to reinscribe it into his own work. Rather than the destruction of one once-renowned society in the twilight of its decline, he sets in contrast the survival of two, in a diptych that is profoundly meaningful, yet less than apocalyptic. On one side, reconfigured around the regal being of Gauvain, remains the flawed replica of a once-glorious temporal order, an order whose decrees, mandates, and customs are no more just or righteous than those who uphold them, an order which still struggles with the evils of this world and remains as vulnerable as it had been to those who would maliciously subvert it in the absence of one exemplary defender. On the other side resides a lineage whose descendants form the nucleus of a community for which exile itself has become a kingdom on earth, a community living collectively under the New Law as "a stranger and a pilgrim in this world."

5

Arthurian intertextuality: crisis and custom

As conceived by Chrétien de Troyes, the Arthurian romance unveils a world ill regulated by its customs, chronically prone to crisis, and repeatedly destabilized in the absence of effective upholders of its institutions. The foregoing chapters have frequently emphasized ways in which *crisis* and *custom* are criteria indispensable for investigating the significance of each of the five works considered as an individual entity. If the inquiry were to cease at this juncture, however, it would fail to weigh the much larger implications of these explorations, because, as we have seen, there is considerable evidence which suggests that each romance, in addition to conveying its own meaning, may also signify as part of a transtextual coherence. A change of perspective will now enable us to measure the importance of crisis and custom to the establishment of that coherence within the *œuvre* as a whole, so that we may view Chrétien's "Arthuriad" as a multitextual totality, one which, as will be emphasized in the Conclusion, owes its literary and socio-cultural uniqueness to his reconceptualization of Arthurian narrative as a powerful vehicle of medieval legal fictions.

THE INTERTEXTUALITY OF CRISIS

Chrétien's romances normally partake of a pattern identified in Chapter 1 (pp. 15ff.) as a *textuality of crisis*. The eponymous hero or couple characteristically develops within a linear format in which crisis organizes two structurally and thematically related series of episodes, one building the conflict that activates the crisis, the other tracing a compensatory movement initiated by disclosures occurring within the crisis.[1] On an individual scale, the critical upheaval within the career of the hero welds the bipartite textuality into a meaningful whole, while giving him access to insight and judgment that entail a qualitative change of orientation.[2] Thus, while his pre-crisis engagements reveal a primary concern with self-centered pursuits – personal esteem, matrimony, tangible acquisitions, and so on – his growth following the crisis typically involves him in the pursuit of objectives lying beyond the self and its immediate satisfaction.

On the communal scale, too, as the foregoing chapters have suggested, crisis is central to Chrétien's romances. Each of them depicts one grave interlude which shakes the very foundations of the Arthurian court. Read together, these interludes of crisis can be viewed intertextually as specific phases within a declining long-term trend. Since *Cligés* ostentatiously effects a severance from the immediately antecedent Arthurian cycle by rewriting the fateful, decisive crisis in that tradition, it takes pride of place in the series of communal crises.

Cligés: By reconceptualizing *the* crisis in the earlier Arthurian tradition represented by Geoffrey and Wace, touched off by Mordret's betrayal of Arthur and the fall of the Arthurian state that ensued, Chrétien reorients the Arthurian matter, substituting a positive outcome for a tragic dénouement, thus rehabilitating the *matière* for new objectives.

Erec et Enide: The crisis in the opening section of *Erec et Enide* places Arthur within a double bind, by virtue of his allegiance to potentially contradictory political forces, one hereditary, the other baronial, each invested with powers of adjudication and sanction. Whenever significant conflicts arise between these two spheres, revisionary demands made upon the legal protocol of the past stand to render him powerless. While the Custom of the White Stag dramatizes the nature of the conflict, the Custom of the Sparrowhawk permits discovery of an acceptable basis for resolution of this initial crisis. The potential for contradiction nonetheless remains.

The *Charrete* and *Yvain*: These two works, which make up the middle of the customal series, provide further illustrations of how Arthur's adherence to custom increases his court's susceptibility to crisis. As in *Erec*, unanticipated demands are brought before the court, though now they concern issues lying well beyond its confines – the contested inheritance of a remote patrimony; the fate not only of Arthur's subjects held captive in a remote realm, but of the queen herself. In each case Arthur's reliance on the formal chivalric procedures prescribed by custom as a potential means of ending the crisis only prolongs it, while augmenting the likelihood of catastrophic losses, either through the injuries mutually inflicted by Yvain and Gauvain in the judicial duel, or through Meleagant's shrewd bargaining for queen and prisoners under terms that invoke the Custom of Logres.

Le Conte du graal: Potential loss also marks the crisis in the opening Arthurian scene of the last romance. As the plenary presence looks on passively, and with alarming indifference, an intruder from afar calls for an adjudicative duel as he lays formal claim to no less than absolute suzerainty over the Arthurian domain itself. Later, when the last remaining episodes of *Le Conte du graal* have been told, the centrifugal principle of Arthurian knighthood, already implicit in the barons' initial resistance in "Li premiers vers," has advanced to its ultimate phase. Having been charged with murder and called away to face a judicial duel, Gauvain is gone. Many other knights have hastened elsewhere, to better abodes or more rewarding ordeals. The once plenary presence has now dwindled to a silent, ineffectual assembly, while only the frightened voices of the sick and the crippled call in vain for Arthur's nephew; anxiety reigns while Arthur wanes. In short, crisis has become a way of life within the Arthurian community.

As an ensemble, these successive Arthurian crises reveal an increase in gravity and a progressive decline. In *Erec* it was merely the prerogatives of customal procedure which were involved; only the harmony and tranquility of the plenary presence was at stake. In the next two works the courts risks being diminished in numbers through the taking of hostages or ritualized carnage. Customal procedure itself is disqualified in *Yvain*, while in its place the judgment of the monarch is dilatory, hesitant, and ultimately arbitrary. In the *Charrete* and *Le Conte du graal*, Arthur's knights are preoccupied with their own objectives, while he remains powerless to counter the jeopardy posed to the court by abuses of its own customs. The most vital aspects of the monarch's purview – his queen, his subjects, his realm – are subjected to challenges from beyond the community; as the Arthur of earlier tradition had lost the queen and the realm through the machinations of Mordret, Meleagant and the Vermilion Knight would between them readily wrest these treasures from Chrétien's monarch.

It is also apparent that the decline of Arthurian society is already inscribed, as a potential development, into the principles venerated from its inception: the double bind which determines the initial problematic in *Erec* also accounts for the crises arising in the three later works in the customal series, while in all four adherence to custom as a dominant mode of governance transforms an otherwise explosive situation into a critical dilemma that vastly compounds its gravity. The later crises are variations on a theme announced from the outset, their increasingly somber scenarios developing as possible worlds from components of the initial situation. In this regard, "Li premiers vers" of *Erec* effectively embodies the latent model for what could appropriately be called Chrétien's *intertextuality* of crisis.

Thus the concept of crisis is implemented in two distinct guises in Chrétien's works: a textuality of crisis that organizes the dynamically unfolding ethical coherence of a chivalric intrigue, and a communal intertextuality of crisis that progressively describes the deterioration of the Arthurian community as we begin with *Cligés* and proceed through the four customal romances. Does a significant relationship exists between the two types? Since the individual crisis typically marks the hero's maximum degree of remoteness from the collective sphere, a major consequence being a sudden and acute awareness both of the idiosyncracy of such a position and of the urgent need for a reintegrative movement, one might expect that the post-crisis development would feature the hero's return to the milieu and values of the Arthurian community.[3] Things are never so simple, however: while prior to his crisis and from the outset of his principal exploits the hero is invariably an Arthurian knight, his development following the crisis takes him beyond this sphere in more than a geographical sense. Despite what is often taken for granted about the conventional solidarity between heroes and kings, the crises of the individual entail no ultimate return, on the part of the hero, to full and absolute harmony with the Arthurian communal sphere.

On the contrary, Chrétien's extensive depictions of two types of crisis, individual and communal, represent with remarkable consistency a considerable divergence of values between the chivalric protagonists and the royal exponent of the anterior order.[4] While successive implementations of a textuality of crisis gradually widen the gap between Arthur and the hero in the first three poems in the customal series, then progressively distance and finally, in the case of Perceval, remove the hero entirely from the Arthurian sphere of values, the intertextuality of crisis undermines the image of the Arthurian court as an adequate basis for an ethic of knighthood, eventually contrasting its relative decadence with a communal ideal founded on spirituality and a retreat from the worldliness of chivalric life. Yet unlike his precursors – and many of his followers – Chrétien clearly envisaged no violent demise for his Arthurian society. Instead of the traditional alternatives of Arthur's mortality, as in Geoffrey, or his indefinite absence, as in Wace, Chrétien foreshadows a twofold eventuality that contrasts the remote remnant at the Grail Castle with the reconstitution of the anterior order in a third generation. Thus, although the two types of crisis might initially seem to have little in common, they merge in a single demonstration of the inadequacy of the Arthurian ideal and the need for a superior chivalric ethos. While the decline of the ideal is measured by the communal upheavals, the series of individual crises culminates in the revealing opposition between Gauvain, the new maker of knights and keeper of the Custom of the Spur, who now becomes the chief representative of the anterior order, and Perceval, whose reorientation sends him in the direction of a superior social order – a peaceable kingdom – wholly unprecedented in the other implementations of the pattern of chivalric crisis.

This complementarity between the two types of crisis throughout the corpus makes it apparent that Chrétien's *œuvre* signifies as a whole. One sees that, in addition to being read as discrete fictive biographies of knights whose individual exploits involve prowess, love, and communal service, these romances must also be read as the separate components of a larger design, one that conveys meaning through the comprehensive dimension created by all five fictions. The intertextuality of crisis is not the sole determinant of this global coherence, however. Customs also, by creating unity *among* as well as *within* individual works in the *œuvre*, help to lend a unique shape and a highly specialized significance to the transtextual design.

CUSTOMS AND THE TRANSTEXTUAL PERSPECTIVE

Intratextual unity

In each romance in the customal series, the significance of customs tends to exceed the limits of isolated episodes, generating suggestive resonances throughout the work as a whole. In "Li premiers vers" of *Erec*, the same structure informs the Custom of the White Stag and the Custom of the Sparrowhawk, and the two customs mirror one another as variant procedures for making the same determination of status.[5] Later, in the penultimate episode, the Joie de la Cort, they are recalled by significant contrasts. Again we find a disrupted monarchy on the one hand, and on the other a knight engaged by custom in prowess on behalf of his lady. She, however, has used the *don contraignant*, yet another type of custom, to compel her champion to defeat and destroy an indeterminate number of adversaries.[6] The relatively benign accommodation of chivalric and courtly aspirations by the Custom of the Sparrowhawk has here become a grim ritual that drains a kingdom of its vitality.[7]

Like *Erec*, the *Charrete* incorporates two highly detailed customs from neighboring regions, one being the Arthurian realm itself. Each custom is formally introduced, well into the romance, as a highly condensed, abstract case. Yet each recalls and anticipates situations within the work as a whole, which is framed by the symmetry between Meleagant's opening attempt to reinforce the Custom of Gorre by maliciously placing it under the jurisdiction of the Custom of Logres, and Lancelot's closing success in abolishing the Custom of Gorre thanks to his prior adherence to the Custom of Logres.[8]

In *Le Chevalier au lion* only one principal custom is repeatedly featured from the outset. The enduring obligation to defend the fountain becomes a dominant preoccupation which determines the work's outer boundaries and shapes the structure of the whole. Like the primary customs in the *Charrete*, the Custom of the Fountain is identified well into the intrigue, yet its pertinence to the narrative is established in the opening episode, by Calogrenant's story.[9] Thereafter it serves as a measure of the hero's early triumphs, then as a determining factor in his personal crisis, and finally as the ultimate objective of his ethical requalification. While the custom is at issue in every major reversal that prolongs the story, it resonates thematically with many later episodes that also associate customs and the attribution of feudal land-holding privileges. Figuratively as well as literally, then, the Perilous Fountain is an *abyme* from whose depths flow the entire romance's dominant thematic concerns and narrative organization.

If the way in which customs are woven into the fabric of Chrétien's fictions is perceptible to the reader through the linking of certain episodes with the brief formal descriptions of customs, this may well reflect twelfth-century modes of literary production according to the reigning clerical poetics of the day. The methodology of the narrative poet trained in rhetoric and dialectic is founded on the amplification of set pieces and episodes from a specific topic.[10] What is known of twelfth-century techniques of composition enhances the likelihood that the wealth of thematic relationships which customs maintain both within and among Chrétien's romances results from consistent application of conscious poetic processes.[11]

Larger narrative segments detailing the circumstances of legal cases in Chrétien's romances may thus have been amplified from arguments based on the customs evoked by these segments. Such a process would have been furthered by the logical organization of each custom according to an "*if . . . then . . .* " kind of format. For example, the Custom of Logres specifies that "*if* a knight accosts an unescorted female, *then* certain sanctions obtain; *if* she is escorted, *then* certain others apply." Or again, the Custom of Gorre prescribes that "*if* one departs, *then* all may do so." In *Erec*, the Custom of the White Stag requires that "*if* the hunter takes the stag, *then* it is he who bestows the honor upon the female of his choice"; the rival custom prescribes that "*if* the knight triumphs in single combat, *then* his lady may take the prize and receive the honor." Likewise in *Yvain*, "*if* an intruder activates the fountain's storm, *then* he is subject to reprisals." Because of its capacity to link circumstances with appropriate sanctions, this type of structure has been identified as a frequent characteristic of legal propositions in general: *if* certain violations of a law are proved, *then* certain penalties are in order.[12] Here we can compare the method of the jurist and that of the narrative poet: while the former prescribes a sanction after reconstructing the circumstances of a case, the latter constructs the episodic circumstantiality of a "case" around the constraints imposed by the custom which serves as a nucleus of the fiction.[13] Thus for the narrative poet the *"if... then ... "* format within the custom could have provided a valuable model for episodic amplification, suggesting possibilities for the depiction of circumstances that logically derive from the format's constraints.

In terms of reception, the format enables readers to match events and situations in the romance with the conditions posed by the customs.[14] The processes of jurisprudence and those in interpretative reception of literature function virtually in unison here, while the coherence of the legal fiction relies on the vital *intra*textual cues that relate depicted circumstances back to customs.[15]

Thus at the level of the individual text, customs help to effect what Chrétien proclaimed early in his career to be a necessary bond between meaning and the aesthetically engaging narrative – between *sens* and the *bele conjointure* (see the Prologue to *Erec et Enide*, vv. 1–22). Consideration of Chrétien's *œuvre* in its entirety also reveals that episodes featuring customs create numerous relationships of resemblance among the romances. For example, the Vermilion Knight's adamant demand to engage in combat for Arthurian lands in *Le Conte du graal* recalls Meleagant's challenge for Arthur's queen in the *Charrete*, and both evoke the role of Angrés in *Cligés*. *Le Conte du graal* is particularly rich in evocations of matters pertaining to customs in earlier works: the two main adventures identified by the Hideous Damsel are evocative of the White Stag and Sparrowhawk customs, and the last extant episode featuring Gauvain is a rewriting of the Joie de la Cort in *Erec*. These examples indicate that while creating suggestive thematic relations among the various works, customs may also figure within a larger coherence that transcends any given text.

Logres: custom and intertextuality

Nowhere is the intertextual range of any given custom more apparent than in the multiple episodic variations on the Custom of Logres. We have seen that its basic "argument" permeates the circumstantial details of many episodes in the *Charrete*, where it is defined. While there are no explicit allusions to the Custom of Logres prior to the *Charrete*, it is anticipated in earlier works by a variety of suggestive thematic detail. The need for protection afforded the solitary female voyager in the first clause of the custom is also emphasized in *Yvain*:

> si pooit estre an grant esmai
> pucele au bois, et sanz conduit,
> par mal tans, et par noire nuit   (vv. 4842–4)

a maiden in the woods without escort could be in deep distress during foul weather in the black of night.

Customs and the transtextual perspective

Or again, Erec stages a provocation to combat that would fall under the custom's second clause: repeatedly he escorts Enide, forcing her to ride ahead of him richly attired, the apparent objective being to lure attacks from roaming marauders so that he may "rehabilitate" his prowess (vv. 2762ff.). Later, to counter the lustful designs of an ardent count, Enide in her turn stages the scenario for her own conquest:

> mes demain anvoiez ceanz
> voz chevaliers et voz sergenz,
> si me feites a force prandre;
> mes sires me voldra desfandre,
> qui molt est fiers et corageus.
> Ou soit a certes ou a geus,
> feites le prandre et afoler
> ou de la teste decoler.
> Trop ai menee ceste vie,
> je n'aim mie la conpaignie
> mon seignor, je n'an quier mantir.
> Je vos voldroie jà santir
> an un lit certes nu a nu. (vv. 3379–91)

but tomorrow send your knights and servants in here and have me taken by force my lord, who is courageous and fierce, will try to defend me. Whether in earnest or in jest, have him seized and wounded or relieved of his head. I'm sick of this life and hate my lord's company, to tell the truth. I'd like to feel you against me in bed, flesh to flesh.

The provocation would involve the count in a "dishonorable" seizure according to the terms of the custom. A second count finds Enide with a seemingly lifeless Erec – a prefiguration of later instances of the *pietà* motif – and yet another variant on the motif of the imperiled female.

The latter in *Cligés* is none other than Fénice when she is kidnapped by forces under the command of an unsuccessful suitor and "won" back by Cligés – for the emperor – in a judicial combat (vv. 3336ff.). By the standards of the Custom of Logres, Cligés' victory would make Fénice *his* intended, but the only custom governing their relationship at this stage is that maintained by Love:

> Vos qui d'Amors vos feites sage,
> Et les costumes et l'usage
> De sa cort maintenez a foi,
> N'onques ne faussastes sa loi,
> Que qu'il vos an doie cheoir,
> Dites se l'en puet nes veoir
> Rien qui par Amor abelisse,
> Que l'en n'an tresaille ou palisse. (vv. 3819–26)

You who are wise in the ways of Love and keep in faith the customs and usage of his court and never broke his law, whatever might befall you, say if one can really see anything that through Love delights and not tremble or grow pale.

In brief, this amatory "custom" affirms that "*if* there is love, *then* there is fear." In *Yvain*, by contrast, fear is generated by suitors like Harpin or Count Alier who would make the female and her domain the prizes of combat, as Lunete had helped Yvain to make a prize of Laudine after his victory over the latter's husband.

While these scattered episodes are not explicitly identified as being under the custom's aegis and do not consistently fulfil its conditions, they combine with numerous others throughout the *œuvre* to underline the issue of *feminine vulnerability*, thus lending added significance to the custom devised, presumably, as a means for countering it. The issue is broached time and again, in remote or informal settings and in scenes of courtly challenge and combat. It looms large from the opening of *Erec*, where Yder's dwarf lashes the queen's attendant, to the lengthy and poignant confession of the Orgueilleuse near the end of *Le Conte du graal*. In the earlier works, the female victims suffer their lot awkwardly, if not in silence. Enide deals with one lecherous count by her guile and cunning, with another by passive resistance and desperate shrieking after a forced marriage. Like her, others are fortunately rescued or vindicated by chivalric intervention: among them are the besieged Lady of Norison, Gauvain's niece tormented by Harpin, Meleagant's harassed sister, the wretched Tent Maiden, the suicidal Blanchefleur, and Greoreas' nameless victim.[16]

In the last of the five works, the Tent Maiden and the Orgueilleuse, the one by showing, the other by telling, together comprise a new and powerful critique of masculine aggression whose closing synthesis is provided by the Orgueilleuse. In *Le Conte du graal* the case involving the Orgueilleus de la Lande and the one concerning the Orgueilleuse de Nogres and her accomplice, the Orgueilleus del Passage, are both inspired by the Custom of Logres. These episodes, one from the adventures of Perceval and the other from those of Gauvain, are related onomastically by the names of the featured villains. Moreover, the word "orgueilleus" rearranges the letters of the word "Logres" into the negative semantic field of *orgueil*. In addition, the noun "Nogres" suggests a *negation* of Logres, that former paragon of justice, while the association of "Logres" with its rhyme-word "ogres," designating the once barbaric occupants of this realm, suggests its currently regressive tendencies toward a state of anarchy.[17]

The twin "Orgueilleus" segments are both interrupted by an account of the hero's first encounter with his principal challenge: the castle of the Fisher King for Perceval; the Roche de Canguin for Gauvain. In terms of structure, moreover, the two segments are virtual mirror-images of one another. A prominent feature in each is the motif, appropriately identified by Antoinette Saly as the *pietà*, of a damsel weeping over the supine figure of a dead or wounded knight; thus Perceval's cousin and her dead lover are doubled by the distraught maiden and the unconscious Greoreas encountered by Gauvain.[18] In both cases, moreover, the recumbent knight has been the victim of the murderous knight in a second couple; this knight, named in each case Orgueilleus, is ultimately defeated by the hero. The second couple is in each instance linked with a major abuse of the Custom of Logres. The Orgueilleus de la Lande had staged situations permitting him to intervene against innocent knights, on the contrived grounds of their being vulnerable according to the custom's second clause; he had used the Tent Maiden as his accomplice when she was "accompanied" by an unwary traveler. Likewise, the Orgueilleuse had staged contrived scenarios, also replicating the custom's second clause, so that her accomplice could legitimately challenge knights escorting her. Thus, while Perceval's adversary had typically engaged in combat and beheading only in situations where "his" female was "accompanied" by an unsuspecting knight, Gauvain's female detractor had led a series of unsuspecting knights "accompanying" her to the knight waiting to defeat and behead them. In both cases, one abuse of the custom engendered another: Perceval's inadvertent violation of the first clause of the custom, pertaining to unescorted females, prompted the Orgueilleus' homicidal abuse under the protection of the second clause, pertaining to females who are escorted; Guiromelant's homicide under conditions specified by clause two motivated the perverse customal enterprise of the Orgueilleuse. The closing synthesis of this critique is provided by the Orgueilleuse, who alone of all the many victims of masculine abuse in these romances expatiates at length on the profound distress that it occasions.

We can readily see here how such a custom can be subverted while maintaining respect for its formal properties. The "Orgueilleus" in each case adheres to the custom's rules while realizing objectives diametrically opposed to those for which the rules were originally prescribed. By using the custom as a model for creating cases in ethical and pragmatic contradiction with the order it ostensibly guarantees, the Orgueilleus de la Lande and the Orgueilleuse de Nogres are in effect inventing "counter-customs" spawned from the very constraints they seek to overturn. Hence, as in the earlier manipulative stratagems of Maboagrain's lady and Meleagant, we find that these episodes involving an "Orgueilleus" are attempts to "work" the Arthurian juridical system from within its own rigid constraints.

While this intensification of details pertaining to the Custom of Logres serves near the end of the *œuvre* to contextualize the issue of feminine vulnerability as a juridical problem, assimilating details from earlier works, its development also emphasizes a fundamental dichotomy of values. The stipulation of a uniformly applicable concept of justice, on the one hand, and the subordination of justice to matters of privilege on the other, is apparent in the two clauses into which the custom is divided. As described in the *Charrete*, these two clauses are suggestive of two distinct strata, as if the custom had evolved over time in a direction favorable to a certain type of abuse. It is implied that the archaic form, reflected in its initial clause, pertained only to the security of a female traveling alone; according to Gauvain, this rule regarding safe-conduct was ratified by Arthur himself (*Le Conte du graal*, vv. 7121ff.). Onto this archaic substratum, it appears, has been grafted a more recent, rather contradictory chivalric clause covering only the outcome of armed challenge: the accompanied female is awarded to the victorious knight. Unlike the earlier stipulation, this clause effectively removes conventional single combat from the public opprobrium in which willful aggression against females had generally been held. Whatever the implied relative vintage of the two conditions covered by the custom, that prescribing chivalric accompaniment in no way ameliorates the situation of the female, whose individual liberty is pre-empted by might as the sole determinant of right.

In the historical behavior of medieval customs, their mechanisms were at times altered to meet the needs or desires of a given community; or again, customs in geographical proximity were sometimes variants of one another, reflecting the contrasting interests of different groups.[19] Among Chrétien's literary customs, an instance of such "drift" is evident in the contrast between the Custom of the White Stag, an old, royal practice designed to renew collective solidarity, and the distant, noble Custom of the Sparrowhawk, which accommodates precisely the kind of chivalric determination of individual privilege proscribed by the Arthurian custom.[20] If "drift" is again what accounts for the internally contradictory quality of the Custom of Logres, the apparent intent of the second clause is exclusion of chivalric combat from the more general constraints pertaining to unaccompanied females, whence another accommodation of chivalry's desire to render justice on its own terms.

In a utopian world, where chivalry's mightiest champions are always the victorious upholders of the rights of women, children, and the unjustly oppressed as prescribed by the fundamental principles of the order of chivalry, such a clause would no doubt seem adequate.[21] In Chrétien's romances, however, such ideals seldom prevail in practice, while episodes depicting the likes of an Orgueilleus or an Orgueilleuse illustrate how readily and, moreover, how wrongly the Custom of Logres might protect the basely motivated "chivalric" aggressor from public disgrace should he be the victor.

In the Custom of Logres we may thus recognize a general proposition which is clearly evident in *Le Chevalier au lion*. As Chapter 3 has shown, the proposition "*If* might, *then* right" – the operative assumption of the Custom of the Fountain – accounts for a global conceptual level in this romance and is recalled in some significant fashion in virtually every episode (above pp. 6off.). In the second, chivalric clause of the Custom of Logres, as well, the determination of right depends solely on the triumph of physical force, as indeed it does also in the customs observed at Laluth, Brandigant, Pesme-Avanture, and the Roche de Canguin.

The remarkable frequency with which juridical institutions are founded on the adjudicative principle that right is exclusively a product of might indicates that this proposition is a matter of primary concern in these fictions.[22] Chrétien's romances unfold as a long meditation, in a multitude of circumstantial settings, on the potential discrepancy between the valorization of might as determinant of right and the problems this widely held attitude encounters in countless conflicts. From these legal fictions a general critique emerges, one which repeatedly emphasizes that it is the ethical integrity of the agents of right, and not merely their overwhelming strength, which is the indispensable factor in the maintenance of a just order.

By disclosing the dichotomy between the logic of juridical propositions and the ethic they fail to uphold, the dominant legal coherence of these works constitutes a powerful critique of a society based on orally maintained custom as a means of upholding justice. The implications for Logres and for the juridical integrity of the Arthurian court are indeed disturbing, for through the gaping loophole in the custom that bears the name of the realm, one can easily recognize the portrait of

Arthur's reign drawn by the widow in the Waste Forest. Behind the numerous examples of "adjudication" by force one perceives that the rightness of might is a principle upon which the anterior order has long relied, as vested in the dynamic component of an Arthurian chivalric order dedicated *in principle* to ensuring a viable relationship between might and right. In the last work in the corpus, as we have seen, the progressive intensification of misgivings with regard to the agency of chivalry culminates in the image of one type of worldly chivalry too frequently at odds with the royal sponsor of right and justice, and another that espouses an ideal of right and justice whose teleology transcends the world. For the one, *chivalric might* remains the operative principle of an idealized *militia saeculi* overseen in its third incarnation by Gauvain, while for the other a *peregrinatio spiritualis* displaces the chivalric model while entering upon a phase of retreat from the conflicts of this world.

As in our previous examination of two types of crises, consideration of the intertextual coherence of custom brings us once again to the instructive contrast between two ideas of social order developed by the final romance in the *œuvre*. We shall now see how the two most prominent types of literary customs depicted by Chrétien help to determine a consistent pattern of structural organization in each romance in the customal series, while also cumulatively moving toward the meaningful closing contrast that unifies Chrétien's Arthurian romances according to a transtextual design.

From plenary presence to remote locus

It remains to be emphasized that the literary customs in Chrétien's Arthurian romances are major determinants of structure and meaning within the individual works in the customal series. Throughout the series, the Custom *in* the Arthurian Opening and the Custom *at* the Remote Locus (see above, pp. 93ff.) help to structure each text and, when read successively, bring into prominence the transtextual design. These two types of custom may be represented in tabular form, as shown below.

	Erec et Enide	*Yvain*	*Charrete*	*Conte du graal*	
Arthurian Opening	White Stag Custom	Fountain Custom	Custom of Logres	Perceval: Combat – Verm. Knight	Gauvain: Combat – Guingam.
Remote Locus	Joie de la Cort	Pesme-Avanture	Custom of Gorre	Grail Castle	La Roche de Canguin

The *Arthurian opening* is a conventional feature of the customal series, occurring at court on the occasion of a plenary presence. Yet while invariably coming to prominence *in* the opening, the customs in this category are not enacted *at* court; apart from the stag hunt, all involve distant combats. Read successively, these openings suggest a progressive decline in Arthur's authoritative administration of the court's procedures. While Arthur revives the White Stag Custom and manages, despite potential for discord, to salvage it from revisionary designs, in successive analogues he is much more passive. His lethargy, idle curiosity, and incomprehension of the fountain's juridical prohibition add up to a less than flattering portrait in the opening of *Yvain*. This ineffectual profile is further developed by the abuses of custom in the openings of the *Charrete* and the Perceval section of *Le Conte du graal*; at the outset of the Gauvain section of that work the king's own nephew, heretofore the paragon of Arthurian values, is being summoned to a judicial duel on charges of homicide.

Decline is also apparent in successive glimpses of the royal entourage. At the beginning of *Erec*, the court teems with 500 eager knights and their noble ladies: the narrator can inventory by name the members of the Round Table but is unable to identify even one-fifteenth of the knights present (vv. 1662ff.); at the couple's wedding Arthur's barons include the kings, dukes and counts "qui de lui tenoient terre" (v. 1876) – the landholding vassals that comprise a distinguished plenary presence (vv. 1884ff.). The court's membership is never again described in such opulent terms. The assembly of supposedly "boen chevalier esleü" (*Yvain*, v. 40) – the "elite" of chivalry – is relegated to the background in *Yvain* and the *Charrete*; they look on idly while Kay displays his habitual discourtesy toward the queen and Calogrenant (*Yvain*, vv. 113–35) and abuses the *don contraignant* to the detriment of the royal couple (*Charrete*, vv. 82ff.). The first Arthurian opening in *Le Conte du graal* finds Arthur dismayed that so many of his knights have departed in pursuit of better opportunities elsewhere, and along with this implication of a decline in the king's capacity for *largesse* goes the serene indifference to the crisis at hand on the part of those who have remained; in the second Arthurian opening, the departures of Perceval and Gauvain coincide with the exodus of dozens more, in a rush toward adventure and promised renown. Collectively, these opening moments provide yet another means of plotting the coordinates of a negative progression. Far from highlighting the harmonious stability of an exemplary feudal community, all blend instances of communal antagonism with examples of the court's propensity to juridical malfunction; hence its vulnerability to challenges both from without and from within.

Custom, which thus ensures that the Arthurian opening will depict the court's ongoing propensity to a failure of *krisis*, or judgment, also provides a catalyst propelling the hero into his principal itinerary. Here again the custom *in* the opening is vital: directly or indirectly, it determines the *circumstances* of the hero's engagement in developments that will take him far beyond the immediate context of the court. The crucial nuance is that regardless of the potential turmoil, disruption, or peril that the custom may represent for the court at the outset, the hero's departure and subsequent initiatives reflect no imperious desire on his part to obviate the conflict in the interest of the court. Other preoccupations – vengeance, love, gain, self-exculpation – are invariably the efficient causes of departure. The opening custom is thus the point at which the values of the hero begin to bifurcate from those of the Arthurian order.

While the Arthurian opening activates the heroic dynamic, the *Remote Locus* awaits the hero as he struggles toward the apogee of his career, confronting him with what will be his *pesme avanture*, his most formidable challenge. In every case, the site of that confrontation is identified with an ongoing, obligatory local practice – a custom – that the hero undertakes to end. Nomenclature varies: the Joie de la Cort is called an "avanture" (*Erec*, vv. 5384; 5416), the procession in the Grail Castle a "merveille" (*Conte du graal*, v. 3202), the Roche de Canguin a locus of "enchantments" (v. 7604).[23] These adjudicative complexes are nonetheless similar in function to their two analogues explicitly identified as sites of customs, Pesme-Avanture and Gorre; Köhler groups all five in a classification pertaining to customs "abolished" by the hero.[24] In each case, in ending an obligatory practice – combat, tribute, captivity, or ritualized anticipation amidst suspended vitality – the hero must strive to rescue a demoralized community from the anguish of a desperate situation or from the tyranny of malevolent abusers.

In terms of the textuality of crisis, abolition of the custom maintained at the Remote Locus represents the hero's principal encounter, as well as the supreme test that affirms his heroic mastery in the last of the compensatory ordeals necessitated after his crisis. A primary consequence of victory is the attribution of *value*. Erec, having transcended his "premier los" and delivered a kingdom from peril, is at last worthy of a second return to the paternal realm, this time as its monarch. Having restored to the lord of a tyrannized castellany his right to *tenir terre* in peace, Yvain will return to performance of the same function in his own domain. Yet significantly, Arthur's symbolic, accessory sanction of Erec in the closing coronation in *Erec et Enide* has no counterpart in *Yvain*, which replaces royal recognition of the hero by the king's inept settlement of contested claims. The breach between the lawgiver and the heroic subject widens even further in the *Charrete*: the Arthurian community is now the primary beneficiary of the hero's victory over the malevolent agent of the Remote Locus, yet public sanction is set aside, ironically, in favor of the queen's covert amatory sanction of her lover. This progressive removal of the hero from the sphere of values represented by the Arthurian court culminates in the bifurcated itineraries of Perceval and Gauvain. The irony of the former's crisis lies in its occurrence at the apogee of his exaltation by the Arthurian court, thus bringing the previously implicit dichotomy of values between hero and king into the foreground and making it the basis for Perceval's move toward a Remote Locus whose values are diametrically opposed to those of the Arthurian standard. Only in the itinerary of Gauvain, as we have seen, do Arthurian values and those of the heroically restored Remote Locus begin to converge, configuring the beginning of a new phase for the anterior order.[25]

The way in which the successive depictions of the Arthurian openings and the Remote Locus progressively blend into a meaningful design leads one to sum up one of the most consequential intertextual aspects of Chrétien's Arthurian fictions by saying that, while Uther and Gauvain are the once and future rulers of Arthur's realm, customs are the once and future fictions of Chrétien's Arthurian world. Whence, in sum, a meaningful global coherence in which customs are chief among the coordinates marking the progressive intertextual decline of the Arthurian ideal. The end of the customal series is inscribed as an ominous possibility in its beginning, in the double bind that determines the initial problematic, shapes the later crises, and ultimately enthrones crisis as a way of life at what eventually remains of the Arthurian court.

This larger significance, inherent in the decline intermittently described across the five works in the ensemble, is also apparent from the tensions generated by the precarious coexistence of two dimensions of textuality. While the intertextual dimension traces the phases of a communal decline, the textuality of crisis ultimately uses the Remote Locus as a means of depicting two types of survival, as well as the implied futurity of a fiction. In the three earlier works in the customal series, the Remote Locus had always been the ultimate milestone in the itinerary of the hero. In the last romance in the ensemble, it identifies two sites at which two lineages will survive to exemplify two radically different modes of existence: at one Remote Locus, the exiled remnant of a tarnished kingdom strives to revive its hegemony as a viable ideal within the world; at the other, exile itself has become an alternative kingdom permanently apart from the world and its ways, in anticipation of the end of time, the ultimate closure. Between these extremes of worldly and spiritual exile lies implicit the inevitability of social change within the secular world – an open question. Nothing will ever change, meanwhile, within the last, frozen frame of this prematurely truncated fictive world. While the anterior order will still struggle awkwardly into the unknown by upholding, through its customs, the superannuated mandates of the past, the order of the grail, poised expectantly somewhere this side of eternity, will, with the custom venerated by its solemn ceremonies, continue to transform the present into a ritualized memory of the future.

Conclusion

Literary customs and the socio-historical question

The foregoing chapters have examined the highly specialized usage of customs as *literary* devices in a given world of medieval *fiction*, indicating their various functions in providing unity and coherence within and among the individual texts that make up that world. Yet precisely because the creator of these devices designated them by the term contemporaneously used in the vernacular to designate certain varieties of feudal legal transactions, he also created the potential for raising issues germane to the concerns of the social historian; at least some measurement of the common ground between fiction and history seems in this case to be a distinct possibility. The student of medieval literature may prefer to remain content with the literary dimension, leaving to medieval historians the question of how Chrétien's literary customs compare to customs within the late twelfth-century socio-historical sphere. Yet we cannot simply dismiss the question. Erich Köhler, who opened it on a modest scale a quarter of a century ago, wisely enclosed the term "coutume" in quotation marks as if to emphasize *contrast* between literary devices and historical phenomena; in so doing, however, he cast only a brief glance at the historical properties of medieval custom reflected in Chrétien's works, while treating the question within the unduly restricted optic of his own socio-historical thesis.[1] Our conclusion will reconsider these issues, in the hope of stimulating further reflection on the ways in which our inquiry into the literary order may have implications for inquiries into the historical order as well.

The formula *lex et consuetudo* – law and custom – recurs in documents dating from as far back as the ninth century; not until the thirteenth do the teaching of Roman and canon law in the universities and the compilation of customals begin to foreshadow the eventual predominance of *lex* over *consuetudo*. By the late twelfth century custom was already deeply ingrained in a wide variety of social transactions. In fact the kind of steadfast reliance on custom evident in Chrétien's poems was to persist within many different social groups until long after the proliferation of customals, for custom prevailed over written law in Europe throughout the Middle Ages.[2] Many different types of transactions were included under the rubric of custom. Seigneurial and ecclesiastical fees, as well as monastic rules, were at times so designated; nobles, vassals, merchants, ecclesiastics, bourgeois, even serfs observed customs that were quite specific to the needs of a restricted and homogeneous community.[3] Likewise in Chrétien's romances we have seen that customs are maintained within circumscribed ethno-political groups, such as the chivalric and noble Custom of the Sparrowhawk at Laluth, the Fountain Custom, or the separate customs at Pesme-Avanture, one maintained by the townspeople outside the castle walls, the other enforced within by the count and his two captors. Chrétien's inventory even includes one instance of custom as tax or fee levied by a commune, as Gauvain discovered at Tintagel.[4] The jurisdictional scope of customs at Arthur's court also varies, from the Custom of the White Stag observed only by the Round Table to the Custom of Logres enforced throughout the realm – and challenged by the custom enforced throughout the realm of Gorre. The Custom of the Spur in *Le Conte du graal* is an example of a practice pertaining to a specific social stratum yet also observed in different locales.

Chrétien's creation of literary situations that compare or contrast in suggestive ways with historical practice undoubtedly determined a certain "effet de réel" ("reality effect") within a courtly public.[5] More specifically, perhaps, the two types of customs prominently developed in the last three works in the series reflect contemporaneous problems in late twelfth-century Champagne, where the personal security of travelers to the numerous fairs held annually in the region and the attribution of feudal property rights were matters of the utmost concern.[6] Yet the prominence of literary customs in these fictions clearly stems from more than a precociously novelistic concern with achieving "mimetic realism." Such an effect is diminished precisely by the customs' inclusion among the explicit indications that these works, far from being authentic reflections of the present, are depictions of a different world belonging to a remote past.[7] Whence, for example, the archaizing flavor of the opening lines of *Yvain*:

> Mes or parlons de cez qui furent,
> si leissons cez qui ancor durent...　　　　(vv. 29–30)

But now let us turn from those still living and speak of those who came before.

Likewise, the narrator in *Le Conte du graal* reminds us that the custom of sending prisoners to Arthur is so unfamiliar to a contemporaneous public as to need a gloss:

> Costume estoit a cel termine
> Sel trovon escrit en la letre...　　　　(vv. 2722–3)

at that time the custom was, as we find it written in the source...

Yet at the same time, rather as in utopian literature or science fiction, the alterity of this remote world makes current political and social problems all the more conspicuous through defamiliarization. Rather than self-consciously replicating specific practices or events in the historical order, Chrétien's fictions place the mechanisms of custom into imaginary, temporally remote yet operative situations that evoke problematic issues within the contemporaneous socio-historical sphere.

No assessment of this aspect of the romances can fail to consider the seminal contribution of Erich Köhler. He evokes those moments when Arthur, obliged to respect custom as the juridical foundation of the realm, is powerless when abuse of a custom threatens the very order it was to have guaranteed; he also argues that custom is used to dramatize a "contradiction between the necessity for a supra-personal order in which chivalry takes shape as a class and the centrifugal forces inherent in chivalry."[8] He maintains that this contradiction, "insoluble" within the context of "socio-historical reality" (p. 395), was turned by Chrétien into a fictive demonstration of "individual perfection" within an ideal community. Thus the "chosen" knight (*élu*) "must himself in his quest for adventure, pass through the three dialectical stages, so as finally to resolve the extant contradiction: separation from the court whose harmony is disrupted; isolation in the quest for adventure (with the conventional motif of refusal to remain at court); and finally the return, culminating in the 'Joy' of harmony restored" (p. 396). While his journey assumes the circular contour of a mythic quest, his stellar profile is likened to that of a "liberator," even of a "redeemer" (p. 396).[9] Thus, the argument runs, whenever the Arthurian "supra-personal" order is threatened, the exemplary protector of the suzerain-monarch intercedes, undertaking a "quest" at whose outcome the custom is either restored to collective usage or "forever abolished" (p. 389).[10]

This emphasis on the "role" of custom in exalting the mediatory chivalric hero is clearly consonant with what Köhler in his earlier book had characterized as Chrétien's "chivalric ideal."[11] Arthur's court is a "locus of Joie" and of "total harmony between ideal and reality," though surrounded by a "demonized reality" which represents "a permanent threat to the ideal order realized at court" (p. 90). In his *aventure*, "the hero of courtly romance undergoes a purifying trial which must bring him to individual perfection," while "this process is also the constant safeguard of a community in jeopardy" (p. 97). The knight, the "guarantor of the *costume*," is engaged in the "eschatological struggle of Good versus Evil" (pp. 108, 110). While in the earlier works love may serve as an "organizing force" of chivalric perfection (p. 206), it yields in *Le Conte du graal* to "the eschatological mission of the chivalric class" (p. 231), the "last" of Chrétien's heroes – Perceval – embarking on an adventure oriented toward "redemption" (p. 259). Arthur's court becomes "the poetic symbol of an ideal kingdom impossible to locate within the real world," while Arthur himself "must be the resplendent incarnation of exemplary humanity represented by his entourage" (p. 38). Yet since this very position of pre-eminence would render him vulnerable were it not for his exemplary knights, he must seek to retain the best of them at court, so as to make it a center of "perfect humanity" (pp. 38–9). This Arthur, instead of incarnating the characteristics of a powerful sovereign aligned with a nascent merchant class, would thus display the features of a feudal suzerain, a *primus inter pares*, his reign optimally expressing the reintegrative aspirations of a lower and middle nobility (pp. 35; 45).[12]

Köhler's surprisingly optimistic view of the so-called "role" of customs in these works in fact reflects, to some extent inaccurately, only the most superficial kinds of circumstances in Chrétien's poems: while the "'Joy' of harmony restored" is indeed what Arthur himself most desires and needs, in the form of a plenary presence to ratify in unanimity the mandates of the anterior order, the expanding corpus suggests that this is what he most lacks. The weakest aspect of Köhler's perspective, however, lies in his idealized view of Chrétien's heroes as mediatory agents.[13] Whereas Köhler characterizes them as steadfast mediators between the court and the "centrifugal tendencies" within chivalry as well as beyond the court, Chrétien consistently depicts them to various degrees as the conscious *exponents* of chivalric individualism. In short, the heroes themselves display "centrifugal tendencies." Nor does Köhler acknowledge the sublime inadvertence with which the various heroes do in fact, despite their own divergent agendas, fulfil short-term Arthurian goals: it is while acting primarily, and often ardently, in their own interests that on occasion they may also, less purposefully or even unintentionally, act in the court's interest as well. Apart from Gauvain who in *Le Conte du graal* explicitly upholds the principle of safe-conduct in the name of the king, these heroes are only rarely depicted as *voluntary* agents in service to the integrity of the Arthurian order.

Moreover, nowhere in Chrétien's corpus is *Arthur* "the symbol of an ideal feudal state represented as the guarantor of a perfect human order and proposed as such."[14] If this characterization is appropriate to the idealized retrospective image of the age of *Uther*, in Chrétien's hands Arthurian story dramatizes the unlikelihood of ever recovering the harmony of that feudal past at its apogee. The age of Chrétien's Arthur is captured as the tension between a backward-looking king wedded to the anterior ideal of a thriving feudal community, and a far more complex contemporaneous world in which the pluralism of values and individual demands demonstrate in myriad ways the obsolescence of the early feudal mode. In the background we find a courtly chivalry that over the course of the ensemble eventually verges on decadence because various kinds of individualism consistently lead to neglect or even subversion of its avowed ideals as a class. The eponymous heroes, meanwhile, never perform the kind of ideal service that would equate them with the extraordinary knights described by Köhler in connection with an idealized literary form.[15] Their conduct exemplifies instead, as we have seen, the problematic dissociation between the dynamic sphere of the hero and the institutional purview of the lawgiver. Rather than reinvest a mythic paradigm in which the two spheres converge, as Köhler would have it, Chrétien progressively compounded the tensions between them.[16] To rephrase the question in terms of the two types of crisis discussed in Chapter 5, Köhler's analysis assumes the existence of positive reciprocity and solidarity between the heroic textuality of crisis and the crises that jeopardize the Arthurian ideal; Chrétien's works, meanwhile, repeatedly emphasize the contrary. In sum, Köhler invented a "role" for customs to strengthen his view of the ideology he abstracted from these romances, whose main objective he took to be that of creating a compensatory fictive world for a crepuscular feudal nobility.[17] Our medieval poet, meanwhile, undertook through the medium of fiction an extended exploration of the mechanisms of customs in numerous hypothetical situations and thus gave his romances a primary "role" in emphasizing their problematic aspects.

Prominent among these is the implication that the customs of an earlier, more homogeneous feudal world no longer elicit the kind of absolute communal assent essential to their effective regulation of social transactions. The foundation and survival of historical customs depended on their success in garnering collective assent within the group that observed them. Later customals emphasize that custom – sometimes in contrast with habitual "usage" – was identified by its obligatory force, perceived within the group. In the *Coutumes de Beauvaisis* of 1283, Philippe de Beaumanoir says that "coutumes sont à tenir," while in seeking some types of judgment "li usaiges seroit de nulle valeur" ("customs are to be maintained ... usage would have no force").[18] The fourteenth-century *Coustumes d'Anjou et de Maine* observes that "coustume est droit" while "usage est fait" ("custom is right ... usage is practice").[19] Taking this emphasis into account, Gilissen has recently defined medieval customs globally as "an ensemble of juridical usages that acquired obligatory force within a given socio-political group, through the repetition of public and peaceful acts during a relatively long span of time."[20] The terms "coutume" and "usage" – the latter being seldom in evidence – are sometimes used synonymously in Chrétien, notably in *Cligés* (vv. 3820, 4487, 4807). Regardless of which is used, however, there is generally a strong implication that an *obligation* obtains.[21] It is apparent from Arthur's comments in *Erec* concerning the potential dangers of invoking "other customs" that respect for this criterion is essential to the solidarity of the group. Such an ideal is seldom upheld, however, in most of the episodes where custom is invoked. Indeed, between Gilissen's definition and Chrétien's depictions of customs the most significant contrast concerns "the repetition of ... *peaceful* acts." Far from demonstrating the capacity of customs to effect a reasonable and *peaceful* judgment, these narratives make the relative prominence and consequentiality of a given custom directly proportional to its capacity to provoke *discord* and engender crisis.

This would seem to be as true of the presumably "good" customs as it is of the obviously "bad" ones. As in Chrétien's romances, customs in the historical order were not uncommonly deemed to be "good" and "reasonable" or else "bad," in which case they were subject to abrogation.[22] In his coronation charter of 1154, for example, Henry II, expressing his concern for the common good of the realm, concedes to his counts, barons, and vassals "all concessions and donations, freedoms and free customs" conceded to them by his grandfather, Henry I, while setting aside and abolishing "for myself and my heirs, all of the bad customs which he set aside and abolished..."[23] Like Henry II, Arthur in his discourse on monarchy in *Erec* intends to preserve only those customs prescribed by his lineal predecessor (vv. 1763ff.). Despite his repeated insistence that such a proclamation is "right" and "true," however, Arthur never asserts that what is "right" and "true" is also *good*; nor does he ever abrogate the "bad" – ineffective or harmful – customs that mar his own reign. As we have frequently observed, it is the hero, not the king, who normally "abolishes" the "bad" customs, as is, with one exception, the case with the Custom *at* the Remote Locus. Regardless of whether they are "good" or "bad," however, the major customs are repeatedly shown to be vulnerable to *divergent interpretations* or *eccentric applications* that would alter their jurisdiction in favor of a faction, such as Arthur's knights, or an individual, like Meleagant or the Orgueilleuse, whose interests are contrary, even perniciously detrimental, to the groups that initially observed them.

Literary customs and the socio-historical question

Thus do we find a considerable pliability and "play" within the mechanisms of these literary customs, and it is this malleability which determines their vulnerability to abuse. Mutability is also a property of customs in the historical order, and there, as in the customs represented in Chrétien's poems, it results from the fact that custom relies for its survival on *oral transmission*. Emphasizing this feature of custom in a positive light, Georges Duby speaks of the role of memory in societies that conclude daily transactions without benefit of writing, evoking rural feudalism as "a world that …, in order to regulate the totality of its social relations, relied not on texts but on memory, especially the collective memory that was custom – a very strict, exacting code, though it was nowhere written down. When it was a question of clarifying a fine point of this law, one necessarily recounted one's recollections. The oral inquiry – the periodic interrogation of members of the community, especially of the elders, as the repositories of an older vintage, considered more valuable because more deeply rooted in the past – constituted one of the major mechanisms for regulating society."[24]

In Chrétien's *œuvre* this "collective memory that was custom" is shown to subsist exclusively in oral assertions made by various voices, the most august being that of Arthur himself. As the unwritten juridical foundation of the Arthurian realm, the custom must be reiterated by a speaking voice.[25] Throughout the corpus we find statements in direct discourse descriptive of customs, uttered by a variety of secondary characters, all auxiliaries of the narrator who also on occasion assumes this juridical function. In all of these instances we may recognize the crucial intervention of the *informant*, by whom the utterance of the law of custom, drawn from an archaic reserve, is integrated into the fiction. This type of utterance carries with it a connotation of its own venerable status, reminiscent of Duby's remarks: "a world … that relied not on texts but on memory," a world that "interrogated the elders," a world for which the "oldest" authority was "the most valuable." Yet what of the status of this attitude in Chrétien's *œuvre*: though venerated by voices *in* the fiction, is it venerated by the fiction itself? From the very outset the shadow of a doubt is cast: in the opening scene of *Erec* the anxious voice of Gauvain attests to a general disregard for the stipulations of the Custom of the White Stag among the knights and noble ladies who make up the Arthurian plenary presence. Pursuing the profound implications latent in that liminal declaration of a rupture between the individual and the collective sphere, this world of fiction repeatedly casts in the role of *abuser* of custom schemers who model their schemes on the conventions of customs in order to turn them away from their legitimate ends. We have seen how emphatically this point is made by the extensive treatment of the Custom of Logres: it is in the custom that takes its name from the Arthurian realm itself that we find the strongest affinities between the evolution of a custom and its misuse, the clearest illustration of its tendency to align law with power irrespective of values.

Thus we are led to recognize a remarkably general state of affairs in Chrétien's *œuvre*: in virtually every passage where a custom is defined, the description of its basic mechanism includes few if any specifications concerning the values required of the individual who invokes it. Rather than prescribe ethical attributes, the custom merely sets forth an obligation to fulfil a certain repertory of narrative functions, thus providing a juridical model founded more on ritualized action than on a set of invariable values. Whence a form of social regulation whose deontology, or applied ethics, is indeterminate and therefore frequently at the mercy of a will to power, while its ontology relies on a highly unstable oral tradition.

In such a negative attitude toward recourse to customal procedure we may discern a shift of mentality.[26] For this representation of customs, whose primary weaknesses lie in their orality and their consequent malleability, is the central preoccupation of a fiction that precedes and anticipates the development of customals, whose *raison d'être* was precisely the establishment of *written* accounts of juridical precedents and procedures.[27] Just as Chrétien's romances illustrate the alarming mutability of customs, the compilation of written customals would attempt to establish a new juridical stability by immobilizing them.[28] On the eve of this major socio-historical development, Chrétien's works constitute an implicit indictment of juridical procedures whose apparently absolute necessity was matched only by their perennially potential inadequacy. As a coherent ensemble, these romances powerfully dramatize the potential inadequacies of custom as an institution for the maintenance of order. As legal fictions, they foreshadow the powerful mutation that was to begin soon thereafter and result in the establishment of written records of juridical precedents and protocols.[29] The shift could be characterized as a move from one mentality according to which "témoins passent lettres" – a well-known feudal formula so often reflected negatively in Chrétien's romances – to another asserting the contrary, that "lettres passent témoins."[30] While thirteenth-century literary-juridical figures and fictions more frequently respect the second formula as they record a new ascendancy of writing over the oral utterance in both literary and legal domains, Chrétien anticipated these developments by making of his fiction a medium by which to challenge the earlier formula, either as a satisfactory basis for litigation or as an adequate guarantor of collective stability.[31]

With respect to the socio-historical sphere, then, we may conclude that Chrétien's Arthurian romances do not aspire to recuperate an idealized feudal community in all of its harmony and integrity; nor do they exemplify, in quasi mythopoeic fashion, either the efficacy of a mechanism for the attainment of courtly chivalric perfection or the ultimate transcendence of the courtly milieu through the disclosure of an eschatological mission for chivalry. An operative feudal ideal is indeed evoked in these works, but only as a component of the paternal realm. Looking backward with a mixture of admiration and anxiety, Arthur clings to the bygone world of Uther, recalled as a peaceful reign whose communally held values ensured the stability of its institutions. The Arthurian world gradually emerges in Chrétien's romances as a dimension beset by conflicts which the legal models of that earlier era are no longer capable of resolving. Some of these disruptive situations in fact stem from malicious enterprises into which the models provided by previously reliable customs have been integrated in a corrupted manner. Despite this extensive and nuanced critique of the obsolescence and vulnerability of customs, there is never any sense that these fictions were conceived primarily as a means of advocating social change. It is never implied that within the social sphere there must occur either a full-scale rehabilitation of an older feudal ideal or major reforms according to some specific political or ecclesiastical doctrine. In evidence is a far more subtle art, one capable of modifying the consciousness of a courtly public. By directing the suggestive power of narrative fiction – the appeal of "lettres" – toward an implicit indictment of customs, the latter could gradually, over the course of the narrative ensemble, come to be perceived as procedures which give undue privilege to the authority of oral utterance – the voice of the "témoin." Thus did Chrétien de Troyes create Arthurian romance as a literary medium for exploring the legal roots of social instability. In this endeavour custom – the crumbling cornerstone of a once noble political edifice – became the chief means of anticipating social change without in any way prescribing it, by demonstrating the fragility and the vulnerability of a fragmenting feudal world.

Notes

INTRODUCTION

1 Geoffrey of Monmouth, *Historia regum Britanniae*, ed. A. Griscom (New York: Longmans Green, 1929); Wace, *La Partie arthurienne du Roman de Brut*, ed. I.D.O. Arnold and M.M. Pelan (Paris: Klincksieck, 1962), vv. 13, 275–90.

2 For fundamental background prior to Chrétien, see J.D. Bruce, *The Evolution of Arthurian Romance from the Beginnings down to the Year 1300* (Baltimore: John Hopkins, 1923); J.S.P. Tatlock, *The Legendary History of Britain: Geoffrey of Monmouth's Historia regum Britanniae and its Early Vernacular Versions* (Berkeley and Los Angeles: University of California Press, 1950); R.S. Loomis, ed., *Arthurian Literature in the Middle Ages: A Collaborative History* (Oxford: Clarendon, 1959); and Jean Frappier, *Chrétien de Troyes, l'homme et l'œuvre* (Paris: Hatier, 1957), pp. 8–65. For Chrétien and later French Arthurian romance consult, in addition to the above, Jean Frappier and Reinhold Grimm, eds., *Le Roman jusqu'à la fin du XIIIe siècle*, Grundriss der Romanischen Literaturen des Mittelalters IV/1, IV, 2 (Heidelberg: Winter, 1978; 1982); Beate Schmolke-Hasselmann, *Der arthurische Versroman von Chrestien bis Froissart: Zur Geschichte einer Gattung* (Tübingen: Niemeyer, 1980); Elspeth Kennedy, *Lancelot and the Grail* (Oxford: Oxford University Press, 1986); *The Legacy of Chrétien de Troyes*, ed. N.J. Lacy *et al.*, vols. I, II (Amsterdam: Rodopi, 1987, 1988). Among recent contributions on the medieval Arthurian tradition: Jean Effinger Jost, *Ten Middle English Arthurian Romances: A Reference Guide* (Boston: Hall, 1986); Christopher Dean, *Arthur of England: English Attitudes to King Arthur and the Knights of the Round Table in the Middle Ages and the Renaissance* (Toronto, Buffalo, London: University of Toronto Press, 1987).

3 For a review of this question, see Margaret Houck, *Sources of the Roman de Brut de Wace* (Berkeley and Los Angeles: University of California Press, 1941); and Karl D. Uitti, *Story, Myth, and Celebration in Old French Narrative Poetry 1050–1200* (Princeton: Princeton University Press, 1973), pp. 146–53.

4 Wace, *La Partie arthurienne du Roman de Brut*, vv. 475–92. Eng. trans. mine.

5 For a survey of the posterity of Wace, see Margaret Pelan, *L'Influence du Brut de Wace sur les romanciers français de son temps* (Paris: Droz, 1931). Alongside Charlemagne and Godefroy de Bouillon, Arthur represents Christianity among the *preux* in the fourteenth-century *Vœux du paon* of Jacques de Longuyon.

6 A useful analysis of medieval depictions of the literary Arthur's conventional weaknesses appears in Chapter Five of Edward Peters, *The Shadow King: Rex Inutilis in Medieval Law and Literature* (New Haven and London: Yale University Press, 1970), pp. 170–209. Erich Köhler, *L'Aventure chevaleresque: Idéal et réalité dans le roman courtois*, trs. E. Kaufholz (Paris: Gallimard, 1974), speaks of the "remarkably fluctuating image" of the literary Arthur (p. 9). See also Barbara Nelson Sargent-Baur, "*Dux bellorum/res militum/roi fainéant*: La transformation d'Arthur au XIIe siècle," *MA*, 90 (1984), pp. 357–73.

7 For an assessment of the question, see Rosemary Morris, *The Character of King Arthur in*

Medieval Literature (Woodbridge, Suffolk and Totowa, NJ: D.S. Brewer and Rowan and Littlefield, 1982).

8 This is variously detailed in the articles appearing in *The Legacy of Chrétien de Troyes*, vol. 1, as well as in more circumscribed areas: Keith Busby, *Gauvain in Old French Literature* (Amsterdam: Rodopi, 1980); Charles Méla, *La Reine et le graal: La "conjointure" dans les romans du graal, de Chrétien de Troyes au "Livre de Lancelot"* (Paris: Seuil, 1984).

9 The contrary assumption concerning the grail leads to excessive generalization in Marc Shell, *Money, Language, and Thought: Literary and Philosophic Economies from the Medieval to the Modern Era* (Berkeley, Los Angeles, and London: University of California Press, 1982). See the review article on this study by Peter Haidu, "Idealism vs. Dialectics in Some Contemporary Theory," *Canadian Review of Comparative Literature* (September, 1986), pp. 424–49.

10 The latter perspective is adopted by Jacques Ribard, "Pour une interprétation théologique de la 'coutume' dans le roman arthurien," in *Mittelalterstudien: Erich Köhler zum Gedenken*, ed. H. Kraus and D. Rieger (Heidelberg: Winter, 1984), pp. 241–8. In similar fashion, Köhler founds a major aspect of his interpretation of Chrétien's later romances on an extrinsic coherence, in the works of Robert de Boron, in *L'Aventure chevaleresque*, pp. 144, 156ff.

11 Recent contributions suggest a renewal of interest in this issue: Sargent-Baur, "*Dux bellorum*," pp. 357–73; P.S. Noble, "Chrétien's Arthur," in *CTT*, pp. 220–37; Dominique Boutet, "Sur l'origine et le sens de la largesse arthurienne," *MA*, 89 (1983), pp. 397–411; and Emmanuèle Baumgartner, "Arthur et les chevaliers envoisiez," *Rom*, 105 (1984), pp. 312–25.

12 See Judson Boyce Allen, *The Ethical Poetic of the Later Middle Ages: A Decorum of Convenient Distinction* (Toronto: University of Toronto Press, 1982); and Kathy Eden, *Poetic and Legal Fiction in the Aristotelian Tradition* (Princeton: Princeton University Press, 1986).

13 R. Howard Bloch, *Medieval French Literature and Law* (Berkeley and Los Angeles: University of California Press, 1977), pp. 108–214. In many Old French romances, Bloch identifies "an implicit legal model ... of the inquisitory deposition," involving the hero in a pattern of "departure, conquest, return, and report" (p. 199). Bloch shows that early evidence of the model is found in Chrétien's romances, which thus anticipate more consequential developments in later Arthurian works. In so doing, moreover, he brings to light further evidence that Chrétien's works embody a significant legal dimension that may involve a number of different perspectives.

14 Erich Köhler, "Le Rôle de la coutume dans les romans de Chrétien de Troyes," *Rom*, 81 (1960), pp. 386–97; idem, *L'Aventure chevaleresque*. The views of Köhler will receive fuller discussion at the outset of Chapter 2 and especially in the Conclusion.

15 The paternal anterior order is thus a part of the fiction's "pre-diegetic" dimension, the "diegetic" universe consisting of narrated events, the "pre-diegetic" of circumstances antecedent to narrated events which presuppose or evoke them. On this distinction, see Gérard Genette, *Nouveau discours du récit* (Paris: Seuil, 1983), p. 13.

16 Unless specified otherwise, citations of the works of Chrétien are from the following editions: *Les Romans de Chrétien de Troyes*, ed. M. Roques (Paris: Champion): *Erec et Enide*, CFMA, 80 (1952); *Le Chevalier de la charrete*, CFMA, 86 (1958); *Le Chevalier au lion (Yvain)*, CFMA, 89 (1960); *Cligés*, ed. A. Micha, CFMA, 84 (1957); *Le Roman de Perceval ou le conte du graal*, ed. W. Roach, TLF, 71 (Geneva: Droz, 1959). Chrétien's works as represented in the CFMA editions reflect conservative editorial fidelity to the scribal profile of Guiot (BN 794). See Tony Hunt, "Chrestien de Troyes: The Textual Problem," *FS*, 33 (1979), pp. 257–71; William W. Kibler, "*Le Chevalier de la charrete* de Mario Roques: Corrections," *Rom*, 105 (1984), pp. 558–64; and David F. Hult,

"Lancelot's Two Steps: A Problem in Textual Criticism," *Spec*, 61 (1986), pp. 836–58. Consultation of editions by Foerster, Reid, and Hilka indicates, however, that the intertextual coherence pertaining to custom and crisis identified in the following chapters is not significantly modified in the light of such a comparative control. On occasion variant readings will nonetheless be entertained by appropriate indications in the footnotes.

17 On the earliest cutomals (or customaries), see Brian Stock, *The Implications of Literacy: Written Language and Models of Interpretation in the Eleventh and Twelfth Centuries* (Princeton: Princeton University Press, 1983), p. 57; see also Bloch, *Literature and Law*, p. 112.

1 *REX QUONDAM*: ARTHURIAN TRADITION AND THE ANTERIOR ORDER

1 English translations from the works of Chrétien are my own. Unless indicated otherwise, translations of brief citations from critical studies are also my own.
2 See also Maddox, "Kinship Alliances in the *Cligés* of Chrétien de Troyes," *Esp*, 12 (1972), pp. 3–12.
3 Cf. Pelan, *L'Influence,* pp. 41ff.; Frappier, *Chrétien de Troyes*, p. 31; and Maddox, "Pseudo-Historical Discourse in Fiction: *Cligés*," in *Essays in Early French Literature Presented to Barbara M. Craig*, ed. N. J. Lacy and J. Nash (Birmingham, AL: Summa, 1982), pp. 9–24.
4 Wace, *Brut*, vv. 13,010–274. See Pelan, *L'Influence*, pp. 41–51; see also Annette B. Hopkins, *The Influence of Wace on the Arthurian Romances of Crestien de Troies* (Chicago: University of Chicago Press, 1913), pp. 35ff.; more recently, David Shirt, "*Cligés*: Realism in Romance," *FMLS*, 13 (1977), pp. 368–80.
5 Pelan, *L'Influence*, p. 41.
6 For later developments, see Valerie M. Lagorio, "The Apocalyptic Mode in the Vulgate Cycle of Arthurian Romances," *PQ*, 57 (1978), pp. 1–22.
7 Harold Bloom, *The Anxiety of Influence: A Theory of Poetry* (Oxford and London: Oxford University Press, 1973).
8 Ibid., p. 14.
9 Ibid., p. 44.
10 On this topos, see Michelle A. Freeman, "Chrétien de Troyes' *Cligés*: A Close Reading of the Prologue," *RR*, 67 (1976), pp. 89–101; idem, *The Poetics of "Translatio Studii" and "Conjointure": Chrétien de Troyes's Cligés* (Lexington, KY: French Forum, 1979). See also Douglas Kelly, "*Translatio studii*: Translation, Adaptation, and Allegory in Medieval French Literature," *PQ*, 57 (1978), pp. 287–310.
11 This is but one among many ironic features that permeate the work. See Peter Haidu, *Aesthetic Distance in Chrétien de Troyes: Irony and Comedy in Cligès and Perceval* (Geneva: Droz, 1968); idem, "Au début du roman, l'ironie," *Poétique*, 36 (1978), pp. 443–66.
12 To F.L. Critchlow, *The Arthurian Kingship in Chrétien de Troyes* (Princeton, NJ: Princeton University Press, 1912), Chrétien's Arthur is the "image of an ideal ruler, some of the traits of which he no doubt gathered out of the reigns of his own period" (p. 11).
13 While denying that Chrétien's Arthurian fiction is utopian, Marie-Louise Ollier has recently weighed the evidence therein of a certain "pratique utopique." See "Utopie et roman arthurien," *CCM*, 27 (1984), pp. 223–32.
14 Erich Köhler, *L'Aventure chevaleresque*, p. 10 and *passim*.
15 R. Howard Bloch, "Wasteland and Round Table: The Historical Significance of Myths of Dearth and Plenty in Old French Romance," *New Literary History*, 11 (1979–80), pp. 255–76, see p. 270.
16 W.T.H. Jackson, "The Arthuricitiy of Marie de France," *RR*, 70 (1979), p. 3. Frappier, having observed that Chrétien's Arthur is not the "glorious conqueror" of earlier

tradition, describes him as "a composite figure combining the traits of a loyal, just, and generous sovereign with an air of fantasy or strangeness that befits the debonair and rather disconcerting king in the wondertale" (*Chrétien de Troyes*, p. 35). There is no elaboration on the "disconcerting" aspect, which, as will be seen, stems less from the character than from his political situation.

17 William A. Nitze, "The Character of Gauvain in the Romances of Chrétien de Troyes," *MP*, 50 (1951–2), p. 222; cf. Katharina Holzermayr, "Le 'Mythe' d'Arthur: La royauté et l'idéologie," *Annales: Economies, Sociétés, Civilisations*, 39 (1984), pp. 480–94: in *Erec* and *Cligés* "Arthur apparaît comme un garant de plus en plus défaillant de l'Ordre universel" (p. 493).

18 Peters, *Shadow King*, p. 173.

19 Morris, *Character of Arthur*, p. 123.

20 Sargent-Baur, "*Dux bellorum*," p. 373.

21 M. Blaess, "The Public and Private Faces of King Arthur's Court in the Works of Chrétien de Troyes," in *CTT*, pp. 238–49, see p. 246.

22 P. Noble, "Chrétien's Arthur," in *CTT*, pp. 220–37, see p. 234.

23 Cf. Pierre Gallais, "Littérature et médiatisation, réflexions sur la genèse du genre romanesque," *Etudes Littéraires*, 4 (1971), pp. 39–73; Gallais says that Chrétien almost "kills" Arthur in *Le Conte du graal*, in order to "evacuate all ideologies and denounce all mediatizations, concluding with the royal one." Cf. Blaess, "Public and Private Faces," pp. 233–4.

24 Köhler, *Aventure chevaleresque*, p. 26.

25 Not unlike the ecclesiastical-patriarchal Prince in John of Salisbury's *Policraticus*. See also John Dickinson, "The Mediaeval Conception of Kingship and Some of its Limitations as Developed in the *Policraticus* of John of Salisbury," *Spec*, 1 (1926), pp. 308–37, and on the duties of kings, pp. 319–21.

26 See Maddox, *Structure and Sacring: The Systematic Kingdom in Chrétien's Erec et Enide* (Lexington, KY: French Forum, 1978), pp. 73–119.

27 Duby, "Les 'jeunes' dans la société aristocratique dans la France du Nord-Ouest au XIIe siècle," in *Hommes et structures du Moyen Age* (Paris and the Hague: Mouton, 1973), pp. 213–25.

28 *Structure and Sacring*, pp. 120–78.

29 See Maddox, "Trois sur deux: Théories de bipartition et de tripartition des œuvres de Chrétien," *Oeuvres et Critiques*, 5 (1981), pp. 91–102.

30 See Haidu's analysis in "The Episode as Semiotic Module in Twelfth-Century Romance," *Poetics Today*, 4 (1983), pp. 655–81, esp. p. 667; and Maddox, "The Awakening: A Key Motif in Chrétien's Romances," in *Sower*, p. 38.

31 See *Cligés*, vv. 3287–3332; on developments preparatory to this scene, see Freeman, *Poetics*, pp. 91–127.

32 Cf. Maurice Accarie, "La Structure du *Chevalier au lion* de Chrétien de Troyes,' *MA*, 84 (1978), pp. 13–34, and Haidu, "Episode," p. 667.

33 See the detailed structural analysis of the poem by Douglas Kelly, *"Sens" and "Conjointure" in the Chevalier de la Charrette* (The Hague: Mouton, 1966), pp. 166–203; and Maddox, "Awakening," p. 38.

34 On the background of what in this study is identified as "textuality of crisis," see Peter Haidu, "Narrativity and Language in Some XIIth-Century Romances," *YFS*, 51 (1974), pp. 133–46; Matilda Tomaryn Bruckner, "Repetition and Variation in Twelfth-Century French Romance," in *The Expansion and Transformation of Courtly Literature*, ed. N.B. Smith and J. Snow (Athens: University of Georgia Press, 1980), pp. 95–114; Robert Hanning, *The Individual in Twelfth-Century Romance* (New Haven and London: Yale University Press, 1977), pp. 194ff.; Maddox, "Trois sur deux"; idem, "Awaken-

ing," pp. 31–51; idem, "The Semiosis of Assimilatio in Medieval Models of Time," *Style*, 20 (1986), pp. 252–71.

35 The actant performs or undergoes an act, conceptualized in terms of functions operative in narrative independently of semantic investment at the figural level by beings, animals, objects or concepts. See *Dict*, vol. 1 pp. 3–4, and A. J. Greimas, "Les Actants, les acteurs, et les figures," in *Du Sens II* (Paris: Seuil, 1983), pp. 49–66.

36 The term "subject" is here understood, not as a constituent of a sentence, in the grammatical sense, but as a transphrastic category, or "actant," within the narrative organization of discourse. Two or more "actors" – as in the case of the couple – may invest this category. See *Dict*, vol. 1, pp. 369–71, 344–75; and H.S.F. Collins, "A Semiotic Approach to Chrétien de Troyes's *Erec et Enide*," *Arthurian Interpretations*, 15 (1984), pp. 25–31.

37 *Dict*, vol. 1, pp. 94–5, 244ff.

38 For an early appraisal of the Arthurian "scene" – "the Haupt-Artusszene" – in Chrétien's romances, see Wilhelm Kellermann, *Aufbaustil und Weltbild Chrestiens von Troyes im Percevalroman* (Halle: Niemeyer, 1936).

39 A.J. Greimas, *Maupassant: La Sémiotique du texte, exercices pratiques* (Paris: Seuil, 1976), p. 62.

40 For example, in his analysis of Maupassant's *Les Deux Amis* (in *La Sémiotique du texte*), Greimas identifies Life, Death, Paris, Prussia and other non-anthropomorphic entities as investments of the role.

41 For example, *Cligés*, vv. 4368, 4374, 4380, 4384, 4527, 5014.

42 Cf. Peter Haidu, "La Valeur: Sémiotique et marxisme," in *Semiotique en jeu: A partir et autour de l'œuvre d'A.J. Greimas*, ed. M. Arrivé and J.C. Coquet (Paris: Hadès-Benjamins, 1987), pp. 261ff.

43 Paul Ricœur, *Temps et récit*. II. *La configuration dans le récit de fiction* (Paris: Seuil, 1984), p. 83.

44 Cf. Sargent-Baur, "*Dux bellorum*," p. 370.

45 But on Lancelot's relationship to Bademagu's daughter, see Evelyn Mullally, "The Order of Composition of *Lancelot* and *Yvain*," *BBSIA*, 36 (1984), pp. 217–29, esp. 222.

46 On the narratee, see Gérard Genette, *Figures III* (Paris: Seuil, 1972), pp. 227, 265–7; and Gerald Prince, "Introduction à l'étude du narrataire," *Poétique*, 14 (1973), pp. 177–96.

47 Bloch, *Medieval French Literature and Law*, p. 199.

48 Ibid., pp. 201–2.

49 On the mediatory function of Erec in the Joie de la Cort, see Maddox, *Structure and Sacring*, pp. 163ff.

50 On the leitmotif of "joie" in *Erec*, see R.R. Bezzola, *Le Sens de l'aventure et de l'amour (Chrétien de Troyes)* (Paris: La Jeune Parque, 1947), pp. 121ff., and Margueritte S. Murphy, "The Allegory of 'Joie' in Chrétien's *Erec et Enide*," in *Allegory, Myth and Symbol*, ed. M.W. Bloomfield (Cambridge, MA and London: Harvard University Press, 1981), pp. 109–27.

51 Bloch, *Medieval French Literature*, p.0201.

52 Cf. Dominique Boutet, "Carrefours idéologiques de la royauté arthurienne," *CCM*, 28 (1985), pp. 3–17, on the knight absent from court: "la perte d'un être" = "la perte d'être" (p. 8).

53 On the role and categories of aspectualization in discourse, see *Dict*, vol. 1, pp. 21–2, and vol. II, pp. 19–24.

54 On the medieval interrelationships of divine, natural, and human law, see John A. Alford, "Literature and Law in Medieval England," *PMLA*, 92 (1977), pp. 941–51.

55 On the hierarchy of modalities and their relationships to acts, see A.J. Greimas, "Pour une théorie des modalités," in *Du Sens II*, pp. 67–91.

56 *Structure and Sacring*, p. 115. We shall return to this matter in the conclusion.
57 See Marc Bloch, *La Société féodale*, 5th edn. (Paris: Albin Michel, 1968), pp. 171–2.
58 On Enide's presentation (vv.0411ff.) and portraiture in twelfth-century vernacular romance, see Alice M. Colby, *The Portrait in Twelfth-Century French Literature* (Geneva: Droz, 1965), and the pertinent passages in Claude Luttrell, *The Creation of the First Arthurian Romance: A Quest* (Evanston: Northwestern University Press, 1974). Cf. *Structure and Sacring*, pp. 179ff.
59 See also Penny Sullivan, "The Presentation of Enide in the *premier vers* of Chrétien's *Erec et Enide*," *MA*, 52 (1983), pp. 77–89.
60 On the distinction between demonstration and probability in Aristotle, the remanifestation of this during the twelfth century, and its pertinence to Chrétien, see D. Maddox, "Opérations cognitives et scandales romanesques: Méléagant et le roi Marc," in *Mélanges en hommage à Jean-Charles Payen* (Caen: Université de Caen, 1989), pp. 235–47.
61 *Structure and Sacring*, pp. 101ff.
62 According to Boutet, Arthur in *Erec*, in his adherence to this imperative handed down from the past, neither governs nor administers and expresses no will or personal opinion. In his submission to custom and usage, he is, according to this view, merely the "guarantor of a code"; see "Carrefours idéologiques," p. 4. This view is unduly reductive, as the foregoing analysis of Arthur's *willful* adherence to the paternal mandate shows.
63 This is an example of what Lucien Dällenbach calls the "récit du récit," the "invention des origines": *Le Récit spéculaire: Essai sur la mise en abyme* (Paris: Seuil, 1977), pp. 119ff.
64 On Arthur as *primus inter pares*, cf. Köhler, *Aventure chevaleresque*, p. 23, and Boutet, "Carrefours idéologiques," pp. 15–17.
65 See Charles Petit-Dutaillis, *La Monarchie féodale en France et en Angleterre (Xe-XIIIe siècle)* (Paris: Albin Michel, 1971), pp. 34; 122; cf. Bloch, *La Société féodale*, p. 529.
66 Cf. R. Howard Bloch, "Wasteland and Round Table," pp. 265–7, and *Etymologies and Genealogies: A Literary Anthropology of the French Middle Ages* (Chicago and London: University of Chicago Press, 1983) pp. 220ff., esp. p. 221: "the Round Table structures an equidistant relation of each to each and to an immovable center. Thus it nullifies quarrels of precedence within a society for which the question of difference – of hierarchy – has become problematic." Bloch's view captures the egalitarian, pacific, and fraternal *ideal* of the Round Table, an ideal still cherished by Chrétien's Arthur, though not necessarily by his knights, for whom "questions of difference" and individual ambition persist despite the Arthurian ideal.

2 SAFELY THROUGH THE REALM: CUSTOMS IN *LE CHEVALIER DE LA CHARRETE*

1 Parts of this chapter appeared in French under the title "Lancelot et le sens de la coutume," *CCM*, 29 (1986), pp. 339–53.
2 See also Maddox, *Structure and Sacring*, pp. 101–9.
3 Although by no means devoid of customs, *Cligés* does not display the same kinds of structural and ideational usage of customal properties as do the four romances in the "customal tetralogy." Passages that contain depictions of or references to a custom include: Alexandre's recourse to the *don contraignant*, vv. 83ff.; the "custom" of lovers who feast their eyes on the beloved, vv. 584ff.; Alexandre's "custom" of visiting the queen's quarters nightly, vv. 1536ff.; the "costumes et usage" of Amor, vv. 3819ff.; the "us et costume" of the flatterer, vv. 4485ff.; the opening of the Oxford tournament according to custom, vv. 4592ff.; it was custom that *all* knights participated in this

tournament, vv. 4804ff.; "by custom" Cligés changed armor daily during the tournament, vv. 4848ff.; the effects of Death are "costumiere," v. 5970, and "acostumé," v. 5772. In general, *Cligés* is set apart by the large number of figurative or idiosyncratic usages of "custom" or its derivatives, particularly in the amatory and personal spheres.

4 Erich Köhler, "Le Rôle de la coutume dans les romans de Chrétien de Troyes," pp. 386–97; the typology appears on p. 387.

5 The ostensible premise of a recent monograph derives from Köhler's passing observation that customs are fundamental to the structuration of Chrétien's romances: Katalin Halasz, *Structures narratives chez Chrétien de Troyes* (Debrecen: Kossuth Lajos Tudomanyegyetem, 1980). Analyzing *Erec* and *Yvain*, the author concludes that custom "indirectly" determines narrative structure (p. 5). The study examines four types of "evenemental units showing parallel structure": single combat, hospitality, festivals, and service offered and rewarded. All are organized around the chivalric enterprise featuring heroic struggle. While rich in insights concerning the four criteria, the study does not alter or rectify Köhler's basic inventory, nor does it provide any account of structural regularities among types of customs that recur in more than one work (cf. the final section of Chapter 5). Among the sporadic evocations of customs in *Erec* and *Yvain*, those pertaining to single combat as custom are the most incisive (e.g., pp. 23; 38–44; 52–5).

6 The early customals, whose flourishing on the Continent postdates the romances of Chrétien by several years, also incorporate a narrative dimension. See Bloch, *Medieval French Literature and Law*, pp. 4ff.

7 The retro-prospective specularity of the custom thus provides a significant link between the diegetic dimension, comprising of narrated episodes, and the custom's pre-diegetic background. The implications of this double perspective are taken up in the first section of Chapter 5.

8 The implications of this option between travel alone or with an escort will be weighed more fully in Chapters 4 and 5. On the woman as object of exchange by virtue of this custom, see Roberta L. Krueger, "Love, Honor, and the Exchange of Women in Yvain: Some Remarks on the Female Reader," *Romance Notes*, 25 (1985), pp. 305–6.

9 These properties of Chrétien's *literary* customs are also reflected in the historical evidence of customs. We shall return to the historical background in the conclusion.

10 Indeed, it figures in Köhler's third category, pertaining to customs "abolished" by the hero. "Rôle," p. 387.

11 Matilda Tomaryn Bruckner has also emphasized this point. See *"Le Chevalier de la charrete (Lancelot),"* in *The Romances of Chrétien de Troyes*, ed. D. Kelly, Armstrong Monographs on Medieval Literature, 21 (Lexington, KY; French Forum, 1984), pp. 164–5, 170–1.

12 Others have called attention to affinities between the Custom of Logres and the opening of the *Charrete*. In "Suicide and Adultery in *Le Chevalier de la charrete*," in *Mel. Lods*, vol. I, pp. 571–87, J.B. Williamson asserts in passing that through Kay's defeat "Artus lost his rights to his Queen" (p. 573); she does not, however, weigh the implications of this scene for the Custom of Gorre nor trace the two customs' pertinence to ensuing developments. In "An Interpreter's Dilemma: Why Are There So Many Interpretations of Chrétien's *Chevalier de la charrete*," *RPh*, 40 (1986), pp. 159–80, M.T. Bruckner links the Customs of Logres and Gorre to the opening as well as to later episodes, especially to that of the Immodest Damsel (see esp. pp. 164–9; 170–1), but she sees the opening problematization of the Custom of Logres as having been resolved by Lancelot in Gorre and thus does not account for the crucial relationship, identified in this chapter, between the first and last scenes of the work.

13 Meleagant's concern with honor is but one of many details which together comprise an

extensive and multi-faceted reflection on the nature of honor and shame, one which runs throughout the work. See David F. Hult, "Lancelot's Shame," *RPh*, 42 (1988), pp. 30–50; Emmanuel J. Mickel, Jr., "The Theme of Honor in Chrétien's *Lancelot*," *ZrP*, 91 (1975), pp. 243–72; Pietro Beltrami, "Racconto mitico e linguaggio lirico: Per l'interpretazione del *Chevalier de la charrete*," *Studi Medievali*, 30 (1984), pp. 5–67.

14 On the background of the *don contraignant* and its occurrences in the works of Chrétien and others, see Jean Frappier, "Le Motif du don contraignant dans la littérature du Moyen Age," *TLL*, 7 (1969), pp. 7–46; and Philippe Ménard, "Le Don en blanc qui lie le donateur, réflexions sur un motif de conte," in *An Arthurian Tapestry: Essays in Memory of Louis Thorpe*, ed. K. Varty (Glasgow: The University Press, 1981), pp. 37–53. On the manipulative mechanisms involved, see D. Maddox, "Roman et manipulation," *Poétique*, 66 (1986), pp. 179–90.

15 Bruckner examines the work's various types of delay and deferral in "*Le Chevalier de la charrete*," pp. 308–18.

16 This scene is analyzed by Karl D. Uitti, *Story, Myth, and Celebration*, pp. 174–83.

17 At times "Procrustean," Lancelot's relationship to beds marks a number of scenes. See Sarah Milhado White, "Lancelot's Beds: Styles of Courtly Intimacy," in *Sower*, pp. 116–26; cf. Norris J. Lacy, *The Craft of Chrétien de Troyes: An Essay on Narrative Art*, Davis Medieval Texts and Studies, 3 (Leyden: Brill, 1980), Chapter 4.

18 See also Bruckner, "Interpreter's Dilemma," who suggests that the Immodest Damsel's staging of an attempted rape evokes the custom: "Lancelot wins the damsel by force of arms against the combined effort of three knights and four *sergeants*. The hostess' *covant* thus moves toward a conflation with the custom of Logres" (p. 166).

19 This detail figures prominently in a "messianic" reading of the *Charrete*. See Jacques Ribard, *Le Chevalier de la charrette: Essai d'interprétation symbolique* (Paris: Nizet, 1972).

20 David Shirt has suggested that the cart may reflect an authorial awareness of an archaic English custom involving the "tumbril" or "scolding cart," in "Chrétien et une coutume anglaise," *Rom*, 94 (1973), pp. 178–95.

21 According to Moshé Lazar, she is Lancelot's principal feminine adjuvant within a series of others: "Lancelot et la *mulier mediatrix*: La Quête de soi à travers la femme," *Esp*, 9 (1969), pp. 243–56.

22 Bruckner ("Interpreter's Dilemma," p. 165) maintains that the first combat between Lancelot and Meleagant defeats the latter's attempt to claim the queen under the custom's jurisdiction: "The Queen is once again at stake. She goes to the victor – this time Lancelot who, after a slight delay, does indeed complete the custom. Their night of love is, according to the custom of Logres, nothing more than Lancelot's just due: having won Guenièvre by force of arms, the knight may do as he pleases, 'sanz honte et sanz blasme!'" If correct, such a reading would perhaps provide Lancelot with a "perfect justification" (p. 165) for his night with the queen, but in fact he does *not* "complete the custom" at this juncture. The issue will remain pending until he beheads Meleagant at the end of the romance. For confirmation of this, see vv. 3890ff.

23 For an analysis of Meleagant's specious evaluation of the evidence of adultery in this scene, see Maddox, "Opérations cognitives et scandales romanesques."

24 On the background of ecclesiastical and monarchic efforts to eliminate trial by combat, see Bloch, *Literature and Law*, pp. 119–21. See also Gustave Cohen, "Le Duel judiciaire chez Chrétien de Troyes," *Annales de l'Université de Paris*, 8 (1933), pp. 510–27, esp. pp. 515ff. See also Huguette Legros, "Quand les jugements de Dieu deviennent artifices littéraires, ou la profanité impunie d'une poétique," in *La Justice au Moyen Age (Sanction ou impunité?)*, *Sénéfiance* 16 (Aix en Provence and Marseille: CUER MA, 1986), pp. 197–212, emphasizing the *Tristan* of Béroul.

25 Like Béroul and Thomas, Chrétien exploits, for the reader's benefit, the dichotomy

between one set of circumstances designated by an oath where no culpability obtains and another, covert set where the actual culpability is not a juridical issue. Cf. Helaine Newstead, "The Equivocal Oath in the Tristan Legend and its Literary History," *RPh*, 22 (1968–9), pp. 463–70; Jean-Charles Payen, "Lancelot contre Tristan: La Conjuration d'un mythe subversif (réflexions sur l'idéologie romanesque au Moyen Age)," in *Mél. LeGentil*, pp. 617–32; and E. Jane Burns, "How Lovers Lie Together: Infidelity and Fictive Discourse in the *Roman de Tristan*," *Tristania*, 8 (1982–3), pp. 15–30.

26 Perhaps more in the *Charrete* than in any of his other works after *Erec*, Chrétien repeatedly indulges in his fondness for inserting divergent interpretive perspectives into the fiction, via secondary characters and groups. See Arthur Franz, "Die reflektierte Handlung im *Cligés*," *ZrP*, 47 (1927), pp. 61–86; and Bruckner, "Interpreter's Dilemma," pp. 174–5.

27 An assumption, one might add, widespread in modern readings of the *Charrete*, the misreadings of critics perhaps being conditioned by the prisoners' misreading of their own situation as being one of freedom.

28 The dwarf provides a small but crucial link between the narrative trajectory of the heroic subject, Lancelot, where he figures actantially as an opponent, and that of Meleagant, the counter-subject, where he serves as an adjuvant. Cf. A.J. Greimas, "Les Actants, les acteurs, et les figures."

29 Other details in the *Charrete* can be associated with identifiable historical practices. In addition to Shirt, "Chrétien et une coutume anglaise," see, in connection with Lancelot's combat with the guardian of the ford (vv. 730ff.), René Louis, "Une coutume d'origine protohistorique: Les Combats sur les gués chez les Celtes et chez les Germains," *Revue Archéologique de l'Est et du Centre-Est*, 5 (1954), pp. 186–93; and Halasz, *Structures narratives*, p. 42.

30 Gaston Paris, "Etudes sur les romans de la Table Ronde: *Lancelot du lac*. II. *Le Conte de la charrette*," *Rom*, 12 (1883), pp. 459–534. Subsequent critical opinions, on either side of the issue, have recently been detailed by Bruckner, "Interpreter's Dilemma," p. 159 n. 1; and Beltrami, "Racconto mitico," who reopens the question at length, as does Gerald Morgan, "The Conflict of Love and Chivalry in *Le Chevalier de la charrete*," *Rom*, 102 (1981), pp. 172–201.

31 Cf. Maurice Accarie, "L'Eternal départ de Lancelot: Roman clos et roman ouvert chez Chrétien de Troyes," in *Mélanges de langue et de littérature médiévales offerts à Alice Plance* (Nice–Paris: Les Belles Lettres, 1984), pp. 1–20.

32 Godefroi's role has remained controversial. See Alison Adams, "Godefroi de Leigni's Continuation of *Lancelot*," *FMLS*, 9 (1974), pp. 295–99; David J. Shirt, "Godefroi de Lagny et la composition de la *Charrette*," *Rom*, 96 (1975), pp. 27–52; Joseph J. Duggan, "Ambiguity in Twelfth-Century French and Provençal Literature: A Problem or a Value?," in *Jean Misrahi Memorial Volume*, ed. H. Runte *et al.* (Columbia, SC: French Literature Publications, 1977), pp. 136–49; and A.V. Borsari, "Lancillotto liberato," *Lectures*, 12 (1983), pp. 55–76.

33 On the open love intrigue in the *Charrete*, see Accarie, "L'Eternel départ," and Bruckner, "Interpreter's Dilemma," pp. 176ff. While "closure" is a product of literary production based on the juridical intrigue, "openness" is ensured by the unresolved amatory intrigue which founds intertextual *mouvance* and the expansible interpretive horizon of critical reception. On the structural coherence of the *Charrete*, see F. Douglas Kelly, *"Sens" and "Conjointure"*, pp. 166ff.; and Z.P. Zaddy, *Chrétien Studies: Problems of Form and Meaning in "Erec", "Yvain", "Cligés", and the Charrete* (Glasgow: The University Press, 1973).

34 On the interpretation of the prologue, see the articles by Jean Rychner: "Le Prologue du *Chevalier de la charrette* et l'interprétation du roman," in *Mél. Lejeune*, vol. II, pp. 1121–35;

"Le Prologue du *Chevalier de la charrette*," *VR*, 26 (1967), pp. 1–23; "Encore le prologue du *Chevalier de la charrette*," *VR*, 31 (1972), pp. 263–71. See also Jean Frappier, "Le Prologue du *Chevalier de la charrette* et son interprétation," *Rom*, 93 (1972), pp. 337–77; and Tony Hunt, "Tradition and Originality in the Prologues of Chrestien de Troyes," *FMLS*, 8 (1972), pp. 320–44.

35 Peter Haidu, "The Episode as Semiotic Module," p. 667.

36 See also Haidu, "Narrativity and Language," and A.R. Press, "Chrétien de Troyes's Laudine: a *Belle Dame sans Mercy?*," *FMLS*, (1983), pp. 158–71.

37 See Catherine Geninasca, "La Sanction dans un conte populaire," *Actes Sémiotiques-Bulletin*, v, 21 (1982), pp. 43–53.

38 Cf. Geninasca, "La Sanction," p. 53.

39 We must disagree with Beltrami, p. 55, concerning Lancelot as a "representative of the Arthurian community" at this point.

40 Cf. the remarks of Rychner, "Le Sujet et la signification du *Chevalier de la charrette*," *VR*, 27 (1968), pp. 50–76, esp. p. 72.

41 Cf. Bruckner, "Interpreter's Dilemma," p. 178.

42 On ritual and narrative logic as understood here, see Maddox, *Structure and Sacring*, pp. 117ff.

43 On games of chess, tables, dice, and the structuration of this work, see Sarah Milhado White, "Lancelot on the Gameboard: The Design of Chrétien's *Charrette*," *FF*, 2 (1977), pp. 99–109.

3 *TENIR TERRE*: CUSTOMS IN *LE CHEVALIER AU LION*

1 Parts of this chapter appeared in French under the title "Yvain et le sens de la coutume," *Rom*, 109 (1988), pp. 1–17. On the fountain's prominence in *Yvain*, see Emmanuèle Baumgartner, "La Fontaine au pin," in *Approches*, pp. 31–46.

2 See the detailed, influential discussion of this episode by Erich Auerbach, *Mimesis: The Representation of Reality in Western Literature*, trans. W. Trask (New York: Doubleday, 1968), Chapter 6.

3 To Roques' reading of v. 278, from the Guiot MS, "tors salvages, ors et lieparz," and Foerster's from the Vatican MS: "tors salvages et espaarz," we prefer "tors salvages, orz et esparz" ("wild bulls, ferocious and scattered"), proposed by Francis Bar, "Sur un passage de Chrétien de Troyes (*Yvain*, vv. 276–285)," in *St. Siciliano*, vol. i, pp. 47–50. On problematic aspects in Guiot, see Brian Woledge, *Commentaire sur Yvain (Le Chevalier au lion) de Chrétien de Troyes* (Geneva: Droz, 1986), vol. i, pp. 17–49; commentary on vv. 1–3411, pp. 51–197.

4 On the herdsman, see Jean Frappier, *Etude sur Yvain ou le Chevalier au lion* (Paris: SEDES, 1969), pp. 147ff.; Pierre Jonin, "Aspects de la vie sociale au XIIe siècle dans *Yvain*," *L'Information Littéraire*, 16 (1964), pp. 47–54, esp. pp. 50ff.; and Eugene Vance, *From Topic to Tale: Logic and Narrativity in the Middle Ages* (Minneapolis: University of Minnesota Press, 1987), pp. 55–65. For analysis of Chrétien's portraiture here and elsewhere, see Alice M. Colby, *Portrait in Twelfth-Century French Literature*.

5 Whence a kind of dystopic etiological myth maintained by local oral tradition. See also comments by Philippe Walter, "L'Ordre et la mémoire du temps: La Fête et le calendrier dans les œuvres narratives françaises de Chrétien de Troyes à *La Mort Artu*," *Perspectives Médiévales*, 14 (1988), pp. 45–9, esp. p. 46.

6 Together, then, Chrétien's depictions of the herdsman and the fountain's defender comprise a fictive evocation of the roots of social order, a kind of reflection on early models within a *longue durée*. Cf. Jacques Attali, *La Figure de Fraser* (Paris: Fayard, 1983).

7 See James C. Laidlaw, "Shame Appeased: On the Structure and the *Sen* of the *Chevalier au lion*," in *CTT*, pp. 195–219.
8 A point well made by Anna-Susanna Matthias, "Yvains Rechtsbrüche," in *ZrP, Sonderband zum 100 jährigen Bestehen* (Tübingen: Niemeyer, 1977), pp. 156–92.
9 For analysis of this scene, see Maddox, "Roman et manipulation."
10 For more on this, see the conclusion.
11 See also the excellent analysis of *Yvain* from the perspective of value by Peter Haidu, "La Valeur: Sémiotique et marxisme."
12 On rhetorical invention, see Douglas Kelly, "La Spécialité dans l'invention des topiques," in *Archéologie du signe*, ed. L. Brind'amour and E. Vance (Toronto: Pontifical Institute of Medieval Studies, 1982), pp. 101–26.
13 See Tony Hunt, "Aristotle, Dialectic, and Courtly Literature," *Viator*, 10 (1979), pp. 95–129, esp. p. 102, and his excellent general study, *Chrétien de Troyes: Yvain (Le Chevalier au lion)* (London: Grant and Cutler, 1986), which emphasizes the "casuistic" nature of Chrétien's romances and the dialectic aspect of rhetoric in Chrétien. See esp. the last chapter, "Sic et Non."
14 One such image, appearing in the Walters Art Gallery, Baltimore, on a fourteenth-century ivory box lid depicting a tournament, is reproduced on the cover of Joan Tasker Grimbert, *Yvain dans le miroir: Une Poétique de la réflexion dans le Chevalier au lion de Chrétien de Troyes* (Amsterdam and Philadelphia: Benjamins, 1988).
15 The principle enjoys a long background of negative commentary. For example, Seneca identifies the proposition *Ius est in armis* as the watchword of villains in *Hercules Furens*, II, i, v. 49.
16 But not without committing significant juridical transgressions. Matthias ("Yvains Rechtsbrüche," pp. 156ff.) includes in this category his violation of communal trust in undertaking a clandestine departure from court; his breach of the *trève de Dieu* on Pentecost; his engagement of Esclados without a formal challenge; cruelty and murder in a combat; and breach of promise regarding a contracted deadline.
17 Cf. Laidlaw, "Shame Appeased," pp. 195ff.
18 On the significance of the work's center, see Frappier, *Etude sur Yvain*, p. 62; Freeman, *The Poetics of "Translatio Studii*," p. 86; Laidlaw, "Shame Appeased," pp. 210ff.; and Halasz, *Structures narratives*, pp. 100ff.
19 Cf. Haidu, "La Valeur," p. 261; idem, "The Episode as Semiotic Module," p. 667.
20 For Grimbert, the structure of the fountain adventure expresses the fundamental movement of reversal typifying the entire world (*Yvain dans le miroir*, p. 79; cf. p. 100). See also Tony Hunt, "The Dialectic of *Yvain*," *MLR*, 72 (1977), pp. 285–99, who finds that "negatively charged" events, motifs, and details later recur with positive connotations (p. 297). Cf. the pertinent concepts of episode- and motif-duplication applied to Chrétien's works by Wolfgang Brand, *Chrétien de Troyes: Zur Dichtungstechnik seiner Romane* (Munich: Fink, 1972); and the macronarrative analysis of *Yvain* by Francis Dubost, "*Le Chevalier au lion*: Une 'conjointure' signifiante," *MA*, 90 (1984), pp. 195–222.
21 Cf. Maurice Accarie, "L'Eternel départ"; see also Grimbert, *Yvain dans le miroir*, pp. 8ff. *passim*.
22 The safe conduct specified by the initial clause of the Custom of Logres brings to mind similar proclamations in connection with the fairs in late twelfth-century Champagne. See Elizabeth Chapin, *Les Villes de foires de Champagne des origines au début du XIVe siècle* (Paris: Champion, 1937), pp. 48ff. On the castellany and property transactions before and after the late thirteenth-century *Coutumier de Champagne*, see Theodore Evergates, *Feudal Society in the Bailliage of Troyes under the Counts of Champagne, 1152–1284* (Baltimore and London: Johns Hopkins, 1975), pp. 37–40, 96–135. See also Eugene Vance,

"Chrétien's *Yvain* and Ideologies of Change and Exchange," *YFS*, 70 (1986), pp. 42-62, esp. p. 48.

23 This crisis has received renewed critical attention: Jacques Le Goff and Pierre Vidal-Naquet, "Lévi-Strauss en Brocéliande," *Critique*, 325 (1974), pp. 541-71; Peter Haidu, "The Hermit's Pottage: Deconstruction and History in *Yvain*," in *Sower*, pp. 127-45; and Vance, *Topic to Tale*, pp. 65-79.

24 This concern in *Yvain* already anticipates a major issue in *Le Conte du graal*. See Sara Sturm-Maddox, "Tenir sa terre en pais: Social Order in the *Brut* and in the *Conte del graal*," *Studies in Philology*, 81 (1984), pp. 28-41.

25 It is from this episode, appropriately, that Frappier identifies Yvain as a "chevalier du droit." *Etude sur Yvain*, pp. 204-6.

26 On Yvain's role as "liberator," see also Faith Lyons, "Le Bâton des champions dans *Yvain*," *Rom*, 91 (1970), pp. 97-101.

27 On Lunete's innocence, see Grimbert, *Yvain dans le miroir*, p. 110.

28 Cf. Gustave Cohen, "Le Duel judiciaire chez Chrétien de Troyes," esp. pp. 516ff.

29 Although transposed into the register of the *merveilleux*, the episode reflects the "socio-historical reality" of the suitor unworthy of a noble daughter, according to Claude Lecouteux, "Harpin de la Montagne (*Yvain*, v. 3770 et ss.)," *CCM*, 30 (1987), pp. 219-25. The author identifies Yvain's encounters with Harpin and the *fils de netun* as "combats with giants," as opposed to the "judiciary combats" against the seneschal and Gauvain, yet the former are also adjudicative and rectify abuses of custom.

30 On custom and hospitality at Pesme Avanture, see Matilda Tomaryn Bruckner, *Narrative Invention in Twelfth-Century French Romance: The Convention of Hospitality (1160-1200)* (Lexington, KY: French Forum, 1980), pp. 140ff.; and Halasz, *Structures narratives*, p. 65.

31 Cf. Nicolo Pasero, "Chrétien, la realtà, l'ideologia: Ancora sul Chastel de Pesme-Aventure (*Yvain*, vv. 5179ss.)," in *Studi in ricordo di Guido Favati* (Genoa: Università degli studi di Genova, 1975), pp. 145-69; Antonio Pioletti, "Lettura dell'episodio del 'Chastel de Pesme-Aventure' (*Yvain*, vv. 5105-5805)," *MR*, 6 (1979), pp. 227-46; and Laidlaw, "Shame Appeased," p. 198.

32 On the etymology of this term, see Frappier, *Etude sur Yvain*, p. 51 n. 1.

33 On reminiscences of the New Testament in this scene, see Philippe Walter, "Moires et mémoires du réel chez Chrétien de Troyes. La Complainte des tisseuses dans *Yvain*," *Littérature*, 59 (1985), pp. 71-84.

34 These episodes are further analyzed as an ensemble in Chapters 4 and 5.

35 Cf. Köhler, *Aventure chevaleresque*, p. 387.

36 On seigneurial customs and the obligations of fief-holders in Champagne in 1172, see Evergates, *Feudal Society*, pp. 61ff.

37 See John Gilissen, *La Coutume*, La Typologie des Sources du Moyen Age Occidental, 41 (Turnhout: Brepols, 1982), pp. 27ff.

38 On the lord of Pesme-Avanture and Arthur as upholders of custom, see also Gérard Brault, "Fonction et sens de l'épisode du Château de Pesme-Aventure dans l'*Yvain* de Chrétien de Troyes," in *Mélanges ... offerts à C. Foulon* (Rennes: Université de Haute Bretagne, 1980), vol. I, pp. 59-64. On the episode's reflection of "economic realities," Jonin, "Aspects," pp. 51ff. On the status of women, see Roberta L. Krueger, "Love, Honor, and the Exchange of Women in *Yvain*," pp. 302-17.

39 Cf. Pioletti, "Lettura," pp. 227ff.; Roberta Krueger, "Reading the *Yvain/Charrete*: Chrétien's Inscribed Audiences at Noauz and Pesme Aventure," *FMLS*, 19 (1983), pp. 172-87, esp. 177ff; and Jean Subrenat, "Pourquoi Yvain et son lion ont-ils affronté les fils de netun?", in *Approches*, pp. 173-93.

40 Cf. Haidu, "Episode," pp. 674-78.

41 Cf. Halasz (*Structures narratives*, p. 23), who points out that all three "lion" adventures

involve abusive violations of the custom of single combat, so that the lion's assistance of Yvain in no way introduces an infraction of that principle into what are already unjust engagements.

42 In his edition of *Yvain*, Roques follows Guiot in specifying a *fortnight* ("quatorze jorz," v. 4797 and "quinzainne," v. 5849) within which the younger sibling is to secure a champion. A divergent reading is preferable: "Ne il n'i avoit mes qu'un jor / De la *quarantainne* a venir." (Wendelin Foerster, *Kristian von Troyes, sämtliche erhaltene Werke*, II, Halle: Niemeyer, 1887, vv. 5854–5.) Apart from adjudications of homicide, in which case a shorter period was specified, the *quarantaine* was a conventional interim. Cf. Cohen, *Duel judiciaire*, p. 524. This is also corroborated by the forty days' delay specified for the combat between Gauvain and Guingambresil in *Le Conte du graal* (Roach ed., v. 4790).

43 For an excellent analysis of the frequently neglected quest for the Knight of the Lion by the younger sister and her proxy, see Grimbert, *Yvain dans le miroir*, pp. 155–62.

44 Considered in terms of the three types of test, or *épreuve*, identified in the wondertale by Greimas and others, Yvain's victory at Norison is suggestive of a "qualifying test" (*épreuve qualifiante*) which signifies his recovery of a former level of adequation. The "lion adventures" would comprise a graduated, threefold "principal test" (*épreuve principale*), while the sanction, or *épreuve glorifiante*, which recognizes the hero and valorizes his status, would occur after his return to Lunete and Laudine. From this perspective, the penultimate Arthurian episode lies considerably outside the heroic pattern of tests. Cf. the article "Epreuve," in *Dict*, vol. I, p. 131.

45 Although Yvain's superiority is indeed implicit. Cf. Busby, *Gauvain in Old French Literature*, p. 37; and Grimbert, *Yvain dans le miroir*, pp. 56; 146; 208 n. 8.

46 G According to Norman custom, a *deraisne* was a single exculpatory oath by a defendant. Cf. A. Esmein, *History of Continental Criminal Procedure*, trans. J. Simpson (Boston: Little Brown, 1913), p. 57. In Béroul's *Tristan*, Iseut's equivocal exculpatory oath is referred to as a "deraisne" (vv. 3252ff. passim) or "desraignement" (vv. 3280ff. passim); cf. Ernest C. York, "Isolt's Trial in Béroul and *La Folie Tristan d'Oxford*," *Medievalia et Humanistica*, 6 (1975), pp. 157–61. By contrast, in Marie de France's *Lanval* (ed. Rychner, Paris: Champion, 1971) "desrainié" (v. 628) describes the hero's successful defense before the barons, after the decisive testimony of his lady. Cf. E.A. Francis, "The Trial in Lanval," *Studies in French Language and Medieval Literature Presented to Professor Mildred K. Pope* (Manchester: University Press, 1939), pp. 115–24. See, in addition, the usages cited in F. Godefroy, *Dictionnaire de l'ancienne langue française et de tous ses dialectes du IXe au XVe siècle* (Paris: Vieweg, 1883), vol. II, pp. 523ff.: "deraisnier," esp. defs. 5–13; and A.J. Greimas, *Dictionnaire de l'ancien français* (Paris: Larousse, 1968), p. 171.

47 This tactic involving self-justification has affinities with a *deraisne* involving the oath of a single individual. Cf. York, "Isolt's Trial," p. 157.

48 Cf. Bloch, *Medieval French Literature and Law*, p. 241: "As the guardian of custom and privilege, the king represented a passive figure destined to maintain the status quo rather than extend his land and power."

49 Although this may be read as only the younger sister's oath (cf. Grimbert, p. 162), it is not identified as such by the narrator, nor is this surprising, for each sister would have made the same utterance binding her champion to the constraints of the *judicium Dei*.

50 Grimbert (*Yvain dans le miroir*) analyzes the scene's oxymoronic features, pp. 110–11, 132–3; on its paradox, see Hunt, "Dialectic," p. 298.

51 Cf. L.T. Topsfield, *Chrétien de Troyes: A Study of the Arthurian Romances* (London and New York: Cambridge University Press, 1981), p. 202: "Although Arthur sees the injustice of her cause, he and his court are entrapped in their ritual of trial by combat ... [Arthur] complies with custom, however unjust, in the same way ... as the lord of the castle of Pesme Aventure. He drifts in indecision..."

52 On the proximity of lyric debates and legal metaphor, see Bloch, *Medieval French Literature and Law*, pp. 149ff.

53 See also the rapprochements of these two episodes by Peter Haidu, "Narrativity and Language," pp. 33–46; and by Grimbert, *Yvain dans le miroir*, pp. 177ff.; and Douglas Kelly, "Le Jeu de la vérité,' in *Approches*, pp. 105–17.

54 See Maddox, "La Discours persuasif au XIIe siècle: La Manipulation épique et dramatique," *MR*, 12 (1987) "FS Alberto Limentani", pp. 55–73. Some readers may find Arthur's ruse closer, in terms of tone, to the fabliaux than to either the *Roland* or the *Jeu d'Adam*. Yet the gravity of the issue and the manner of its resolution are indicative of a serious underlying concern not typical of the fabliaux.

55 For Grimbert, the older sister's negative reaction to the judgment is "de bien mauvais augure," while the scene in general seems designed to minimize the magnitude of the quarrel and "trivialiser la justice" (*Yvain dans le miroir*, p. 56); Arthur's manner of settlement also inspires a certain "malaise" (p. 97).

56 Jonin, "Aspects," pp. 47–50.

57 Ibid., p. 48: the "droit d'aînesse" was accorded to the eldest daughter when there were no male heirs.

58 Although specific cases are not cited.

59 Ibid., p. 50.

60 See Maddox, "'E Baldewin mun filz': La Parenté dans la *Chanson de Roland*," *VIII Congreso de la Société Rencesvals* (Pamplona: Institución Príncipe de Viana, 1981), pp. 299–304, esp. 300, 303 n. 14.

61 Implicit within this scene is evidence of the need to formalize procedures of inquest as an alternative to either chivalric "battle" or royal litigation. This is the closest Chrétien comes to a reflection of historical developments in this direction. On the development of inquest and literary configurations thereof, see Bloch, *Medieval French Literature and Law*, pp. 108–61, 189ff.

62 P.Y. Badel sees the medieval Arthur as exemplary of the medieval "good judge," meriting the title of "roi droiturier" because of his "scrupulous respect for customs." *Introduction à la vie littéraire du Moyen Age* (Paris: Bordas, 1969), p. 27. Yet this conventional view is in fact challenged by Chrétien's portrayal, here and elsewhere, of Arthur as a *victim* of his scrupulous respect for customs.

63 In addition to Jonin, see Frappier, who says that in this episode Chrétien presents "the model of a good king in the process of rendering justice with finesse as well as firmness and sensitivity" (*Etude sur Yvain*, p. 138). Cf. Robert Hanning: "In the brave new Arthurian world, ... Arthur, no longer the mindless, irresponsible monarch of earlier episodes, becomes instead a just, perceptive, and therefore powerful king." "The Social Significance of Twelfth-Century Chivalric Romance," *Medievalia et Humanistica*, n. s. 3 (1972), pp. 3–29, see p. 68.

64 On parallels between Yvain's growth and that of the narrator, see Karl D. Uitti, "Narrative and Commentary: Chrétien's Devious Narrator in *Yvain*," *RPh*, 33 (1979), pp. 160–7.

65 Grimbert, *Yvain dans le miroir*, p. 97, and her final chapter, pp. 171–81.

66 Ibid., pp. 171ff.

4 *REXQUE FUTURUS*: THE ANTERIOR ORDER IN *LE CONTE DU GRAAL*

1 The Gauvain episodes have been attributed to a continuator: P.-A. Becker, "Von den Erzählern neben und nach Crestien de Troyes," *ZrP*, 55 (1935), pp. 400–16, restricts Chrétien's authorship to vv. 1–3427, through Perceval's first visit to the Grail Castle; Stefan Hofer, *Chrétien de Troyes, Leben und Werke des altfranzösischen Epikers* (Cologne:

Graz, 1954), pp. 211–14, attributes Perceval's adventures, including the hermitage episode, to Chrétien, while identifying the rest as the work of a continuator. Martín de Riquer argues that two originally independent romances, both unfinished, were ineptly conjoined by a later hand: "Perceval y Gauvain en *Li Contes del graal*," *Filologia Romanza*, 4 (1957), pp. 119–47. D.D.R. Owen, *The Evolution of the Grail Legend* (Edinburgh and London: Oliver and Boyd, 1968), pp. 156ff., proposes that Chrétien left incomplete a *Perceval* and a *Gauvain* that were welded together with a religious emphasis involving interpolation of the hermit episode. See also Leo Pollmann, *Chrétien de Troyes und der Conte del graal* (Tübingen: Niemeyer, 1965).

2 See Jean Frappier, "Sur la composition du *Conte du graal*," *MA*, 64 (1958), pp. 67–102, and idem, "Note complémentaire sur la composition du *Conte du graal*," *Rom*, 81 (1960), pp. 308–37, who answers M. de Riquer; Erich Köhler, "Zur Diskussion über die Einheit von Chrestiens *Li Contes del graal*," *ZrP*, 75 (1959), pp. 523–39; Maurice Delbouille, "Chrétien de Troyes et 'le livre du graal'," *TLL*, 6 (1968), pp. 7–35; Peter Haidu, *Aesthetic Distance in Chrétien de Troyes*, pp. 113–259; Paule Le Rider, *Le Chevalier dans le Conte du graal de Chrétien de Troyes* (Paris: CDU, 1978); Jacqueline Cerquiglini *et al.*, "D'Une quête à l'autre: De Perceval à Gauvain, ou la forme d'une différence," in *Mél. Lods*, pp. 269–96; David G. Hoggan, "Le Péché de Perceval: Pour l'authenticité de l'épisode de l'ermite dans le *Conte du graal* de Chrétien de Troyes," *Rom*, 93 (1972), pp. 50–76, 224–75; Antonio Pioletti, *Forme del racconto arturiano: Peredur, Perceval, Bel Inconnu, Carduino* (Naples: Liguori, 1984), pp. 81–135; Guy Vial, *Le Conte du graal: Sens et unité. La Première continuation: Texte et contenu* (Geneva: Droz, 1987), pp. 9–98.

3 Cf. *Erec*, vv. 149ff.; *Yvain*, vv. 42ff.; *Charrete*, vv. 70ff.

4 Whence also resonance between this episode and that of the rival sisters of Noire Espine in *Yvain*, vv. 5804ff.

5 On the allusion to Rion, see Maurice Delbouille, "Les *hanches* du Roi-Pêcheur et la genèse du *Conte du graal*," in *Festschrift Walter von Wartburg*, ed. K. Baldinger (Tübingen: Niemeyer, 1968), pp. 358–79, esp. 371–5; and Madeleine Blaess, "Perceval et les 'illes de mer'," in *Mél. Lods*, pp. 69–77.

6 See the detailed reading of this passage by Haidu, *Aesthetic Distance*, pp. 118–26. This opening emphasizes a concern with "signs and the interpretation of signs" which runs through much of the work, according to Rupert T. Pickens, *The Welsh Knight: Paradoxicality in Chrétien's Conte del graal* (Lexington, KY: French Forum, 1977), p. 138. Cf. Bloch, *Etymologies and Genealogies*, p. 205: "the socialization that Perceval undergoes is indistinguishable from the process of learning the signs that make him capable of reading knightly culture."

7 Whence a fundamental lack which serves as a catalyst. Cf. Charles Méla, "Perceval," *YFS*, 55–6 (1979), pp. 253–79.

8 For more on the relationship between the fictive subject and the figure of the father, see the essays in *The Fictive Father: Lacanian Readings of the Text*, ed. R. Con Davis (Amherst: University of Massachusetts Press, 1981).

9 "Genealogical" disruption likewise resulted; see Bloch, *Etymologies and Genealogies*, p. 202. On the consequences of "interrupted communication" in this regard, see Claude Lévi-Strauss, "Anthropologie sociale," *Annuaire du Collège de France*, 74 (1974), pp. 303–9; idem, "De Chrétien de Troyes à Richard Wagner," *Programmheft der Bayreuther Festspiele*, 1 (1975), pp. 1–9, 60–7; see also Sara Sturm-Maddox, "Lévi-Strauss in the Waste Forest," *Esp*, 18 (1978), pp. 82–94.

10 On this outlook, see R.G. Collingwood, *The Idea of History* (Oxford: Clarendon, 1946), pp. 52–6; and Rudolf Bultmann, *The Presence of Eternity: History and Eschatology* (New York: Harper, 1957), pp. 36–62. Erich Köhler finds an eschatological perspective in *Le Conte du graal*. See *L'Aventure chevaleresque*, pp. 147ff., 209ff.

11 Only *Cligés* and *Perceval* depict the hero's initial arrival at Arthur's court.

12 On Chrétien's role as represented by this prologue, see Pickens, "*Le Conte du graal (Perceval)*," in *The Romances of Chrétien de Troyes*, ed. Kelly, pp. 232–86; on the relationship between prologue and romance, see ibid., pp. 241–59; and Alina Clej, "La Parole et le royaume: Une variation romanesque sur un thème évangélique dans *Li Contes del graal* de Chrétien de Troyes," *RR*, 78 (1987), pp. 271–90. On the lack of rapport between prologue and romance, see Tony Hunt, "The Prologue to Chrestien's *Li Contes del graal*," *Rom*, 92 (1971), pp. 359–79.

13 The "developmental" aspects of Perceval's presentation have sometimes restricted attention to the situation of the "individual" in this work while distracting from the precarious situation of the court. The view of *Le Conte du graal* as a hero-centered *Bildungsroman* is especially reductive, in that it relies primarily on the presentation of Perceval while neglecting Gauvain and takes inadequate account of the Arthurian juridico-social problematic. Exponents of such a view include David C. Fowler, *Prowess and Charity in the Perceval of Chrétien de Troyes* (Seattle: University of Washington Press, 1959), and Jacques Ribard, *Chrétien de Troyes: Le Conte du graal* (Paris: Hatier, 1976).

14 Sara Sturm-Maddox, "'Tenir sa terre en pais'" p. 36.

15 On the nature of the wound and its implications, see Frappier, "La Blessure du Roi-Pêcheur dans le *Conte du graal*," in *Misrahi Memorial Volume*, pp. 181–96.

16 For critical background, see J. Frappier, *Chrétien de Troyes et le mythe du graal: Etude sur Perceval ou le Conte du graal*, 2nd edn (Paris: SEDES, 1979), with a bibliographical supplement by Jean Dufournet. See also Frappier, "Le graal et ses feux divergents," *RPh*, 24 (1970–1), pp. 373–440; and Heinz-Jürgen Wolf, "Zu Stand und Problematik der Graalforschung," *Romanische Forschungen*, 78 (1966), pp. 399–418.

17 See Frappier, "Le Graal et la chevalerie," *Rom*, 75 (1954), pp. 165–210, esp. 171–6.

18 Ribard, for example, sees a ternary, "éducatif" development in Perceval, from chivalry to love to a religious enlightenment: "L'Ecriture romanesque de Chrétien de Troyes d'après le *Perceval*," *Marche Romane*, 25 (1975), pp. 71–81, as does Stanton de V. Hoffman, "The Structure of the *Conte del graal*," *RR*, 52 (1961), pp. 81–98.

19 For Bloch, this is the first in a hierarchy of "misreadings" that comprise "an upside-down Bildungsroman" (*Etymologies*, p. 204).

20 Completion of such training marked the noble youth's passage from *puer* to *miles*, while the newly armed and dubbed knight was often characterized as *juvenis*. Cf. Duby, "Les 'jeunes'," pp. 213ff. If the knight was typically "jeune" between dubbing and paternity (ibid., p. 214), the term would apply to Perceval throughout his depiction in *Le Conte du graal*.

21 See Jean Flori, "Pour une histoire de la chevalerie: L'Adoubement dans les romans de Chrétien de Troyes," *Rom*, 100 (1979), pp. 21–53; and Barbara Nelson Sargent-Baur, "Promotion to Knighthood in the Romances of Chrétien de Troyes," *RPh*, 37 (1983–4), pp. 393–408. Induction into knighthood shows some conformity with the definitive properties of custom. Cf. John Gilissen, *La Coutume*, Typologie des Sources du Moyen Age Occidental, 41 (Turnhout: Brepols, 1982), pp. 20–32. Its literary-historical development moves from non-written procedures involving simply arming, to more prescriptive, written formats. (Cf. Flori, "Pour une histoire," p. 32ff., and Georges Duby, "Les Chevaliers," in Duby and R. Mandrou, *Histoire de la civilisation française* [Paris: Colin, 1968], pp. 52–68.) The ceremony's formative phase, during the eleventh and twelfth centuries, introduced a variety of components (e.g. ablution, prayerful vigil, mass, conferment of sword and other accoutrements, accolade), not all of which are detailed by Chrétien (cf. *Erec*, vv. 6596ff.; *Cligés*, vv. 1107ff.; *Conte du graal*, vv. 9171ff.). Emphasis on the custom of the spur at this juncture assumes a more profound significance later on (vv. 9171ff.), as we shall see. It does not appear in Chrétien's other

works, and according to Flori, fastening of the spur is rare in earlier descriptions of *adoubement*. For an early example, see *La Chanson d'Aspremont*, ed. Brandin (Paris, 1924), vv. 7480ff.

22 See also the analysis of this episode by François Suard, "Place et signification de l'épisode Blanchefleur dans le *Conte du graal* de Chrétien de Troyes," in *Mél. LeGentil*, pp. 803–10.

23 "Apovri et *deshireté* | Et *escillié* furent a tort | Li gentil home aprés la mort | Uterpandragon..." (vv. 442–5).

24 In this regard, Perceval's accession to the status of *miles* is accompanied by a blending of the two types of chivalric service reflected separately in the exploits of Lancelot and Yvain.

25 These two customs are identified by Köhler as ones that Arthur "must observe." "Le Rôle de la coutume," p. 387.

26 In other words, he is now at that point where, according to Georges Duby, the *jeune* characteristically relinquished his itinerant life for lordship and a more sedentary existence. See "Les 'jeunes'," p. 214.

27 Köhler ascribes them to his third category, customs "abolished" by the hero ("Le Rôle de la coutume," p. 387). On other features of this category, see Pierre Gallais, "Littérature et médiatisation," pp. 39–73, and Alexandre Micha, "Le Pays inconnu dans l'œuvre de Chrétien de Troyes," in *St. Siciliano*, vol. II, pp. 785–92.

28 On entry into Gorre, see Douglas Kelly, "Two Problems in Chrétien's *Charrette*: The Boundary of Gorre and the Use of *novele*," *Neophilologus*, 48 (1964), pp. 115–21.

29 As we saw in the previous chapter, his inconclusive combat with Gauvain brings him also no additional growth or glory while providing an extensive critique of the juridical functioning of Arthur's court.

30 Further analysis of the Custom at the Remote Locus appears in the final section of Chapter 5.

31 We shall return to this matter in the final section of this chapter.

32 Perceval's "sin," broached here and later on by the hermit, has remained a controversial issue among scholars. See Amelia A. Rutledge, "Perceval's Sin: Critical Perspectives," *Œuvres et Critiques*, 5 (1980–1), pp. 53–60.

33 On the *preudome*, see Köhler, *L'Aventure chevaleresque*, pp. 149–59.

34 The maiden's repeated "refrains" admonishing flight are particularly reminiscent of the *pastourelle*. On the background of this lyric genre, see Michel Zink, *La Pastourelle, poésie et folklore au Moyen Age* (Paris: Bordas, 1972); see also Kathryn Gravdal, "Camouflaging Rape: The Rhetoric of Sexual Violence in the Medieval Pastourelle," *RR*, 76 (1985), pp. 361–73; and Kenneth Varty, "The Giving and Withholding of Consent in Late Twelfth-Century French Literature," *Renaissance and Modern Studies*, 12 (1986), pp. 27–49, on non-consenting relationships in Chrétien's romances.

35 On this form of inference, see Maddox, "Opérations cognitives et scandales romanesques," in *Mélanges en hommage à Jean-Charles Payen* (Caen: Université de Caen, 1989), 235–47.

36 The implications of this dichotomy are weighed in Chapter 5.

37 It seems plausible that, like the cousin's attribution of Perceval's first failure at the Grail Castle to his unrecognized sin of abandoning his mother, this detail might eventually have been explained – perhaps by Triboët himself – in terms of a previous lapse on Perceval's part: his own lesser infraction of the Custom of Logres through dishonorable treatment of the Tent Maiden. Like his abandonment of his mother *in extremis*, this early transgression inflicted suffering of which he long remained unaware. In the one case, the stain on his virtue left him unable to ask the requisite questions. In the other, according to this projection, it precluded his use of the Fisher King's sword.

38 This scene enjoys a rich background of commentary, including: Grace Armstrong, "The Scene of the Blood Drops on the Snow: A Crucial Narrative Moment in the *Conte du graal*," *KRQ*, 19 (1972), pp. 127–47; Daniel Poirion, "Du sang sur la neige: Nature et fonction de l'image dans le *Conte du graal*," *Voices of Conscience: Essays in Memory of James D. Powell and Rosemary Hodgins*, ed. R.J. Cormier (Philadelphia: Temple University Press, 1976), pp. 143–65; Michelle A. Freeman, "Problems of Romance Composition: Ovid, Chrétien de Troyes and the *Romance of the Rose*," *RPh*, 30 (1976–7), pp. 158–68; Pierre Gallais, "Le Sang sur la neige (le conte et le rêve)," *CCM*, 21 (1978), pp. 37–42; Henri Rey-Flaud, "Le Sang sur la neige," *Littérature*, 37 (1980), pp. 15–24.

39 See Sara Sturm-Maddox, "King Arthur's Prophetic Fool: Prospection in the *Conte du graal*," *Marche Romane*, 29 (1979), pp. 101–8.

40 On the larger resonance of this phrase, see Sturm-Maddox, "'Tenir sa terre en pais'," pp. 36ff.

41 Cf. *Policraticus: The Statesman's Book of John of Salisbury*, trans. J. Dickinson (New York: Knopf, 1927), viii.

42 See the pertinent comments by Charles Méla, *Blanchefleur et le saint homme, ou la semblance des reliques* (Paris: Seuil, 1979), pp. 40ff.

43 See Maddox, *Structure and Sacring*, pp. 73–119.

44 On the contrast between the Arthurian court at this juncture and the "Grail axis," see Pickens, *The Welsh Knight*, p. 141.

45 On the conventional deferral of forty days, see Cohen, "Le Duel judiciaire chez Chrétien de Troyes," p. 524.

46 See Elizabeth Chapin, *Les Villes de foires*, pp. 135ff., 152–9, 284–6; and Theodore Evergates, *Feudal Society in the Bailliage of Troyes*, pp. 42–59.

47 For further on this episode, see Jeanne Lods, "*La pucelle as manches petites*," in *Mélanges de philologie et de littératures romanes offerts à Jeanne Wathelet-Willem*, ed. J. de Caluwé (Liège: Marche Romane, 1978), pp. 357–79.

48 On parallels and contrasts with Perceval's adventures, see Antoinette Saly, "Beaurepaire et Escavalon," *TLL*, 16 (1978), pp. 469–81; idem, "L'Itinéraire intérieur dans le *Perceval* de Chrétien de Troyes et la structure de la quête de Gauvain," in *Voyage, quête, pèlerinage, dans la littérature et la civilisation médiévales* (Aix-en-Provence and Paris: CUERMA and Champion, 1976), pp. 353–61; and Haidu, *Aesthetic Distance*, pp. 113–259.

49 See Per Nykrog, "Two Creators of Narrative Form in Twelfth-Century France: Gautier d'Arras and Chrétien de Troyes," *Spec*, 48 (1973), pp. 258–76.

50 Both are identified by Saly as instances of the *pietà* motif, in "La Récurrence des motifs en symétrie inverse et la structure du *Perceval* de Chrétien de Troyes," *TLL*, 21 (1983), pp. 21–41.

51 Rosemary Morris has recently reviewed the question of toponymy here and elsewhere in Chrétien, in "Aspects of Time and Place in the French Arthurian Verse Romances," *FS*, 42 (1988), pp. 257–77.

52 This detailed summary is helpful in anticipation of subsequent events that will clarify it in detail.

53 On the reiterative motif of "crossing," see Keith Busby, "Reculer pour mieux avancer: L'Itinéraire de Gauvain dans le *Conte du graal*," in *CTg*, pp. 17–26.

54 He had already indicated a willingness to take her with him, though not by force (v. 6698).

55 In its wake, the vengeful stratagem of the Orgueilleuse, inspired by the Custom of Logres, had nourished two accessory customs. In addition to the one maintained by the homicidal guardian of the passage, the ferryman had been accustomed to claiming, as his "fief," the horses of the knights felled by the guardian (vv. 7371ff.). On the latter, see de Riquer, "Un aspecto jurídico en *Li Contes del graal*," *Rom*, 82 (1961), pp. 403–5.

56 Whence a pacific contrast with the law of talion applied to Lunete's abusers in *Yvain* (vv. 4560ff.).

57 The transformation of the Orgueilleuse after disclosure of the source of her deviant behavior should figure in a nuanced account of Chrétien's treatment of feminine characters. Cf. Marie-Noëlle Lefay-Toury, "Roman breton et mythes courtois: L'Evolution du personnage féminin dans les romans de Chrétien de Troyes," *CCM*, 15 (1972), pp. 193–204, 283–93; and June Hall McCash, "Marie de Champagne's 'Cuer d'ome et cors de fame': Aspects of Feminism and Misogyny in the Twelfth Century," in *Spirit of the Court: Selected Proceedings of the Fourth Congress of the International Courtly Literature Society Toronto, 1983*, ed. G. Burgess and R. Taylor (Cambridge: Brewer, 1985), pp. 234–45. On Chrétien's sympathy for females subjected to aggression, see D.D.R. Owen, "Theme and Variations: Sexual Aggression in Chrétien de Troyes," *FMLS*, 21 (1985), pp. 376–86. See also Varty, "Consent," pp. 27ff.

58 For a general comparison of the chivalric qualities of the two, see Le Rider, *Le Chevalier dans le Conte du graal*, though with a less than satisfactory evaluation of the Gauvain section; see also Norris J. Lacy, "Gauvain and the Crisis of Chivalry in the *Conte del graal*," in *Sower*, pp. 155–64. Haidu, *Aesthetic Distance*, provides extensive analysis of parallels, citing those between the Orgueilleus segments, pp. 251ff., as do Saly, "Récurrence," and Roger Dragonetti, *La Vie de la lettre au Moyen Age (Le Conte du graal)* (Paris: Seuil, 1980), pp. 169ff. It would nonetheless appear that the extensive relationship between these episodes and the Custom of Logres has been overlooked in previous studies.

59 On the possible numerical significance of this encounter, see Ribard, "Ecriture," pp. 78ff.; and Harry F. Williams, "The Numbers Game in Chrétien's *Conte du graal (Perceval),*" *Symposium*, 31 (1977), pp. 59–73.

60 On the "penitential" aspects of this scene within the context of Perceval's development, see David G. Hoggan, "Le Péché de Perceval," pp. 50–76, 244–75; and Bonnie Buettner, "The Good Friday Scene in Chrétien de Troyes' *Perceval*," *Trad*, 36 (1980), pp. 415–26; cf. Jean-Charles Payen, "Encore la pratique religieuse dans le *Conte du graal*," in *CTg*, pp. 121–32.

61 On genealogical features, see G.D. West, "Grail Problems, II: The Grail Family in the Old French Verse Romances," *RPh*, 25 (1971), pp. 53–73, esp. 54–58; D. Poirion, "L'Ombre mythique de Perceval dans le *Conte du graal*," *CCM*, 16 (1973), pp. 191–8; and J.G. Gouttebroze, "Famille et structures de la parenté dans l'œuvre de Chrétien de Troyes," *Europe*, 642 (1982), pp. 77–95.

62 Frequently discussed by critics, the central role of interrogation in the *Conte du graal* has recently been reconsidered by E. Jane Burns, "Quest and Questioning in the *Conte du graal*," *RPh*, 41 (1988), pp. 251–66.

63 Poirion speaks of a "foundation myth" reflecting the desire for an alternative to the "despotic, virile and territorial" concerns of feudalism. "Ombre," pp. 197ff.

64 John of Salisbury, *Policraticus*, viii, 17.

65 Cf. Köhler, *Aventure chevaleresque*, ch. 3, and, on John of Salisbury's critique of a worldly chivalry, pp. 57ff.

66 Cf. *Aventure chevaleresque*, pp. 258ff. On eschatological aspects, see also Harry F. Williams, "The Hidden Meaning of Chrétien's *Conte du graal*," in *Diakonia: Studies in Honor of Robert J. Taylor*, ed. J. Halton and J.P. Williman (Washington, DC: Catholic University of America Press, 1986), pp. 145–57.

67 *Aventure chevaleresque*, pp. 234ff.

68 The nature and significance of the lance that bleeds has caused much ink to flow. On unresolved questions pertaining thereto, see Philippe Ménard, "Problèmes et mystères du *Conte du graal*," in *CTg*, pp. 61–76, esp. pp. 70ff.

69 His task, as Vial reminds us (*Le Conte du graal: Sens et unité*, p. 19), is not to seek either grail or lance, but rather to heal the maimed king by asking the requisite questions.

70 We should also remember that the lance does *not* figure in the grail procession itself but precedes it (vv. 3190-205, 3213ff.). See also Frappier, "Le Cortège du graal,' in *Lumières du graal*, ed. Nelli, pp. 175-221, esp. 192; and Vial, *Sens et unité*, pp. 80ff.

71 On romanesque symmetry, see Fern Farnham, "Romanesque Design in the *Song of Roland*," *RPh*, 18 (1964-5), pp. 143-64; Charles Altman, "Interpreting Romanesque Narrative: Conques and the *Roland*," *Olifant*, 5 (1977), pp. 4-28; Stephen G. Nichols, Jr., *Romanesque Signs: Early Medieval Narrative and Iconography* (New Haven and London: Yale University Press, 1983), pp. 158ff.

72 For *both* heroes, and not just Perceval as in Lévi-Strauss' conception, the principal encounter would be with an answer awaiting the question capable of eliciting it so as to restore "interrupted communication" within a lineage. Cf. "Anthropologie sociale," pp. 307ff.

73 According to Perceval's mother (vv. 435-58), the death of Uther had occurred perhaps a dozen years earlier; the grail has sustained the old king for a dozen years as well (v. 6429). Yet Ygerne's retreat took place sixty years earlier (vv. 8743ff.). On this discrepant view of the time elapsed since Uther's death, see de Riquer, "Perceval y Gauvain," p. 147; and Frappier, "Composition," p. 87. That the Roche de Canguin is located in a "land of the dead," the Other World, or a dimension in which time is "suspended," has frequently been suggested (e.g. Frappier, "Composition"; Hoffman, "Structure," p. 96; Busby, "Reculer," p. 20; Régine Colliot, "Le Voyage de Gauvain à la Roche Champguin chez Chrétien de Troyes et Wolfram d'Eschenbach," in *Voyage, quête, pèlerinage*, pp. 325-38, esp. 326; Lucienne Carasso-Bulow, *The Merveilleux in Chrétien de Troyes' Romances* (Geneva: Droz, 1976), p. 111; and Vial, *Sens et unité*, p. 33. This issue may well remain undecidable, but its status is not crucial to the genealogical and socio-political coherence of the episode, nor to that of Gauvain's symbolic functions therein.

74 See Poirion, *Le Merveilleux dans la littérature française du Moyen Age* (Paris: Presses Universitaires de France, 1982); and Carasso-Bulow, *The Merveilleux*, pp. 109-10.

75 Perhaps a test organized by Ygerne, according to Ronald M. Spensley, "Gauvain's Castle of Marvels Adventure in the *Conte del graal*," *MA*, 42 (1973), pp. 32-7.

76 See the pertinent comments by Hoffman, "Structure," p. 97; and Vial, *Sens et unité*, p. 21.

77 The first six monarchs in the Capetian dynasty associated sons to the throne during their own reigns so as to make the crown hereditary as well as elective. See R. Van Waard, "*Le Couronnement de Louis* et le principe de l'hérédité de la couronne," *Neophilologus*, 30 (1946), 52-8; and Jean-Pierre Boyard, *Le Sacre des rois* (Paris: La Colombe, 1964). Certainly more is at issue in this episode than Gauvain's becoming, in Frappier's words, "the prince of a gynaeceum: charming and pathetic royalty" (*Etude sur Perceval*, p. 129). The idea that Gauvain would be the most likely heir of Arthur's throne becomes more explicit after Chrétien. In the cyclic prose *Lancelot*, the barons elect Gauvain king of Logres when Arthur's prolonged absence (occasioned by his captivity, as it turns out) creates anxieties about a monarchy with no ruler. See *Lancelot, roman en prose*, ed. A. Micha (Geneva: Droz, 1978), vol. I, ch. VII, 1-7, pp. 110-13.

78 As for the unresolved matter of the lance, if Gauvain were to have returned with it, the instrument of retribution against Arthur's kingdom, weakened and on the verge of collapse from the ravages of injustice rampant after the death of Uther, would be in the hands of Gauvain's captors and thus the chief enemies of Arthur's court. Gauvain refuses the oath obliging him to return with it, and swears instead only to seek it, thus removing the obligation to deliver the instrument of Logres' doom. While Gauvain's return to Escavalon for captivity or combat are plausible projections for the completed work, his eventual return with the lance seems much less likely. Implausible is Leslie

Topsfield's opinion that Gauvain's quest for the lance "will make him and his like into the destroyers of Arthur's realm..." (*Chrétien de Troyes: A Study of the Arthurian Romances*, p. 276). Also improbable is the notion that Perceval's eventual success at the Grail Castle would contrast with the Arthurian realm's fall, as Köhler believed (*Aventure chevaleresque*, pp. 232ff.).

79 Cf. Sturm-Maddox, "King Arthur's Prophetic Fool," pp. 101ff.

5 ARTHURIAN INTERTEXTUALITY: CRISIS AND CUSTOM

1 As indicated in Chapter 1, this pattern is developed with particular consistency in the four romances of the customal series. Although *Cligés* displays certain eccentricities with regard to it, certain of its properties are nonetheless retained in this romance as well.

2 On this aspect of crisis, see also Norris J. Lacy, *The Craft of Chrétien de Troyes*, Chapter one, "The Crisis and the Quest," and Maddox, "Trois sur deux."

3 As does Erich Köhler, "Le Rôle de la coutume," pp. 395ff.

4 Although Erec ultimately rescues the Pandragonian custom from a divisive, revisionary modification, he is but the involuntary agent of this outcome. Lancelot's private obsession is not with the court's security, and though he does finally end its long crisis, he kills Meleagant only to exact personal vengeance. Yvain's crisis is provoked, worked through, and ultimately resolved within a context apart from the gravest problems faced by the court, and this romance supplants an heroic solution to its major crisis. Perceval only inadvertently ends the last of the major Arthurian crises, and with total indifference to the imperiled state of the court.

5 The transformational behavior of these two customs is akin to features Claude Lévi-Strauss has identified in mythic narratives from homogeneous cultures. See *The Raw and the Cooked*, trans. J. and D. Weightman (New York and Evanston: Harper and Row, 1969), pp. 130ff.

6 Elsewhere I have suggested that the custom of the *don contraignant* is one of the most complex figures of manipulation in Chrétien's works; see my "Roman et manipulation." In every instance, the individual who has recourse to this stratagem seeks to obtain a *don*, whether this be a tangible object or permission to complete some task or action; the demand, however, solicits a "blank check," as it were, the nature of the sometimes rashly accorded benefit being disclosed later on. (Cf. *Erec*, vv. 531ff.; *Charrete*, vv. 82ff.; *Yvain*, vv. 2549ff.; *Cligés*, vv. 81ff.) Recourse to the *don contraignant* privileges transactional form over content. Moreover, implicit in the granting of the request is the presumption that the noblest attitudes will prevail: mutual respect, free will, honorable motives. Instances of the *don contraignant* frequently depict the unfortunate consequences of such blind authorizations and emphasize that their ethical qualities depend entirely upon the instigator's motives; there is more than a hint that the tacitly obligatory usage involved in such a supposedly "courtly" ritual is inadequate to the needs of the society that nonetheless continues to venerate it. See also Frappier, "Le Motif du don contraignant"; Philippe Ménard, "Le Don en blanc."

7 As in "Li premiers vers," Erec's initiatives provide a means of reconciling couple and court, though his abolition of the destructive custom at Brandigant occurs on a higher, voluntary plane that contrasts with his earlier self-interested involvement in the custom at Laluth. See Sara Sturm-Maddox, "The 'Joie de la Cort': Thematic Unity in Chrétien's *Erec et Enide*," *Rom*, 103 (1982), pp. 513–28; and Maddox, *Structure and Sacring*.

8 It is apparent that the two main customs in the *Charrete* comprise an authentic *mise en abyme* of the entire work, if by this term is understood, following Lucien Dällenbach, an element internally reflecting "the totality of the story by singulative, iterative, or specious reduplication." See *Le Récit spéculaire*.

9 We are again in the domain of fiction that contains interior reduplications, i.e.,

"specular" or "reflexive" passages, as in *mise en abyme*. See Marie-Louise Ollier, "Le Discours en 'abyme' ou la narration équivoque," *MR*, 1 (1974), pp. 351–64, esp. p. 363.

10 Matthew of Vendôme describes invention as a threefold process. See Edmond Faral, *Les Arts poétiques du XIIe et du XIIIe siècle* (Paris: Champion, 1924), pp. 109–93. The poet selects a particular topic (*locus* or *topos*) capable of clarifying the poetic *matière*, then invents an *argumentum* in the *locus*; this determines, in the words of Douglas Kelly, "the content of that clarification according to one's conception of the work; the argument thus serves to interpret the material and make it plausible," leading in turn to the *amplificatio* of the *argumentum* as it is fed into the developing poetic matter. D. Kelly, "La Spécialité dans l'invention des topiques," p. 104. Eugene Vance has recently attempted to show how a dialectical topic accounts for much of the conceptual organization of *Yvain*. In the composition of romance, he suggests, a topic allowed a poet to invent an argument in his *matière* and then to amplify it "into a much larger fictive narrative in whose 'circumstances' there still pertains, no matter how abundant or various its content, a coherent structure based on one topical 'truth'". *From Topic to Tale*, p. 54.

11 Consideration of the potential importance of customs to Chrétien's narrative invention also reveals a close relationship between poetic technique and a developmental ethical coherence within the textual ensemble. It is thus not inappropriate to speak of an "ethical poetic" whose substance of content features customs as the bases of legal fictions. On ethics and medieval poetic theory see Judson Boyce Allen, *The Ethical Poetic of the Later Middle Ages*; on legal fictions, see Kathy Eden, *Poetic and Legal Fictions in the Aristotelian Tradition*, pp. 45–61.

12 A. J. Greimas and Eric Landowski, "Analyse sémiotique d'un discours juridique," in *Sémiotique et sciences sociales* (Paris: Seuil, 1976), pp. 79–128, esp. p. 88; see also D. Maddox, *Semiotics of Deceit: The Pathelin Era* (Lewisburg, PA: Bucknell University Press, 1984), pp. 95–108.

13 The basic "*if . . . then . . .*" type of syntax could thus have permitted invention of an argument within the customal topic from which to produce amplifications of varying dimensions, from the juridical interlace of "Li premiers vers" of *Erec* to the global narrative dimensions of the *Charrete* grounded in the customal loci of Logres and Gorre. In *Yvain* the fountain custom is conceivably a locus whose amplification organizes the heroic itinerary and determines the initial and terminal boundaries of the entire narrative while also founding the arguments of numerous secondary episodes. In *Le Conte du graal*, finally, the Custom of Logres could perhaps have provided the locus for the arguments amplified in the twin "Orgueilleus" episodes.

14 It also marks the boundaries within which characters who maliciously manipulate customs must remain if they are to use their formal rigor as a means of subverting justice. Whence, for example, the importance of the clause stipulating that "*if* she is accompanied. . ." to the vindictive stratagems of the Orgueilleus de la Lande and the Orgueilleuse.

15 The custom is thus a vital determinant of Chrétien's customal romances as *legal* fictions that depict hypothetical cases which lead to the formation of judgments as a component of reception. Cf. Eden, *Poetic and Legal Fiction*, Chapter one.

16 See Owen, "Theme and Variations," for a review of pertinent episodes in all of the romances; and Dietmar Rieger, "Le Motif du viol dans la littérature de la France médiévale, entre norme courtoise et réalité courtoise," *CCM*, 31 (1988), pp. 241–67.

17 Others have shown that Chrétien was fond of such verbal play to emphasize a more profound coherence. On the onomastic aspect of "orgueilleus," see Haidu, *Aesthetic Distance*, pp. 251ff. On the play of signifiers in Chrétien, see Dragonetti, *Vie de la lettre*, and Charles Méla, "'La lettre tue': Cryptographie du graal," *CCM*, 26 (1983), pp. 209–21.

Notes to pages 126–34

18 Antoinette Saly," La Récurrence des motifs en symétrie inverse'; see also Dragonetti, *Vie de la lettre*, pp. 169ff., and Haidu, *Aesthetic Distance*, pp. 251ff.
19 See Bloch, *La Société féodale*, pp. 170–5; and Gilissen, *La Coutume* pp. 33ff., 55. On the later geography of French customs, see Jean Yver, *Essai de géographie coutumière* (Paris: Sirey, 1966), and Emmanuel Le Roy Ladurie, "Système de la coutume," in *Le Térritoire de l'historien* (Paris: Gallimard, 1973), pp. 222–51.
20 See Maddox, *Structure and Sacring*, pp. 101ff.
21 These principles are set forth cogently in Bernard of Clairvaux's *De Laude Novae Militiae*. See Köhler, *Aventure chevaleresque*, pp. 112 et passim; and Le Rider, *Le Chevalier dans le Conte du graal*, pp. 319ff. See also the principles enumerated in the *Ordene de chevalerie*, ed. K. Busby (Amsterdam and Philadelphia: Benjamins, 1983), pp. 86–95.
22 Chrétien was by no means the first to emphasize the ethical weakness of the proposition *Ius est in armis* – might determines right – and its adaptability to the ends of tyranny; a case in point is the attitude of the Creon of Sophocles' *Antigone*. More generally, Seneca observed that *Ius est in armis* is the operative proposition of many a villain (*Hercules Furens*, Act II, scene I, v. 49). In a similar vein, *Le Chevalier au lion* repeatedly depicts behavior based on this audacious proposition, underlining its overwhelming appeal as a basis for the assertion of authority and the maintenance of order while illustrating in a variety of ways the limitations of its validity. For Chrétien, as for Seneca, it is ultimately amplified as a *rhetorical* argument, one founded not on universality or necessity, but on *opinion*. As such, it is revealed to be a specious assertion emanating from the domain of speculation, or *logica probabilis*.
23 Pierre Gallais emphasizes the affinities among these episodes in "Littérature et médiatisation," pp. 52ff.
24 Köhler, "Rôle," p. 389.
25 We can see, then, that only Gauvain among Chrétien's heroes comes close to replicating the convergence of Arthurian values with heroic agency attributed to all of them by Köhler, "Rôle," pp. 395–7.

CONCLUSION. LITERARY CUSTOMS AND THE SOCIO-HISTORICAL QUESTION

1 "Le Rôle de la 'coutume'."
2 Especially in the areas now represented by France, Switzerland, Belgium, the Low Countries, and Scandinavia, according to John Gilissen, *La Coutume*, pp. 42ff. See also Paul Ourliac, "Coutume et mémoire: Les coutumes françaises au XIIIe siècle," in *Jeux de mémoire: Aspects de la mnémotechnie médiévale*, ed. B. Roy and P. Zumthor (Montréal: Les Presses de l'Université de Montréal; Paris: Vrin, 1985), pp. 111–22, esp. p. 112.
3 See Gilissen, *La Coutume*, pp. 22–4.
4 Cf. Ourliac, "Coutume et mémoire," pp. 113–14.
5 For a discussion of this concept in fiction, see Roland Barthes, "L'Effet de réel," *Communications*, 11 (1968), pp. 84–9.
6 The Custom of Logres addresses the problem of safe-conduct; so did the Counts of Champagne, who accorded it to those who transported merchandise to the regional fairs. See René Crozet, *Histoire de Champagne* (Paris: Boivin, 1933), p. 87; and Chapin, *Les Villes de foires de Champagne*, esp. pp. 48–9, for a charter issued by Henry the Liberal in 1154 for the fair on the Feast of the Innocents at Lagny. Henry granted usages according to the same "liberties and customs" as conceded by Thibaut V and his predecessors, as well as safe-conduct to merchants (BN, ms. lat. 9902, fol 24 ro). See also pp. 282ff. In relation to problems of land-holding in Chrétien, see Evergates, *Feudal Society*, pp. 60–95; Judith L. Kellogg, "Economic and Social Tensions Reflected in the

Romance of Chrétien de Troyes," *RPh*, 39 (1985), pp. 1–21; pp. 5ff.; Eugene Vance, "Signs of the City: Medieval Poetry as Detour," *New Literary History*, 4 (1972–3), pp. 557–74; and idem, "Chrétien's *Yvain* and the Ideologies of Change and Exchange."

7 Where longevity is concerned, some customs – White Stag, Logres, single combat, and so on – emanate from the remote past, while the inception of others – like the one in Laudine's realm or those at Brandigant, Pesme-Avanture, the Roche de Canguin, and in Gorre – can still be recalled. Concerning longevity of customs, see Gilissen, *La Coutume*, pp. 29–30.

8 "Rôle," p. 396.

9 Köhler's distillation of the ideal hero as a selfless defender of the realm here comes closer to the hero of the Oxford *Roland* than to any of Chrétien's featured heroic figures.

10 Köhler is not alone among critics who have advanced abstract, idealized views of the "heroic process" in Chrétien. Cf. Kellermann, *Aufbaustil und Weltbild*, p. 168; H. Emmel, *Formprobleme des Artusromans und der Graldichtung* (Berne: Francke, 1951), pp. 34ff., on "Artuskreis"; P. Zumthor, *Essai de poétique médiévale* (Paris: Seuil, 1973), p. 351, whose comments on adventure, reintegration, and "histoire finalisée" echo Köhler's views; R. Hanning, "Social Significance," p. 14; idem, *The Individual . . . Romance* pp. 203ff.; Frappier, *Chrétien de Troyes*, on the "normative function of the Arthurian community," p. 214; K. Boklund, "On the Spatial and Cultural Characteristics of Courtly Romance," *Semiotica*, 20 (1977), pp. 1–37, esp. p. 31; M.-L. Ollier, "Utopie et roman arthurien," p. 228.

11 Köhler, *Aventure chevaleresque*.

12 In the contemporaneous historical arena, this ideal would have been more commensurate with the concerns of the princely houses of Blois, Champagne, and Flanders (p. 26) and the political designs of Anglo-Norman and Angevin royalty (p. 303) than with the evolving Capetian monarchy (pp. 19ff.).

13 He maintains that, through his "adventure," the hero attains full "self-comprehension" and "harmonizes the reality of his existence with his ideal image of it," thus re-establishing the "ordo" and "individual perfection" upon which "the order of an ideal feudal state depends" ("Rôle," p. 396). The Arthurian knight becomes the "master" of the custom, "for through his person and his adventure the disjunction between individual interests and those of the community ceases" (p. 392).

14 *Aventure chevaleresque*, p. 26.

15 Others have recently questioned an idealized view of the relationship between literary form and the social order. R. Howard Bloch, noting that Köhler and others have seen the court as "a fixed locus of justice and peace from which the ideal knight ventures in his conquest of himself and of the uncontrolled nonchivalric forces that surround it, all prior to a final reintegration within a strengthened chivalric order at the end of the archetypal quest," calls "into question such easy passage from a set of privileged moral values undeniably chivalric in character to essential literary form." *Medieval French Literature and Law*, pp. 198–9. See also Kellogg, "Economic and Social Tensions"; Katharina Holzermayr, "Le 'Mythe' d'Arthur," p. 439; Barbara Nelson Sargent-Baur, "*Dux bellorum/rex militum/roi fainéant*," p. 371 n. Köhler reviewed the earliest objections to his views in a lengthy supplement to the second edition: *Aventure chevaleresque*, pp. 299ff.

16 Contrast Köhler: the "imminent dialectical contradiction . . . in the ideal kingdom of Arthurian fiction brought to a final harmony by the hero" ("Rôle," p. 395).

17 "Through the medium of a fictive universal history, Arthur represents the legitimation of the deepest aspirations of the feudal courts" (*Aventure chevaleresque*, p. 37). In Chrétien Köhler identifies a literary reaction against a monarchy allied with an antifeudal bourgeoisie.

18 Philippe de Beaumanoir, *Coutumes de Beauvaisis*, ed. A. Salmon (Paris: Picard, 1899–1900), vol. I, p. 347, no. 684.
19 Claude Liger, *Coustumes d'Anjou et de Maine*, ed. C.J. Beautemps-Beaupré (Paris: Sirey, 1899), I, p. 454, no. 1200. Cf. Ourliac, "Coutume et mémoire," p. 112: "C'est l'ancienneté qui permet de la distinguer de l'usage, de l'habitude, de l'opinion..."
20 On longevity of customs, Gilissen, *La Coutume*, p. 20; see Ourliac, "Coutume et memoire," pp. 111 n.; 117.
21 Köhler does not sufficiently emphasize this point. His treatment of the historical aspect of customs is confined to a tripartite classification of their "medieval" signification: "1. usage, habitual practice; 2. right established by usage; 3. tax, fee" ("Rôle," p. 387).
22 It was not uncommon for dukes and counts, upon their investiture, to uphold "good" customs and abrogate "bad" ones. See Elisabeth Magnou-Mortier, "Les Mauvaises Coutumes en Auvergne, Bourgogne méridionale, Languedoc et Provence au XIe siècle: Un Moyen d'analyse sociale," in *Structures Féodales et féodalisme dans l'Occident Méditerranéen Xe–XIIIe siècles* (Paris, NRS 1980), pp. 135–72.
23 Cited in Petit-Dutaillis, *La Monarchie féodale*, p. 109.
24 Georges Duby, "Mémoires sans historien," *Nouvelle Revue de Psychanalyse*, 15 (1977), reprinted in *Mâle moyen âge* (Paris: Flammarion, 1988), pp. 210–21, see p. 212. See also Ourliac, "Coutume et mémoire," pp. 117–18.
25 Chrétien's representation of the orality of customs is related to what Paul Zumthor has identified as the "intervocality" of medieval poetic discourse and supports his argument that the "literary" romance did not stifle orality. See *La Lettre et la voix: De la "littérature" médiévale* (Paris: Seuil, 1987), pp. 107–29, 155–77; 299–322.
26 An overworked term, *mentalité* has nonetheless been placed in a stable perspective by Jacques Le Goff, "Les Mentalités, une histoire ambiguë," in J. Le Goff *et al.*, *Faire de l'histoire. III. Nouveaux objets* (Paris: Gallimard, 1974), pp. 106–29. Among the properties ascribed to the concept are the collective dimension of the mentality, its manifestations in quotidian contexts, its transcendence of individual historical subjects, and its capacity to link high and low strata of a culture. For a study which espouses this view while showing its pertinence to a specific corpus, see Carlo Ginzburg, *The Cheese and the Worms: The Cosmos of a Sixteenth-Century Miller*, trans. by J. and A. Tedeschi (Baltimore and London: Johns Hopkins, 1980).
27 The earliest to have survived dates from between 1191 and 1204, according to Brian Stock, *The Implications of Literacy*, p. 57. Cf. Ourliac, "Coutume et mémoire," p. 116. Among others from the thirteenth century: the *Summa de legibus Normanniae* (1235–8); the *Conseil à un ami* of Pierre de Fontaines (1253–8); the *Facet* of Saint-Amand (1265); and the *Coutumes de Beauvaisis* of Beaumanoir (1279–83). Cf. Bloch, *Medieval French Literature and Law*: "The customal represented an attempt to collect and codify prevailing usage by writing it down. Unlike the more theoretical discussions of law by late thirteenth-century jurists such as Beaumanoir, the oldest customary compilations served as a supposedly accurate transcription of that which was assumed to have always been in the hopes that it might continue to be" (p. 4). "Devoid of an explicit philosophy of law, the early customal is dominated by the relation of particular situations" (p. 5).
28 As the Old French proverb would have it: "Coustume se remue." Cit. in *Proverbes français antérieurs au XVe siècle*, ed. J. Morawski (Paris: Champion, 1925), p. 16. Brian Stock speaks of the "immobilization" of customs when these were finally written into the customals: *Implications*, p. 56.
29 The development of customals might well be thought of in terms of Stock's notion of "textual communities," constituted and modified by texts and those who master them. See *Implications*, pp. 88ff. In a similar vein, Chrétien's fictive use of customs to develop a critique of contemporaneous institutions and procedures could be seen as an effort to

condition his own public as a courtly textual community. Cf. Vance, *Topic to Tale*, p. 107. As for the public's active interpretative involvement in the juridical coherence of Chrétien's legal fictions, one thinks of Matilda Tomaryn Bruckner's discussion of Old French romance as "case" involving an hypothetical play on norms. See *Narrative Invention in Twelfth-Century French Romance*, pp. 182ff.

30 Formulae cited by Gilissen (*La Coutume*, p. 55), who provides an analysis of the nature and content of early customals, pp. 80–92.

31 Chrétien's adaptation of the "languages of romance" toward this end might well figure among the developments already cited in Michel Zink's excellent study, "Une mutation de la conscience littéraire: Le Langage romanesque à travers des exemples français du XIIe siècle," *CCM*, 24 (1981), pp. 3–27.

Bibliography

In this bibliography of books and articles will also be found editions of the romances of Chrétien de Troyes not referred to in the text or notes. Additional bibliographical resources on the works of Chrétien de Troyes include the *Bibliographical Bulletin of the International Arthurian Society (BBIAS)*; F.D. Kelly, *Chrétien de Troyes: An Analytic Bibliography*, Research Bibliographies and checklists, 17 (London: Grant and Cutler, 1976); R. Bossuat, *Manuel bibliographique de la littérature française du moyen âge* (Melun, 1951); *Supplément (1949–1953)* (Paris, 1955); *Second supplément (1954–1960)* (Paris, 1961); *Troisième supplément (1960–1980)* (Paris, 1986); the pertinent sections in *The Year's Work in Modern Language Studies*; the *MLA Bibliography*; and the *Bibliographie der französischen Literaturwissenschaft*, ed. O. Klapp (1960–   ).

Accarie, M. "La Structure du *Chevalier au lion* de Chrétien de Troyes," *MA*, 84 (1978), 13–34.
— "L'Eternel départ de Lancelot: Roman clos et roman ouvert chez Chrétien de Troyes," in *Mélanges de langue et de litterature médiévales offerts à Alice Planche*. Nice–Paris; Les Belles Lettres, 1984.
Adams, A. "Godefroi de Leigni's Continuation of *Lancelot*," *FMLS*, 9 (1974), 295–9.
Alford, J.A. "Literature and Law in Medieval England,"*PMLA*, 92 (1977), 941–51.
Allen, J.B. *The Ethical Poetic of the Later Middle Ages: A Decorum of Convenient Distinction.* Toronto: University of Toronto Press, 1982.
Altman, C. "Interpreting Romanesque Narrative: Conques and the *Roland*," *Olifant*, 5 (1977), 4–28.
Armstrong, G. "The Scene of the Blood Drops on the Snow: A Crucial Narrative Moment in the *Conte du graal*," *KRQ*, 19 (1972), 127–47.
Attali, J. *La Figure de Fraser*. Paris: Fayard, 1984.
Auerbach, E. *Mimesis: The Representation of Reality in Western Literature*, trans. W. Trask. New York: Doubleday, 1968.
Badel, P.Y. *Introduction à la vie littéraire du Moyen Age*. Paris: Bordas, 1984.
Bar, F. "Sur un passage de Chrétien de Troyes (*Yvain*, vv. 276–285)," in *St. Siciliano*, I, 47–50.
Barthes, R. "L'Effet de réel," *Communications*, 11 (1968), 84–9.
Baumgartner, E. "Arthur et les chevaliers envoisiez," *Rom*, 105 (1984), 312–25.
— "La Fontaine au pin," in *Approches*, 31–46.
Beaumanoir, P. de. *Coutumes de Beauvaisis*, ed. A. Salmon. Paris: Picard, 1899–1900.
Becker, P.-A. "Von den Erzählern neben und nach Chrestien de Troyes," *ZrP*, 55 (1935), 257–92, 385–445, 513–60; 56 (1936), 241–74.
Beltrami, P. "Racconto mitico e linguaggio lirico: Per l'interpretazione del *Chevalier de la charrete*," *Studi Medievali*, 30 (1984), 5–67.
Bezzola, R.R. *Le Sens de l'aventure et de l'amour (Chrétien de Troyes)*. Paris: La Jeune Parque, 1947.

Bibliography

Blaess, M. "Perceval et les 'illes de mer'," in *Mél. Lods*, 69–77.

"The Public and Private Faces of King Arthur's Court in the Works of Chrétien de Troyes," in *CTT*, 238–49.

Bloch, M. *La Société féodale*, 5th edn. Paris: Albin Michel, 1968.

Bloch, R.H. *Etymologies and Genealogies: A Literary Anthropology of the French Middle Ages.* Chicago and London: University of Chicago Press, 1983.

Medieval French Literature and Law. Berkeley and Los Angeles: University of California Press, 1977.

"Wasteland and Round Table: The Historical Significance of Myths of Dearth and Plenty in Old French Romance," *New Literary History*, 11 (1979–80), 255–76.

Bloom, H. *The Anxiety of Influence: A Theory of Poetry.* Oxford and London: Oxford University Press, 1973.

Boklund, K.M. "On the Spatial and Cultural Characteristics of Courtly Romance," *Semiotica*, 20 (1977), 1–37.

Borsari, A.V. "Lancillotto liberato," *Lectures*, 12 (1983), 55–76.

Boutet, D. "Carrefours idéologiques de la royauté arthurienne," *CCM*, 28 (1985), 3–17.

"Sur l'origine et le sens de la largesse arthurienne," *MA*, 89 (1983), 397–411.

Boyard, J.-P. *Le Sacre des Rois.* Paris: La Colombe, 1964.

Brand, W. *Chrétien de Troyes: Zur Dichtungstechnik seiner Romane.* Munich: Fink, 1972.

Brault, G. "Fonction et sens de l'épisode du Château de Pesme-Aventure dans l'*Yvain* de Chrétien de Troyes," in *Mélanges de langue et littérature françaises du Moyen Age et de la Renaissance offerts à Charles Foulon*, 1. Rennes: Université de Haute Bretagne, 1980, 59–64.

Bruce, J.D. *The Evolution of Arthurian Romance from the Beginnings down to the Year 1300.* Baltimore: John Hopkins, 1923.

Bruckner, M.T. "*Le Chevalier de la charrete (Lancelot)*," in *The Romances of Chrétien de Troyes*, ed. D. Kelly, Armstrong Monographs on Medieval Literature, 21. Lexington, KY: French Forum, 1984, 132–81.

Narrative Invention in Twelfth-Century French Romance: The Convention of Hospitality (1160–1200). Lexington, KY: French Forum, 1980.

"Repetition and Variation in Twelfth-Century French Romance,' in *The Expansion and Transformation of Courtly Literature*, ed. N.B. Smith and J.T. Snow. Athens: University of Georgia Press, 1980, 95–114.

"An Interpreter's Dilemma: Why Are There So Many Interpretations of Chrétien's *Chevalier de la charrete?*," *RPh*, 40 (1986), 159–80.

Buettner, B. "The Good Friday Scene in Chrétien de Troyes' *Perceval*," *Trad*, 36 (1980), 415–26.

Burns, E.J. "How Lovers Lie Together: Infidelity and Fictive Discourse in the *Roman de Tristan*," *Tristania*, 8 (1982–3), 15–30.

"Quest and Questioning in the *Conte du graal*," *RPh*, 41 (1988), 251–66.

Busby, K. *Gauvain in Old French Literature.* Amsterdam: Rodopi, 1980.

ed. *Raoul de Hodenc, "Le Roman des eles": Ordene de chevalerie.* Amsterdam and Philadelphia: Benjamins, 1983.

"Reculer pour mieux avancer: L'Itinéraire de Gauvain dans le *Conte du graal*," in *CTg*, 17–26.

Carasso-Bulow, L. *The Merveilleux in Chrétien de Troyes' Romances.* Geneva: Droz, 1976.

Cerquiglini, J., *et al.* "D'Une quête à l'autre: De Perceval à Gauvain, ou la forme d'une différence," in *Mél. Lods*, 269–96.

Chapin, E. *Les Villes de foires de Champagne des origines au début du XIVe siècle.* Paris: Champion, 1937.

Clej, A. "La Parole et le royaume: Une variation romanesque sur un thème évangélique dans

Bibliography

Li Contes del graal de Chrétien de Troyes," RR, 78 (1987), 271–90.

Cohen, G. "Le Duel judiciaire chez Chrétien de Troyes," Annales de l'Université de Paris, 8 (1933), 510–27.

Colby, A.M. The Portrait in Twelfth-Century French Literature: An Example of the Stylistic Originality of Chrétien de Troyes. Geneva: Droz, 1965.

Collins, H.S.F. "A Semiotic Approach to Chrétien de Troyes's Erec et Enide," Arthurian Interpretations, 15 (1984), 25–31.

Colliot, R. "Le Voyage de Gauvain à la Roche Champguin chez Chrétien de Troyes et Wolfram d'Eschenbach," in Voyage, quête, pèlerinage, dans la littérature et la civilisation médiévales. Aix-en-Provance and Paris: CUERMA and Champion, 1976.

Critchlow, F.L. The Arthurian Kingship in Chrétien de Troyes. Princeton, NJ: Princeton University Press, 1912.

Crozet, R. Histoire de Champagne. Paris: Boivin, 1933.

Dällenbach, L. Le Récit spéculaire: Essai sur la mise en abyme. Paris: Seuil, 1977.

Davis, R.C. The Fictive Father: Lacanian Readings of the Text. Amherst: University of Massachusetts Press, 1981.

Dean, C. Arthur of England: English Attitudes to King Arthur and the Knights of the Round Table in the Middle Ages and the Renaissance. Toronto, Buffalo, London: University of Toronto Press, 1987.

Delbouille, M. "Chrétien de Troyes et 'le livre du graal'," TLL, 6 (1968), 7–35.

"Les hanches du Roi-Pêcheur et la genèse du Conte du graal," in Festschrift Walter von Warburg zum 80. Geburtstag, ed. K. Baldinger, Tübingen: Niemeyer, 1968, 358–79.

Dickinson, J. "The Mediaeval Conception of Kingship and Some of its Limitations as Developed in the Policraticus of John of Salisbury," Spec, 1 (1926), 308–37.

Dragonetti, R. La Vie de la lettre au Moyen Age (Le Conte du graal). Paris: Seuil, 1980

Dubost, F. "Le Chevalier au lion: Une 'conjointure' signifiante," MA, 90 (1984), 195–222.

Duby, G. "Les Chevaliers," in Duby and R. Mandrou, Histoire de la civilisation française. Paris: Colin, 1968, 52–68.

"Les 'jeunes' dans la société aristocratique dans la France du Nord-Ouest au XIIe siècle," in Hommes et structures du Moyen Age. Paris and The Hague: Mouton, 1973, 213–25.

"Mémoires sans historien," Nouvelle Revue de Psychanalyse, 15 (1977), reprinted in Mâle moyen âge. Paris: Flammarion, 1988, 210–21.

Duggan, J.J. "Ambiguity in Twelfth-Century French and Provençal Literature: A Problem or a Value?" in Jean Misrahi Memorial Volume, ed. H.R. Runte et al. Columbia, SC: French Literature Publications, 1977, 136–49.

Eden, K. Poetic and Legal Fiction in the Aristotelian Tradition. Princeton: Princeton University Press, 1986.

Emmel, H. Formprobleme des Artusromans und der Graldichtung. Berne: Francke, 1951.

Esmein, A. History of Continental Criminal Procedure, trans. J. Simpson. Boston: Little Brown, 1913.

Evergates, T. Feudal Society in the Bailliage of Troyes under the Counts of Champagne, 1152–1284. Baltimore and London: Johns Hopkins, 1975.

Farnham, F. "Romanesque Design in the Song of Roland," RPh, 18 (1964–5), 143–64.

Flori, J. "Pour une histoire de la chevalerie: L'Adoubement dans les romans de Chrétien de Troyes," Rom, 100 (1979), 21–53.

Foerster, W. ed. Kristian von Troyes. Erec und Enide. Halle: Niemeyer, 1896.

Kristian von Troyes. Cligés. Halle: Niemeyer, 1901.

Christian von Troyes. Sämtliche erhaltene Werke. II. Der Loewenritter. IV. Der Karrenritter (Lancelot) und das Wilhelmsleben (Guillaume d'Angleterre). Halle: Niemeyer, 1887–99.

Fowler, D.C. Prowess and Charity in the Perceval of Chrétien de Troyes. Seattle: University of Washington Press, 1959.

Bibliography

Francis, E.A. "The Trial in Lanval," in *Studies in French Language and Medieval Literature Presented to Professor Mildred K. Pope*. Manchester: Manchester University Press, 1939, 115–24.

Franz, A. "Die reflektierte Handlung im *Cligés*," *ZrP*, 47 (1927), 61–86.

Frappier, J. "La Blessure du Roi-Pêcheur dans le *Conte du graal*," in *Misrahi Memorial Volume*, 181–96.

Chrétien de Troyes: L'Homme et l'œuvre. Paris: Hatier, 1957.

Chrétien de Troyes et le mythe du graal: Etude sur Perceval ou le Conte du graal. Paris: SEDES, 1979.

"Le Cortège du graal," in *Lumières de graal*, ed. R. Nelli, Paris: Cahiers du Sud, 1951, 175–221.

Etude sur Yvain ou le Chevalier au lion. Paris: SEDES, 1969.

"Le Graal et la chevalerie," *Rom*, 75 (1954), 165–210.

"Le Graal et ses feux divergents," *RPh*, 24 (1970–1), 373–440.

"Le Motif du don contraignant dans la littérature du Moyen Age," *TLL*, 7 (1969), 7–46.

"Note complémentaire sur la composition du *Conte du graal*," *Rom*, 81 (1960), 308–37.

"Le Prologue du *Chevalier de la charrette* et son interprétation," *Rom*, 93 (1972), 337–77.

"Sur la composition du *Conte du graal*," *MA*, 64 (1958), 67–102.

Frappier, J. and Reinhold Grimm, eds. *Le Roman jusqu'à la fin du XIIIe siècle*, Grundriss der Romanischen Literaturen des Mittelalters IV/1, IV, 2. Heidelberg: Winter, 1978, 1982.

Freeman, M.A. "Chrétien de Troyes' *Cligés*: A Close Reading of the Prologue," *RR*, 67 (1976), 89–101.

The Poetics of "Translatio Studii" and "Conjointure": Chrétien de Troyes's Cligés. Lexington, KY: French Forum, 1979.

"Problems of Romance Composition: Ovid, Chrétien de Troyes and the *Romance of the Rose*," *RPh*, 30 (1976–7), 158–68.

Gallais, P. "Littérature et médiatisation, réflexions sur la genèse du genre romanesque," *Etudes Littéraires*, 4 (1971), 39–73.

"Le Sang sur la neige (le conte et le rêve)," *CCM*, 21 (1978), 37–42.

Genette, G. *Figures III*. Paris: Seuil, 1972.

Nouveau discours du récit. Paris: Seuil, 1983.

Geninasca, C. "La Sanction dans un conte populaire," *Actes Sémiotiques-Bulletin*, V, 21 (1982), 43–53.

Geoffrey of Monmouth, *Historia regum Britanniae. A Variant Version Edited From Manuscripts*. Cambridge, MA: The Mediaeval Academy of America, 1951.

Historia regum Britanniae, ed. A. Griscom. New York: Longman's Green, 1929.

Historia regum Britanniae, in E. Faral, *La Légende arthurienne*. Paris: Champion, 1929.

Gilissen, J. *La Coutume*. Typologie des Sources du Moyen Age Occidental, 41. Turnhout: Brepols, 1982.

Godefroy, F. *Dictionnaire de l'ancienne langue française et de tous ses dialectes du IXe au XVe siècle*. Paris: Vieweg, 1883.

Gouttebroze, J.G. "Famille et structures de la parenté dans l'œuvre de Chrétien de Troyes," *Europe*, 642 (1982), 77–95.

Gravdal, K. "Camouflaging Rape: The Rhetoric of Sexual Violence in the Medieval Pastourelle," *RR*, 76 (1985), 361–73.

Greimas, A.J. "Les Actants, les acteurs, et les figures," in *Du Sens II*. Paris: Seuil, 1983, 49–66.

Dictionnaire de l'ancien français. Paris: Larousse, 1968.

Maupassant: La Sémiotique du texte, exercices pratiques. Paris: Seuil, 1976.

"Pour une théorie des modalités," in *Du Sens II*. Paris: Seuil, 1983, 67–91.

Greimas, A.J. and E. Landowski. "Analyse sémiotique d'un discours juridique," in *Sémiotique et sciences sociales*. Paris: Seuil, 1976, 79–128.

Bibliography

Grimbert, J.T. *Yvain dans le miroir: Une Poétique de la réflexion dans le Chevalier au lion de Chrétien de Troyes*. Amsterdam and Philadelphia: Benjamins, 1988.

Haidu, P. *Aesthetic Distance in Chrétien de Troyes: Irony and Comedy in Cligés and Perceval*. Geneva: Droz, 1968.

"Au début du roman, l'ironie," *Poétique*, 36 (1978), 443–66.

"The Episode as Semiotic Module in Twelfth-Century Romance," *Poetics Today*, 4 (1983), 655–81.

"The Hermit's Pottage: Deconstruction and History in *Yvain*," in *Sower*, 127–45.

"Idealism vs. Dialectics in Some Contemporary Theory," *Canadian Review of Comparative Literature* (September, 1986), 424–49.

"Narrativity and Language in Some XIIth-Century Romances," *YFS*, 51 (1974), 133–46.

"La Valeur: Sémiotique et marxisme," in *Semiotique en jeu: A partir et autour de l'œuvre d'A.J. Greimas*, ed. M. Arrivé and J.C. Coquet. Paris: Hadès-Benjamins, 1987, 247–63.

Halasz, K. *Structures narratives chez Chrétien de Troyes*. Debrecen: Kossuth Lajos Tudomanyegyetem, 1980.

Hanning, R. *The Individual in Twelfth-Century Romance*. New Haven and London: Yale University Press, 1977.

"The Social Significance of Twelfth-Century Chivalric Romance," *Medievalia et Humanistica*, n. s. 3 (1972), 3–29.

Hofer, S. *Chrétien de Troyes, Leben und Werke des altfranzösischen Epikers*. Cologne: Graz, 1954.

Hoffman, S. de V. "The Structure of the *Conte del graal*," *RR*, 52 (1961), 81–98.

Hoggan, D.G. "Le Péché de Perceval: Pour l'authenticité de l'épisode de l'ermite dans le *Conte du graal* de Chrétien de Troyes," *Rom*, 93 (1972), 50–76, 244–75.

Holzermayr, K. "Le 'Mythe' d'Arthur: La royauté et l'idéologie," *Annales: Economies, Sociétés, Civilisations*, 39 (1984), 480–94.

Hopkins, A.B. *The Influence of Wace on the Arthurian Romances of Crestien de Troies*. Chicago: University of Chicago Press, 1913.

Houck, M. *Sources of the Roman de Brut de Wace*. Berkeley and Los Angeles: University of California Press, 1941.

Hult, D.F. "Lancelot's Shame," *RPh*, 42 (1988), 30–50.

"Lancelot's Two Steps: A Problem in Textual Criticism," *Spec*, 61 (1986), 836–58.

Hunt, T. "Aristotle, Dialectic, and Courtly Literature," *Viator*, 10 (1979), 95–129.

"Chrestien de Troyes: The Textual Problem," *FS*, 33 (1979), 257–71.

Chrétien de Troyes: Yvain (Le Chevalier au lion). London: Grant and Cutler, 1986.

"The Dialectic of *Yvain*," *MLR*, 72 (1977), 285–99.

"The Prologue to Chrestien's *Li Contes del graal*," *Rom*, 92 (1971), 359–79.

"Tradition and Originality in the Prologues of Chrestien de Troyes," *FMLS*, 8 (1972), 320–44.

Jackson, W.T.H. "The Arthuricity of Marie de France," *RR*, 70 (1979), 1–17.

John of Salisbury. *Policraticus: The Statesman's Book of John of Salisbury*, trans. J. Dickinson. New York: Knopf, 1927.

Jonin, P. "Aspects de la vie sociale au XIIe siècle dans *Yvain*," *L'Information Littéraire*, 16 (1964), 47–54.

Jost, J.E. *Ten Middle English Arthurian Romances: A Reference Guide*. Boston: Hall, 1986.

Kellermann, W. *Aufbaustil und Weltbild Chrestiens von Troyes im Percevalroman*. Halle: Niemeyer, 1936.

Kellogg, J.L. "Economic and Social Tensions Reflected in the Romance of Chrétien de Tròyes," *RPh*, 39 (1985), 1–21.

Kelly, D. *"Sens" and "Conjointure" in the Chevalier de la Charrette*. The Hague: Mouton, 1966.

"La Spécialité dans l'invention des topiques," in *Archéologie du signe*, ed. L. Brind'amour and E. Vance. Toronto: Pontifical Institute of Medieval Studies, 1982, 101–26.

Bibliography

"Le Jeu de la vérité," in *Approches*, 105–17.

"*Translatio studii*: Translation, Adaptation, and Allegory in Medieval French Literature," *PQ*, 57 (1978), 287–310.

"Two Problems in Chrétien's *Charrette*: The Boundary of Gorre and the Use of *novele*," *Neophilologus*, 48 (1964), 115–21.

Kennedy, E. *Lancelot and the Grail*. Oxford: Oxford University Press, 1986.

Kibler, W.W. "*Le Chevalier de la charrete* de Mario Roques: Corrections," *Rom*, 105 (1984), 558–64.

Köhler, E. *Ideal und Wirklichkeit in der höfischen Epik. Studien zur Form der frühen Artus- und Graldichtung*, ZfrP, Beiheft 97, Tübingen: Niemeyer, 1956. Tr. E. Kaufholz, *L'Aventure chevaleresque: Idéal et réalité dans le roman courtois*. Paris: Gallimard, 1974.

"Le Rôle de la coutume dans les romans de Chrétien de Troyes," *Rom*, 81 (1960), 386–97.

"Zur Diskussion über die Einheit von Chrestiens *Li Contes del graal*," *ZrP*, 75 (1959), 523–39.

Krueger, R.L. "Love, Honor, and the Exchange of Women in *Yvain*: Some Remarks on the Female Reader," *Romance Notes*, 25 (1985), 302–17.

"Reading the *Yvain/Charrete*: Chrétien's Inscribed Audiences at Noauz and Pesme Aventure," *FMLS*, 19 (1983), 172–87.

Lacy, N.J. *The Craft of Chrétien de Troyes: An Essay on Narrative Art*, Davis Medieval Texts and Studies, 3 Leyden: Brill, 1980.

"Gauvain and the Crisis of Chivalry in the *Conte del graal*," in *Sower*, 155–64.

Lacy, N.J. *et al.*, eds. *The Legacy of Chrétien de Troyes*, I, II. Amsterdam: Rodopi, 1987, 1988.

Lagorio, V.M. "The Apocalyptic Mode in the Vulgate Cycle of Arthurian Romances," *PQ*, 57 (1978), 1–22.

Laidlaw, J.C. "Shame Appeased: On the Structure and the *Sen* of the *Chevalier au lion*," in *CTT*, 195–219.

Lazar, M. "Lancelot et la *mulier mediatrix*: La Quête de soi à travers la femme," *Esp*, 9 (1969), 243–56.

Lecouteux, C. "Harpin de la Montagne (*Yvain*, v. 3770 et ss.)," *CCM*, 30 (1987), 219–25.

Lefay-Toury, M.-N. "Roman breton et mythes courtois: L'Evolution du personnage féminin dans les romans de Chrétien de Troyes," *CCM*, 15 (1972), 193–204, 283–93.

Le Goff, J. "Les Mentalités, une histoire ambiguë," in J. Le Goff *et al. Faire de l'histoire*. III. *Nouveaux objets*. Paris: Gallimard, 1974, 106–29.

Le Goff, J. and P. Vidal-Naquet. "Lévi-Strauss en Brocéliande," *Critique*, 325 (1974), 541–71.

Legros, H. "Quand les jugements de Dieu deviennent artifices littéraires, ou la profanité impunie d'une poétique," in *La Justice au Moyen Age (Sanction ou impunité?)*, *Sénéfiance* 16 (Aix en Provence and Marseille: CUER MA, 1986), 197–212.

Le Rider, P. *Le Chevalier dans le Conte du graal de Chrétien de Troyes*. Paris: CDU, 1978.

Le Roy Ladurie, E. "Système de la coutume," in *Le Territoire de l'historien*. Paris: Gallimard, 1973, 222–51.

Lévi-Strauss, C. "Anthropologie sociale," *Annuaire du Collège de France*, 74 (1974), 303–9.

"De Chrétien de Troyes à Richard Wagner," *Programmheft der Bayreuther Festspiele*, I (1975), 1–9, 60–7.

Liger, C. *Coustumes d'Anjou et de Maine*, ed. C.J. Beautemps-Beaupré. Paris: Sirey, 1899.

Lods, J. "*La pucelle as manches petites*," in *Mélanges de philologie et de littérature romanes offerts à Jeanne Wathelet-Willem*, ed. J. de Caluwé. Liège: Marche Romane, 1978, 357–79.

Loomis, R.S., ed. *Arthurian Literature in the Middle Ages: A Collaborative History*. Oxford: Clarendon, 1959.

Louis, R. "Une coutume d'origine protohistorique: Les Combats sur les gués chez les Celtes et chez les Germains," *Revue Archéologique de l'Est et du Centre-Est*, 5 (1954), 186–93.

Bibliography

Luttrell, C. *The Creation of the First Arthurian Romance: A Quest*. Evanston: Northwestern University Press, 1974.

Lyons, F. "Le Bâton des champions dans *Yvain*," *Rom*, 91 (1970), 97–101.

Maddox, D. "'E Baldewin mun filz': La Parenté dans la *Chanson de Roland*," *VIII Congreso de la Société Rencesvals*. Pamplona: Institución Príncipe de Viana, 1981, 299–304.

"Le Discours persuasif au XIIe siècle: La Manipulation épique et dramatique," *MR*, 12 (1987) (Festschrift Alberto Limentani), 55–73.

"Kinship Alliances in the *Cligés* of Chrétien de Troyes," *Esp*, 12 (1972), 3–12.

"Opérations cognitives et scandales romanesques: Méléagant et le roi Marc," in *Mélanges en hommage à Jean-Charles Payen*. Caen: Université de Caen, 1989, 235–47.

"Pseudo-Historical Discourse in Fiction: *Cligés*," in *Essays in Early French Literature Presented to Barbara M. Craig*, ed. N.J. Lacy and J. Nash. Birmingham, AL: Summa, 1982, 9–24.

"Roman et manipulation," *Poétique*, 66 (1986), 179–90.

Semiotics of Deceit: The Pathelin Era. Lewisburg, PA: Bucknell University Press, 1984.

Structure and Sacring: The Systematic Kingdom in Chrétien's Erec et Enide. Lexington, KY: French Forum, 1978.

"The Awakening: A Key Motif in Chrétien's Romances," in *Sower*, 31–51.

"The Semiosis of Assimilatio in Medieval Models of Time," *Style*, 20 (1986), 252–71.

"Trois sur deux: Théories de bipartition et de tripartition des œuvres de Chrétien," *Oeuvres et Critiques*, 5 (1981), 91–102.

Magnou-Mortier, E. "Les Mauvaises Coutumes en Auvergne, Bourgogne méridionale, Languedoc et Provence au XIe siècle: Un Moyen d'analyse sociale," in *Structures féodales et féodalisme dans l'Occident Méditerranéen (Xe–XIIIe siècles)*. Paris: CNRS, 1980, 135–72.

Matthias, A.-S. "Yvains, Rechtsbrüche," in *ZrP. Sonderband zum 100 jährigen Bestehen*. Tübingen: Niemeyer, 1977, 156–92.

McCash, J.H. "Marie de Champagne's 'Cuer d'ome et cors de fame': Aspects of Feminism and Misogyny in the Twelfth Century," in *Spirit of the Court: Selected Proceedings of the Fourth Congress of the International Courtly Literature Society Toronto, 1983*, ed. G. Burgess and R. Taylor, Cambridge: Brewer, 1985, 234–45.

Méla, C. *Blanchefleur et le saint homme, ou la semblance des reliques*. Paris: Seuil, 1979.

"'La lettre tue': Cryptographie du graal," *CCM*, 26 (1983), 209–21.

"Perceval," *YFS*, 55–6 (1979), 253–79.

La Reine et le graal: La "conjointure" dans les romans du Graal, de Chrétien de Troyes au "Livre de Lancelot". Paris: Seuil, 1984.

Ménard, P. "Le Don en blanc qui lie le donateur, réflexions sur un motif du conte," in *An Arthurian Tapestry, Essays in Memory of Lewis Thorpe*, ed. K. Varty. Glasgow: The University Press, 1981, 37–53.

"Problèmes et mystères du *Conte du graal*," in *CTg*, 61–76.

Micha, A. "Le Pays inconnu dans l'œuvre de Chrétien de Troyes," in *St. Siciliano*, II, 785–92.

Mickel, E.J., Jr. "The Theme of Honor in Chrétien's *Lancelot*," *ZrP*, 91 (1975), 243–72.

Morgan, G. "The Conflict of Love and Chivalry in *Le Chevalier de la charrete*," *Rom*, 102 (1981), 172–201.

Morris, R. "Aspects of Time and Place in the French Arthurian Verse Romances," *FS*, 42 (1988), 257–77.

The Character of King Arthur in Medieval Literature. Woodbridge, Suffolk and Totowa, NJ: D.S. Brewer and Rowan and Littlefield, 1982.

Murphy, M.S. "The Allegory of 'Joie' in Chrétien's *Erec et Enide*," in *Allegory, Myth and Symbol*, ed. M.W. Bloomfield. Cambridge, MA and London: Harvard University Press, 1981, 109–27.

Bibliography

Newstead, H. "The Equivocal Oath in the Tristan Legend and its Literary History," *RPh*, 22 (1968–9), 463–70.

Nichols, S.G., Jr. *Romanesque Signs: Early Medieval Narrative and Iconography*. New Haven and London: Yale University Press, 1983.

Nitze, W.A. "The Character of Gauvain in the Romances of Chrétien de Troyes," *MP*, 50 (1952–3), 219–25.

Noble, P. "Chrétien's Arthur," in *CTT*, 220–37.

Nykrog, P. "Two Creators of Narrative Form in Twelfth-Century France: Gautier d'Arras and Chrétien de Troyes," *Spec*, 48 (1973), 258–76.

Ollier, M.L. "Le Discours en 'abyme' ou la narration équivoque," *MR*, 1 (1974), 351–64.
"Utopie et roman arthurien," *CCM*, 27 (1984), 223–32.

Ourliac, P. "Coutume et mémoire: Les coutumes françaises au XIIIe siècle," in *Jeux de mémoire: Aspects de la mnémotechnie médiévale*, ed. B. Roy and P. Zumthor. Montréal: Les Presses de l'Université de Montréal; Paris: Vrin, 1985, 111–22.

Owen, D.D.R. *The Evolution of the Grail Legend*. Edinburgh and London: Oliver and Boyd, 1968.
"Theme and Variations: Sexual Aggression in Chrétien de Troyes," *FMLS*, 21 (1985), 376–86.

Paris, G. "Etudes sur les romans de la Table Ronde: *Lancelot du lac*. II. *Le Conte de la charrette*," *Rom*, 12 (1883), 459–534.

Pasero, N. "Chrétien, La realtà, L'ideologia: Ancora sul Chastel de Pesme-Aventure (*Yvain*, vv. 5179 ss.)," in *Studi in ricordo di Guido Favati*, Genoa: Università degli Studi di Genova, 1975, 145–69.

Payen, J.-C. "Encore la pratique religieuse dans le *Conte du graal*," in *CTg*, 121–32.
"Lancelot contre Tristan: La Conjuration d'un mythe subversif (réflexions sur l'idéologie romanesque au Moyen Age)," in *Mél. LeGentil*, 617–32.

Pelan, M. *L'Influence du Brut de Wace sur les romanciers français de son temps*. Paris: Droz, 1931.

Peters, E. *The Shadow King: Rex Inutilis in Medieval Law and Literature*. New Haven and London: Yale University Press, 1970.

Petit-Dutaillis, C. *La Monarchie féodale en France et en Angleterre (Xe–XIIIe siècle)*. Paris: Albin Michel, 1971.

Pickens, R.T. "*Le Conte du graal (Perceval)*," in *The Romances of Chrétien de Troyes*, ed. Kelly, 232–86.
The Welsh Knight: Paradoxicality in Chrétien's Conte del Graal. Lexington, KY: French Forum, 1977.

Pioletti, A. *Forme del racconto arturiano: Peredur, Perceval, Bel Inconnu, Carduino*. Naples: Liguori, 1984.
"Lettura dell'episodio del 'Chastel de Pesme-Aventure' (*Yvain*, vv. 5105–5805)," *MR*, 6 (1979), 227–46.

Poirion, D. "Du sang sur la neige: Nature et fonction de l'image dans le *Conte du graal*," in *Voices of Conscience: Essays in Memory of James D. Powell and Rosemary Hodgins*, ed. R.J. Cormier. Philadelphia: Temple University Press, 1976, 143–65.
Le Merveilleux dans la littérature française du Moyen Age. Paris: Presses Universitaires de France, 1982.
"L'Ombre mythique de Perceval dans le *Conte du graal*," *CCM*, 16 (1973), 191–8.

Pollmann, L. *Chrétien de Troyes und der Conte del graal*. Tübingen: Niemeyer, 1965.

Press, A.R. "Chrétien de Troyes's Laudine: A *Belle Dame sans Mercy*?" *FMLS*, 19 (1983), 158–71.

Prince, G. "Introduction à l'étude du narrataire," *Poétique*, 14 (1973), 177–96.

Rey-Flaud, H. "Le Sang sur la neige," *Littérature*, 37 (1980), 15–24.

Ribard, Jacques. *Le Chevalier de la charrette: Essai d'interprétation symbolique*. Paris: Nizet, 1972.

Bibliography

Chrétien de Troyes: Le Conte du graal. Paris: Hatier, 1976.

"L'Ecriture romanesque de Chrétien de Troyes d'après le *Perceval*," *Marche Romane*, 25 (1975), 71–81.

"Pour une interprétation théologique de la 'coutume' dans le roman arthurien," in *Mittelalterstudien: Erich Köhler zum Gedenken*, ed. H. Kraus and D. Rieger. Heidelberg: Winter, 1984, 241–8.

Ricœur, P. *Temps et recit*. II. *La configuration dans le récit de fiction*. Paris: Seuil, 1984.

Rieger, D. "Le Motif du viol dans la littérature de la France médiévale, entre norme courtoise et réalité courtoise," *CCM*, 31 (1988), 241–67.

Riquer, M. de. "Perceval y Gauvain en *Li Contes del graal*," *Filologia Romanza*, 4 (1957), 119–47.

"Un aspecto jurídico en *Li Contes del graal*," *Rom*, 82 (1961), 403–5.

Rutledge, A.A. "Perceval's Sin: Critical Perspectives," *Œuvres et Critiques*, 5 (1980–1), 53–60.

Rychner, J. "Encore le prologue du *Chevalier de la charrette*," *VR*, 31 (1972), 263–71.

"Le Prologue du *Chevalier de la charrette*," *VR*, 26 (1967), 1–23.

"Le Prologue du *Chevalier de la charrette* et l'interprétation du roman," in *Mél. Lejeune*, II, 1121–35.

"Le Sujet et la signification du *Chevalier de la charrette*," *VR*, 27 (1968), 50–76.

Saly, A. "Beaurepaire et Escavalon," *TLL*, 16 (1978), 469–81.

"L'Itinéraire intérieur dans le *Perceval* de Chrétien de Troyes et la structure de la quête de Gauvain," in *Voyage, quête, pèlerinage*, 353–61.

"La Récurrence des motifs en symétrie inverse et la structure du *Perceval* de Chrétien de Troyes," *TLL*, 21 (1983), 21–41.

Sargent-Baur, B.N. "*Dux bellorum/res militum/roi fainéant*: La transformation d'Arthur au XIIe siècle," *MA*, 90 (1984), 357–73.

"Promotion to Knighthood in the Romances of Chrétien de Troyes," *RPh*, 37 (1983–4), 393–408.

Schmolke-Hasselmann, B. *Der arthurische Versroman von Chrestien bis Froissart: Zur Geschichte einer Gattung*. Tübingen: Niemeyer, 1980.

Shell, M. *Money, Language, and Thought: Literary and Philosophic Economies from the Medieval to the Modern Era*. Berkeley, Los Angeles, and London: University of California Press, 1982.

Shirt, D. "Chrétien et une coutume anglaise," *Rom*, 94 (1973), 178–95.

"*Cligès*: Realism in Romance," *FMLS*, 13 (1977), 368–80.

"Godefroi de Lagny et la composition de la *Charrette*," *Rom*, 96 (1975), 27–52.

Spensley, R.M. "Gauvain's Castle of Marvels Adventure in the *Conte del graal*," *MA*, 42 (1973), 32–7.

Stock, B. *The Implications of Literacy: Written Language and Models of Interpretation in the Eleventh and Twelfth Centuries*. Princeton: Princeton University Press, 1983.

Sturm-Maddox, S. "The 'Joie de la Cort': Thematic Unity in Chrétien's *Erec et Enide*," *Rom*, 103 (1982), 513–28.

"King Arthur's Prophetic Fool: Prospection in the *Conte du graal*," *Marche Romane*, 29 (1979), 101–8.

"Lévi-Strauss in the Waste Forest," *Esp*, 18 (1978), 82–94.

"'Tenir sa terre en pais': Social Order in the *Brut* and in the *Conte del graal*," *Studies in Philology*, 81 (1984), 28–41.

Suard, F. "Place et signification de l'épisode Blanchefleur dans le *Conte du graal* de Chrétien de Troyes," in *Mél. LeGentil*, 803–10.

Subrenat, J. "Pourquoi Yvain et son lion ont-ils affronté les fils de netun?" in *Approches*, 173–93.

Bibliography

Sullivan, P. "The Presentation of Enide in the *premier vers* of Chrétien's *Erec et Enide*," *MA*, 52 (1983), 77–89.

Tatlock, J.S.P., *The Legendary History of Britain: Geoffrey of Monmouth's Historia regum Britanniae and its Early Vernacular Versions*. Berkeley and Los Angeles: University of California Press, 1950.

Topsfield, L.T. *Chrétien de Troyes: A Study of the Arthurian Romances*. London and New York: Cambridge University Press, 1981.

Uitti, K.D. "Narrative and Commentary: Chrétien's Devious Narrator in *Yvain*," *RPh*, 33 (1979), 160–7.

Story, Myth, and Celebration in Old French Narrative Poetry 1050–1200. Princeton: Princeton University Press, 1973.

Vance, E. "Chrétien's *Yvain* and the Ideologies of Change and Exchange," *YFS*, 70 (1986), 42–62.

From Topic to Tale: Logic and Narrativity in the Middle Ages. Minneapolis: University of Minnesota Press, 1987.

"Signs of the City: Medieval Poetry as Detour," *New Literary History*, 4 (1973), 557–74.

Van Waard, R. "*Le Couronnement de Louis* et le principe de l'hérédité de la couronne," *Neophilologus*, 30 (1946), 52–8.

Varty, K. "The Giving and Withholding of Consent in Late Twelfth-Century French Literature," *Renaissance and Modern Studies*, 12 (1986), 27–49.

Vial, G. *Le Conte du graal: Sens et Unité. La Première continuation: Texte et contenu*. Geneva: Droz, 1987.

Walter, P. "Moires et mémoires du réel chez Chrétien de Troyes. La Complainte des tisseuses dans *Yvain*," *Littératures*, 59 (1985), 71–84.

"L'Ordre et la mémoire du temps: La Fête et le calendrier dans les œuvres narratives françaises de Chrétien de Troyes à *La Mort Artu*," *Perspectives Médiévales*, 14 (1988), 45–9.

West, G.D. "Grail Problems, II: The Grail Family in the Old French Verse Romances," *RPh*, 25 (1971), 53–73.

White, S.M. "Lancelot's Beds: Styles of Courtly Intimacy," in *Sower*, 116–26.

"Lancelot on the Gameboard: The Design of Chrétien's *Charrette*," *FF*, 2 (1977), 99–109.

Williams, H.F. "The Hidden Meaning of Chrétien's *Conte du graal*," in *Diakonia: Studies in Honor of Robert T. Mayer*, ed. T. Halton and J.P. Williman. Washington, DC: Catholic University of America Press, 1986, 145–57.

"The Numbers Game in Chrétien's *Conte du graal (Perceval)*," *Symposium*, 31 (1977), 59–73.

Williamson, J.B. "Suicide and Adultery in *Le Chevalier de la charrete*," *Mél. Lods*, I, 571–87.

Woledge, B. *Commentaire sur Yvain (Le Chevalier au lion) de Chrétien de Troyes. I. vv. 1–3411*. Geneva: Droz, 1986.

Wolf, H.-J. "Zu Stand und Problematik der Graalforschung," *Romanische Forschungen*, 78 (1966), 399–418.

York, E.C. "Isolt's Trial in Béroul and *La Folie Tristan d'Oxford*," *Medievalia et Humanistica*, 6 (1975), 157–61.

Yver, J. *Essai de géographie coutumière*. Paris: Sirey, 1966.

Zaddy, Z.P. *Chrétien Studies: Problems of Form and Meaning in "Erec", "Yvain", "Cligés", and the Charrete*. Glasgow: The University Press, 1973.

Zink, M. *La Pastourelle, poésie et folklore au Moyen Age*. Paris: Bordas, 1972.

"Une mutation de la conscience littéraire: Le Langage romanesque à travers des exemples français du XIIe siècle," *CCM*, 24 (1981), 3–27.

Zumthor, P. *Essai de poétique médiévale*. Paris: Seuil, 1973.

La Lettre et la voix: De la 'littérature' médiévale. Paris: Seuil, 1987.

Index

Index

Index

Index